THE 1940s HOUSE

THE 1940s HOUSE

Juliet Gardiner

Foreword by Norman Longmate

First published in 2000 by Channel 4 Books,
This edition published 2002 by Channel 4 Books,
an imprint of Pan Macmillan Ltd,
20 New Wharf Road, London N1 9RR,
Basingstoke and Oxford

Associated companies throughout the world.

www.panmacmillan.com

ISBN 0 7522 6514 8

Text © Juliet Gardiner, 2000
Foreword © Norman Longmate, 2000

9 8 7 6 5 4 3 2 1

A CIP catalogue record for this book is available from the British Library.

Design by Isobel Gillan
Special Photography © Simon Roberts/Growbag
Colour reproduction by Speedscan Ltd
Printed in the UK by Bath Press

CONTENTS

FOREWORD

The Second World War is one of the great dividing lines in our history. The people who lived through it feel different to those who did not. Those who experienced that unique mixture of expectation and disappointment, fear and relief, deprivation and satisfaction, excitement and boredom, still – if they are honest – consider themselves superior to those born too late to remember the strange, unique years from 1939 to 1945. It is an attitude that becomes even more marked as the survivors' numbers dwindle and the words 'You remember how it was during the war…' no longer produce the same response.

To attempt to re-create those war years was a challenging enterprise. The period is indeed remembered by millions, but those memories may not always be accurate. The war is familiar, indirectly, to many more people through innumerable books, films and television programmes, but sometimes misleadingly. Those who lived through the war inevitably tend to think that their own memories were universal. If, thanks to a kindly shopkeeper, they had never gone short of tobacco – one of the most stressful experiences for 'our' family – they may find it hard to believe that anyone else had done so. If they had lived in the large area of the country free from flying bombs, they may find it difficult to appreciate the impact of these on the lives of people in south-east England. Everyone, though, had to suffer shortages of food, fuel and clothes, and here surely a sigh of recognition will go up from many older people as they identify with Lyn's struggles to satisfy the appetite of two hungry small boys.

'Wish us luck as you wave us goodbye': loaded with luggage, the Hymers' taxi leaves their Victorian terrace in Yorkshire on the first stage of their journey back to the 1940s.

1940s
HOUSE

The 1900 House had shown how effective a technique it could be to install a modern family in a property of an earlier period, dressing them in the clothes of the time and exposing them to all the inconveniences of what now seem primitive living conditions. The 1940s house proved hardly less traumatic for its occupants. What emerges over and over again in the family's reactions – and what, I confess, surprised me – is the extent to which it was the disadvantages of their new environment, rather than its specifically wartime aspects, which made the deepest impact. It was not merely the grown-ups who were affected by the lack of fridge and vacuum cleaner, washing machine and microwave. At the 'end of term' party, when the 'War Cabinet' was allowed to meet the members of the family, one of the boys remarked that it was the change in the methods of food preparation that had most impressed him.

The sheer drudgery of life in the late 1930s and early 1940s has been overshadowed by the additional privations of the war, but, especially for those on low income, without domestic help, it was very real. What is often forgotten, in recalling those mainly grey – though occasionally colourful – years is that, especially at the beginning of the war, the shortest commodity of all was money. Full employment (even if one's husband was in the forces) meant that people could at least buy all their rations, and it was the combination of rationing and, for millions, a higher, regular income that brought about the great 'fair shares' revolution.

It was decided that 'our' family, while certainly not hard-up by 1940s standards, should be far from well-off. (The 'War Cabinet' agreed early on: no car, no telephone, a minimum of electrical appliances.) A rigorous eye was kept on the increase in the cost of living and the Hymers could not simply buy their way out of difficulty by resorting to the black market. In fact, the overwhelming majority of citizens honoured the rationing system and if, occasionally, a clothing coupon changed hands for money, the nation was no worse off. The way in which the war could affect one in unexpected ways was neatly brought home when Michael was fined for a blackout offence. I also delighted in the Hymers' squeamishness, typical of many wartime families, in refusing to have a pet that could in time be converted into that favourite wartime delicacy (its meat sometimes allegedly passed off by expensive restaurants as chicken) – rabbit pie.

Clearly, if the experiment was to be convincing, all depended on two factors: the house and the family. When I first entered 17 Braemar Gardens I truly felt, in the clichéd words, that I had stepped back in time. This was not indeed the house I had lived in during the war (which, gaslit and with an outside toilet, was far humbler), but the house in which I had aspired to live, as many of my better-off friends actually did. The choice was, I felt, inspired, the redecoration and provision of equipment masterly. And for our purposes, the area – 'neutral' at the start of the war, plagued by flying bombs towards the end – was just right. As for the family, the way in which they entered into the spirit of the enterprise will be evident to everyone who reads this book.

There were, inevitably, limitations to what could be achieved. The Hymers did not, as so many families did during the war, live under the perpetual shadow of having a loved one absent in the forces. They did not, when they went out, have to stumble through the blackout, or squeeze themselves into a perpetually overcrowded train, or have to waste hours trying to buy a toothbrush or a saucepan – though wherever possible we made their 'wartime' lives as realistic as we could. Above all they knew that in nine weeks the All Clear would sound for the last time and that the war did not stretch on ahead into an unknown future.

But the 1940s house was the nearest we could get to what it had really been like, putting real people into what had once been a real setting. Many wartime housewives will surely identify with Lyn's dilemma, described in Chapter 14. Should she retreat to the Anderson shelter when the siren sounded or try and salvage the meal she was preparing, having confused ginger with curry powder? No survivor of the war will be surprised that the kitchen won. And all of us will echo her final verdict. That this living history lesson can only increase one's admiration for those who lived then.

NORMAN LONGMATE

CHAPTER 1

CALL-UP PAPERS

'War is about to be declared. A modern family has volunteered to experience life on the home front in Britain during the Second World War. They're about to spend two months living in the 1940s house', runs the commentary to the Channel 4 series as images of wartime – gas masks, searchlights, ration books, an Anderson shelter – flash up on the screen.

It was on 22 February 2000 that the Hymers family of Otley near Leeds in West Yorkshire found out that 'We are officially the 1940s family!' That like the Bowler family before them they were to travel back in time, for the delectation of a new millennium television audience. But unlike the Bowlers, who had found themselves in a 1900 house, for the Hymers the time capsule stopped only a little more than half a century back: they were to telescope the Second World War from September 1939 to May 1945 into nine weeks. It was to be as authentic an experience as possible, given that they would not be enduring the ever-present danger of actual war. What they would experience were the hardships, the constrictions and the uncertainties of those wartime years.

In 2000, fifty-five years after the end of the war, even those people too young to have experienced it directly have an idea of what it was like to live through it. They may have older relatives or friends who have shared their memories of life on the home front. And of course there are the masses of films, television programmes and books that draw inexhaustible inspiration from those wartime years. Films such as *Mrs Miniver* and *Hope and Glory* reflect the domestic experience; on television there

'We're going to miss you'. Ben and Thomas leave their grandparents' Yorkshire home, bedecked with flags strung up by their neighbours in farewell to the 1940s family, on 16 April 2000.

are sitcoms such as the endlessly popular *Dad's Army* along with documentaries investigating seemingly every element of wartime life. As well as diaries and memoirs about the home front, there are novels that drew on the experience, such as Elizabeth Bowen's *The Heat of the Day* or Evelyn Waugh's *Put Out More Flags*. And the music of the time – from Glenn Miller to Vera Lynn – remains potent for many people.

Kirstie Hymers, dressed for her wartime experience, in her parents 50s-diner-style kitchen in Otley.

So the wartime experience suffuses our culture still – and stirs up questions. What did Spam really taste like? How hard was it to spin out a week's rations when each person got only an ounce of cheese and two ounces of tea per week, and lemons were a distant memory? Could you have lived with the blackout, coped in the confines of an Anderson shelter? And, on the lighter side, how good would you have been at the jitterbug?

Such is the interest in the home front in the Second World War, and the admiration for those who courageously endured its hardships, that when the call went out – 'Could you be the 1940s family?' – over 300 families volunteered to live the 'wartime experience'.

But somehow from this rush of applicants the Hymers stood out as being the right family for the experience. It's a three-generation family: Michael is fifty-two, his wife Lyn is fifty, and their daughter Kirstie is twenty-nine, a single parent bringing up her two sons, Ben (ten) and Thomas (seven). Michael and Lyn have another daughter, Jodie, recently married to Iain, who was not able to move in to the 1940s house with the rest of the family, but was keenly interested in the project and came to visit. Lyn has lived in the market town of Otley all her life and had never been to London, nor had her grandsons, and the only time that Kirstie had been was on a school trip.

Lyn and Michael live in a large terraced house at the edge of the Pennine Way. It's typically Victorian, built of solid dark stone, but inside it's an historical galaxy from the Edwardian bathroom and Victorian 'parlour' to the 1950s kitchen-diner resplendent with a big red fridge and cardboard cut-out of James Dean by the

1940s HOUSE

back door. 'The house is evidence that we can't agree on anything,' says Lyn, but the dining room where Michael spends a lot of time shows not only his obsession with the 1940s (even if it has got a 1951 Festival of Britain door complete with his own crafted version of Abram Games's logo) but also how that has rubbed off on to the rest of the family. The room is packed with 40s memorabilia, from the achingly authentic to the frankly kitsch – from a 'yacht' single-bar electric fire, Winston Churchill handkerchiefs and 1940s board games, to books and magazines and a wind-up gramophone that regularly floods the house with such haunting wartime melodies as 'Lili Marlene', 'Run, Rabbit, Run' and 'There'll Always Be an England'.

Michael, an engineer, is now an executive in charge of production at a small local firm that manufactures aeroplane parts among other precision equipment, but it was at his first job in a factory that he became interested in the Second World War. The experience of the war was still very present in many of the men's lives and they talked a lot about how it had been. 'It always sounded great from what they were saying. I know it wouldn't all have been like that, but the way they described it made it sound fantastic,' he recalled.

Looking forward to going backwards: Lyn and Michael Hymers on the morning they left Yorkshire for the 1940s house in Kent.

Kirstie looking pensive as the family wait for their taxi.

It was Michael's longing for a 'real' experience of wartime that made his family resolve to make a bid to be the '1940s family'. But it wasn't a simple matter of indulging Michael: rather, as Lyn explained, the family was insistent that he should learn what it had really been like in the war years; they wanted him to lose his rose-tinted view of the period. She wanted him to stop 'once and for all going on and on about how it was better then and how we should all live like that now'. Indeed, Michael had been known to drag Lyn round a supermarket trying to persuade her that she should buy only wartime rations and that they should have an austerity binge right there in their 50s kitchen in Otley. 'I wanted to prove my dad wrong,' said their daughter Kirstie, with feeling.

Lyn, who had worked as a tax investigator but took early retirement to devote time to her family, friends and her many other interests, had her own reasons for wanting to be a 1940s housewife. 'I like to party and I can't cook. We almost live on pre-packaged foods and takeaways,' she admitted, 'so I want to prove to the family that I can do it. That I will be a good mother in the circumstances and cook and sew and all those things. That I could survive the hardships.'

Her daughter Kirstie sees it as a challenge for her mother too: 'I can't wait to see Mum trying to wheedle more than her due rations from the shopkeeper… she spends a criminal amount of money on food and throws so much of it away. I want to challenge her to cook and live off rations.'

But despite Kirstie's wish to pull her mother into line and disabuse her father of his nostalgic view of the 1940s, it was her own curiosity about the period that was an

important reason why she wanted to 'live the wartime experience' with her parents. Michael's enthusiasm had inspired her and she wanted to know all about the home front. 'We only seem to know half the story. I want to know why did they do that? Why did that happen? Every time I ask my dad I never get a proper answer. That's why I want to do it, to find out the whole story.' But there was another reason: as a single mother – her husband had left her when she was pregnant with Thomas – Kirstie felt that her confidence had taken a dive and that the challenge of helping manage a 1940s household – in front of a television camera – would rebuild her assurance and make her more confident with people, better able to face new situations.

The Hymers are a close family – Kirstie and her children live near her parents' home in Otley – and the emotional bonds are tight, which means a lot of warmth and laughter and some fierce arguments too. But they are also an intensely democratic family – everything is talked through thoroughly, family meetings are called and held round the dining table, everyone has their say, and somehow a consensus is hammered out, or whatever is being proposed just doesn't happen. 'There is no way that we would have volunteered to do this if everyone was not 100 per cent sure about it,' explained Lyn. And that meant Ben and Thomas too.

The boys signed up straightaway, even though it meant a new school 'for the duration' and sharing the house with their grandparents. Ben already loved to play 'Grampy's board games' from the 1940s, and he also harboured the dream of a real leather football with laces and everything. And Ben had already thought up a cunning scheme. If there was an Anderson shelter at the house – and from all Michael had told him he imagined that there would be – he could envisage family tensions erupting in that cramped space, so he was planning to put in a swear box and make his fortune. Thomas shared his brother's enthusiasm even though he was only seven: he hoped that it would mean that the grown-ups would have fewer distractions and there would be more 'quality time' when the whole family could sit down and play games or read to him.

After all the applications, interviews and discussions, Wall To Wall, the production company making the series for Channel 4, decided the Hymers family just had to be the one to move into the 1940s house. The family impressed everybody with their articulate enthusiasm for the period (shared in varying degrees of intensity, it has to be said), their well-thought-out reasons why they wanted to put themselves through the experience of wartime conditions, and their 'wicked' sense of humour. Director Caroline Ross Pirie and producer Simon Shaw took the train to Yorkshire to break the good news. Once the customary champagne bottles had been cracked open, Caroline and Simon set off back to London. And as the news sunk in, the Hymers began to think what it would really mean.

Lyn was concerned about leaving friends to whom she had become an emotional support, always there for a coffee or a glass of wine, or 'at the end of the phone day or night' to hear their problems, and she regretted that her other daughter Jodie and her husband could not move in too. Kirstie was concerned about the boys' schooling, and about leaving her close friend, Vicki. Michael had concerns about his work – how was he going to negotiate time off? He couldn't just down tools for two months. The boys wondered how it would be without television, video games, Pokémon cards, crisps, fizzy drinks, trainers – the list was endless. That reminded Lyn and Kirstie that they were both soap addicts – *Emmerdale* structured their day, and then there was *EastEnders* that couldn't be missed either. Lyn worried about the lack of face creams – she spent a fortune on those to ward off the wrinkles – and how was she going to manage her hair, which she hennaed a flame red? And what about shoes? She always wore flip-flops – smart ones for evening functions – and lived in leggings. Then there was Michael's beard – Lyn couldn't remember him without one. Michael didn't feel too happy about scratchy Izal toilet paper when they were all used to soft tissue.

Labelled for despatch.
Ben Hymers, age ten.

The overwhelming feeling was one of excited anticipation – even if this was shot through with anxiety – and the family went into training the very next day. Lyn got up early and made a cauldron of porridge 'which delighted the children. Poor things, they are so deprived of home cooking.' In the afternoon the whole family 'played 1940s band music, and had a very jolly time. Thomas played the spoon and cheese grater and Ben played a crisp drum.' It was Michael's birthday in a couple of days, so Lyn decided to spend £60 on a pathéscope to show Mickey Mouse films from the 1930s – they hung a pillow case from the mantelpiece to serve as a screen. Michael was learning the saxophone so he decided that he simply had to have a 1930s sax and his teacher promised to look out for one. 'We all hope he is unsuccessful,' confided Lyn.

Michael spent time rooting through the attic and came out with lots of 1930s books he'd bought over the years that the family might find helpful in the 1940s house – cookery books, and a *Daily Express* tome called *The Home of To-day: Its Choice, Planning, Equipment and Organisation* that he had picked up somewhere

for 50p. It was to prove an invaluable standby, a map to navigate the unknown terrain ahead. A grandly titled section on 'household management' included hints on 'home laundry work', 'marketing and purchasing' (rationing was going to blow that out of the window), a recipe section (which wasn't going to be much use in that respect either, with its Mrs Beeton-like call for half a lobster, four yolks of egg, half a pint of cream, a quarter of a pound of chocolate), and a 'home arts and crafts' section. But it also had irrelevant advice on 'servants, management of', 'geese, rearing of' – which no one was keen to try – a daunting section on 'children, training of' and suggestions for furnishing a smoking room that just made Lyn worry all over again about her 'ciggies'.

Both Lyn and Kirstie were heavy smokers – twenty-a-day addicts – and the prospect of cigarette shortages worried them considerably. But Kirstie could secretly see some benefit from the situation: cigarettes could become a new currency, she joked, giving her a hold over her mother. 'Do that, or let me have this, and I'll give you my cigarette allocation – or some of it.' Or maybe this would be the opportunity to give up altogether, though realistically both women doubted if the strains of wartime living were likely to be conducive to that particular sacrifice.

Lyn started to try out recipes from Marguerite Patten's re-creation of wartime recipes *We'll Eat Again*. The family watched a video that Michael had unearthed from his attic archive: the 1943 Lauder and Gilliat film *Millions Like Us*, all about another

Named and numbered.
Thomas Hymers, age seven.

family at war. They loved the frocks and hairstyles and giggled about the hats. Long before it was time to leave, the family found that they didn't want to watch television any more (at least the adults didn't) and that, amazingly for a family of keen football fans, 'We just couldn't get into the England v. Argentina match.'

On 7 March the Hymers had medical examinations at the University of Leeds, both to make sure that they were fit enough to undertake the experiment and also to monitor how they fared living on wartime rations. They were weighed, had their blood pressure taken, their cholesterol levels measured. Would it be proved true that, denied many rich foods, eggs, cream, butter, chocolate and other sweet things, and with limited meat supplies and less refined flour, people had been fitter in the war than either before or after?

Then it was a long train journey to London to be kitted up in 1940s outfits. Lyn was unhappy about the whalebone corsets ('no better than living in the 1900 house') and she wrote furiously in her diary: 'That bra is to me what lack of shampoo was to Joyce Bowler [in the 1900 house]. I hate it and it hurts. I DON'T WANT TO DO IT.'

During the eight weeks between knowing that they were to be the 1940s family and actually moving into the house, everyone was volatile as excitement for the project jostled with apprehension about how they would cope. Lyn's feelings alternated more than those of the rest of the family – or perhaps she just articulated them more. But she was enthusiastic again after watching another video, this time of John Boorman's semi-autobiographical film *Hope and Glory*, all about the war as seen from the perspective of a nine-year-old boy. She was soon tying her hair up 1940s-style in a turban scarf and waltzing through 'a little light housework' to the rhythm of Glenn Miller, Vera Lynn and 'the totally tuneless Gracie Fields', though her favourite was an early 30s number, 'Gather lip rouge while you may' – which she began to suspected might be prophetic: 'You'll never feel much younger,/Why not appease the hunger/ while you may./Let yourself be led astray/While you are still worth leading.' She also found herself gorging on 'huge quantities of things I know will be rationed – bacon, chocolate, anything greasy. I bought double cream, single cream, whipping cream and ice-cream. I didn't buy anything to put it on, so I'll probably bin it all in a few days – I just felt I needed to have it!'

The situation was not helped when Kirstie tripped over the piles of 1940s books Michael had brought out of the attic and fell down the stairs. Her mother took her to hospital where fortunately nothing was found to be broken, but Lyn felt guilty that concern for her daughter had come second to her first thought: 'We won't be able to do the 1940s house!' Then Ben had an accident at school and he was on crutches too for the family's final trip to London to get kitted up before moving in. 'We haven't even started our wartime experience, but with two of us already on crutches, we look as if we've been through the war already,' Lyn reflected.

The week before the Hymers left Otley for West Wickham in Kent, where the 1940s house was being equipped for their arrival, Lyn confided to her diary: 'I feel very emotional now our departure is drawing near. The small worries have gone – I no longer care about the hair, clothes or make-up. They seem incidental. I am worried about the people I am leaving behind and I have so much to do, finances to sort out, housework to do – big time.' (Lyn confessed to having twenty-seven unironed shirts in her laundry basket: 'I so hate ironing that when Michael needs a shirt, he goes out and buys a new one.') 'The pressure seems to be mounting. Michael seems to be slipping more and more into the 1940s – it's all he talks about. What if he wants to stay there forever?'

There was one concern that transcended all others and that was never to leave Lyn or any other member of the '1940s family'. That was their responsibility to the 'real' wartime experience. To the millions of people who had endured not just the hardships of war but its terrible dangers too – death, injury, loss of family and friends, of home and possessions, the ever-present fears and uncertainties, and the weariness and exhaustion. 'I felt scared,' wrote Lyn, 'very scared. And I think it's because the Second World War had such an enormous impact on so many people's lives and I would hate them to feel that we had trivialized their pain and suffering in any way.' She continued, 'We know that the war is still very emotive for many people. We all resolved to keep in mind at all times the fact that people in Britain died during the blitz and later raids and that whatever our deprivations will be, they will be small indeed by comparison. We want to do it to be a sort of tribute to the sufferings of the wartime families – even if we find that we can't cope at least we will be able to say of the war generations, "We admire you, you were bloody marvellous, and this is our tribute to you."'

Operation 1940: the television crew – cameraman Rob Goldie and sound recordist Steve Bowden – film the Hymers family's departure from Otley. And the neighbours turn out to watch.

CHAPTER 2

WAR BEGINS AT HOME

'We are the 1940s family,' chanted Ben and Thomas Hymers gleefully, looking like the Bisto kids, and the family all talked ceaselessly about 'when we move into the 1940s house'. But where was this house that was to provide the setting for living the home front experience, that had to be taken back in time, stripped of the accretions of more than half a century and put on a war footing?

It was not going to be a film set. It was to be an ordinary family house facing the extraordinary conditions of war: home to the five members of the Hymers family for nine weeks. The brief had been to find a house that had been built between the wars when an increasing number of families were buying their own homes rather than renting. It should be suitable for a middle-class family with a modest income where the father was a white-collar worker, working in a bank perhaps, an insurance agent, or maybe a local shopkeeper or an engineer like Michael Hymers. The mother would not usually work outside the home in peacetime, though when the children were older she might do some voluntary work. As there would be only one income, the family had to budget carefully and the house, though comfortable, was not a palace of excess.

The location was very important: an area had to be found where there had been interwar development and where the war had impacted significantly on the lives of its inhabitants. It was not to be a place that was devastated by the blitz, such as Coventry or the East End of London, but nor was it to be where bombers overhead were a rare occurrence.

'Our wartime home.' The front room at 17 Braemar Gardens, decorated and furnished by Lia Cramer. The moquette-covered golden-syrup tin footstool is in the foreground.

At the end of the First World War the Prime Minister, Lloyd George, had fought the election on the slogan promising 'homes fit for heroes' to a nation exhausted by five years of war. But it hadn't happened. The so-called 'Geddes Axe' had fallen in 1922 and the local authorities' programme of house building in the cities, the clearing away of malodorous slums and tenements, slowed down. But since interest rates had fallen after the financial crises of the late 1920s and early 1930s, local authorities and building societies were able to offer mortgages on favourable terms to would-be owner-occupiers who by 1939 accounted for around a third of all householders. Speculative builders cashed in on this increased demand for private housing, buying up vacant land and demolishing large houses that no one could afford to run any more, to build sprawling estates of desirable residences for sale, mainly on the fringes of towns and cities.

West Wickham in Kent fitted the profile perfectly. Today it's not very different from how it was in 1939. Of course, the shops have changed ownership, supermarkets have arrived, there's much more traffic and there are pockets of post-war development, but screw up your eyes to block out the cars parked bumper to bumper along the kerbs, and mountain bikes and skateboards tossed against hedges and fences, then the town still looks very much as it must have done in 1939. The curved streets run off the High Street, with their rows of mock Tudor, half-timbered, often pebbledashed houses, some still with mullioned leaded windows, most with neat square front gardens.

In the mid-eighteenth century Gilbert West, a poet, writer and friend of Lord Chatham (who frequently rode over from Hayes to visit him at Wickham Manor), was so inspired by this 'most pleasant and rural' village that he penned a paean to his West Wickham abode:

> Not wrapt in smoky London's sulphurous clouds,
> And not far distant, stands my rural cot;
> Neither obnoxious to intruding crowds,
> Nor for the good a friendly too remote.
>
> And when too much repose brings on the spleen,
> Or the gay city's idle pleasures cloy,
> Swift as my changing wish I change the scene,
> And now the country, now the town enjoy.

By the end of the First World War, West Wickham was still a rural Kentish village with a population of 1,300; by the late 1930s it had expanded to a bustling suburban town of 20,000 inhabitants. The High Street had been widened and new shops had been built to cater to the needs of the fast-growing population. There was a post office

providing an enviable seven-day-a-week delivery service – and open on weekdays from 8 a.m. to 7.30 p.m. A cinema, the Plaza, with an Art Deco foyer and rows of plush seats, was opened next to the post office in 1933; there were six pubs in the town, and in 1928 the clearing banks opened a branch in the High Street. This was the same year that main drainage supplanted cesspits in West Wickham and 'stinky Harry', the driver of the collection lorry, was put out of business.

Transport improved in the interwar years: West Wickham was on a bus route to nearby Croydon and buses ran into London too; when the railway was electrified in 1925, West Wickham became a place where those who needed to commute to 'town' could contemplate buying a house since 'the journey to London takes thirty minutes' and cost £1 14s for a monthly season ticket or 11d for a workman's (third class) day return.

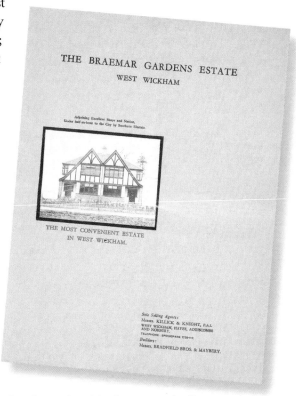

Brochure advertising houses on the Braemar Gardens Estate: 'the most convenient estate in West Wickham' in 1932.

Braemar Gardens was built in 1932 by the builders Bradfield Bros and Maybery, part of a residential development advertised as being 'unrivalled for convenience, being but a few minutes of excellent shops in the High Street and West Wickham Station, from whence the City is reached in under half an hour by a good service of Electric Trains. The entire estate is composed of gravel soil, and is within easy walking distance of such well known beauty spots as Wickham Woods, Hayes and Keston Common.' The houses were advertised as being 'progressive in design, solid in construction, and without parallel for real value. The deep timbered gables, and general aspect of these semi-detached houses give a pleasing air of dignity and real homeliness. Inside, close inspection will reveal how ingeniously they have been designed to lighten labour and increase comfort.'

No. 17 Braemar Gardens was offered for sale at £875 freehold. A 90 per cent mortgage could be arranged, which would mean repayments of about £1 3s 7d a week spread over twenty-one years. Rates and water rates would add 5s 6d a week, and it was expected that the houses would be purchased by a 'black-coated worker' (or what we today would call – increasingly misleadingly – a white-collar worker):

a clerk, minor civil servant (indeed, the brochure produced about the Braemar Estate promised that 'special terms' were available for civil servants) or a shop manager, and also that a scattering of the 'artisan class' (manual labourers or factory workers) might aspire to own a house there too.

During the war 17 Braemar Gardens was left empty, as were a number of houses in the road. Its owners may have left West Wickham either for a place of greater safety or to follow work that was relocated for the same reason; or perhaps they had been obliged to take up essential war work in some other part of the country. The empty house was then requisitioned by the local authority, probably as housing for bombed-out Londoners; during part of that time it was occupied by an elderly couple, Mr and Mrs Dixon. Albert Dixon, who died in April 1944, was a retired clerk. But in 1999, 17 Braemar Gardens was on the market again, this time for £187,000.

West Wickham had already been identified as an ideal area, but what about the house? To the delight of the production team and particularly of Lia Cramer, the art director who was charged with recreating the 1940s house, No. 17 was structurally much as it would have been when it was built – and when war broke out in 1939. Unlike some of the houses in the street, it had no added conservatory or loft extension, and still had its original 'diamond leaded glazed windows with opening top lights' as the original sales material for Braemar Gardens specified. Nor had any major structural changes been carried out, no knock-throughs to make a single room from the separate dining and sitting rooms, no modern kitchen extension, no bathroom makeover with power shower added; even the original stained-glass panels were still intact in the front door and in the stair window. A fitted kitchen had been installed and the original French windows leading from the dining room into the garden had been replaced by a modern, double-glazed door; there were fitted carpets throughout, and the decoration was distinctly in the 1980s vernacular rather than 1930s. But apart from that, the house had all the necessary potential for the role it was going to be called upon to play.

'It was fantastic,' recalls Lia Cramer. 'It was the perfect street, a curve of houses all looking the same, and there was even the twitch of net curtains as we rolled up to start demodernizing.

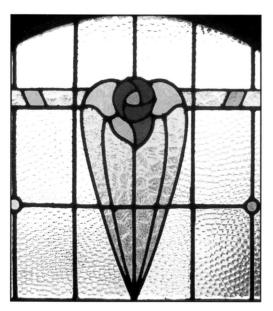

No. 17 still retained many of its original features – including the stained-glass panel in the front door.

We started by getting the builders to rip out everything post-war – fireplaces were opened up if they had been blocked up in the onward march of the radiator and carpets were pulled up.' There was a patio, very much a 1970s feature, an idea brought back from all those al fresco meals people were enjoying on 'continental holidays' that were beyond the imagination of the ordinary family to whom the 1940s Braemar Gardens was going to be home. This had to go, and anyway there were plans for the garden. 'We had a stroke of luck,' said Lia, 'when we found that the original French windows had been used to build the shed, so we were able to put those back.'

Some astute detective work by Lia located a section of original lino laid at another address in Braemar Gardens when the houses were built and the prize was carefully carried back to No. 17 – where it crumbled as soon as the builders tried to lay it. So Lia had to use a reproduction lino on the kitchen and bathroom floors; in the rest of the house, rugs were laid on stained wood.

Once the house had been returned to how it would had been when it was first built in 1932, Lia set about decorating it. There was considerable interest in interior decorating in the 1920s and 30s among those who had moved out of rented accommodation and for the first time had their very own homes to decorate as they wanted, rather than having to put up with a landlord's taste. Two magazines still on sale today, *Homes and Gardens* (founded 1919) and *Ideal Home* (1920), featured 'real-life' interiors showing how more affluent families were decorating their newly built suburban houses – a lifestyle statement to aspire to in West Wickham as in Edmonton, Southgate or Sydenham.

For Lia, 'The most important thing was to get the paint colour right. That was the background and everything else would be determined by that.' She consulted a range of the magazines of the period, looked at estate agents' selling brochures, catalogues, postcards and any other illustrations she could find of the exterior and interior of similar houses to 17 Braemar Gardens, and was surprised how bright the colours were. 'I'd always thought that pre-war colours were rather drab, but that was far from the case – though of course with coal fires everywhere, the grit and dust they generated tended to militate against too pale or pastel colours.' She then went to the Victoria and Albert Museum in London's South Kensington – which is, after all, a 'museum of the decorative arts' – and looked at their paint samples for the period. Houses in the 1930s were generally decorated with what was usually called distemper, though this covered a multitude of different paints. These ranged from a chalk and water mix often used on ceilings, to oil-based paints not dissimilar to our modern-day emulsion, which often used rabbit glue or something similar to bind it together. Such paint is not generally available any more, so Lia needed to match the V&A colours with modern-day equivalents.

The 'back reception room' which the Hymers family used as their
dining room – returned to 1940s style.

'Once I found the green that we used for the outside woodwork and the front gate and the brown we used on quite a lot of the interior woodwork, everything else fell in place,' said Lia. 'It was very much the fashion to have different colours in every room rather than the white on white so many people seem to want today, and again I had some good luck.' Careful scraping revealed a palimpsest of the past, fragments of paint and wallpaper coming to light in some of the rooms. 'There was blue in the front bedroom, a fragment of green in the boys' bedroom and pink in the small front bedroom which would be where Kirstie would sleep, so that's what I went with.'

The dining room was green too, and the living room was hung with oatmeal-coloured wallpaper. Lia had the kitchen, bathroom and loo painted in the appropriate cream and eau-de-nil oil-based paints of the period. 'The fact that the original black-and-white tile borders were still in place in the kitchen and bathroom helped make it look authentic straightaway,' she said. 'And then I had a real find – rolls of soft green and brown wallpaper with what were called "autumn tints", swirly "Jacobean" patterns, which was absolutely right for the house, so I had that in the hall and landing and spent a wonderful time choosing wallpaper borders for the dining room and the living room. Trevor Howsam has a huge collection of 1930s wallpaper

borders in his warehouse in Boston in Lincolnshire and, once these had been stuck on as geometric framing, the house really began to say "1930s" and it was time to start furnishing and equipping it.'

Though the action was going to take place in the 1940s, the house would have been decorated in 1930s style, as Lia explained. 'When the original owners moved in they might have brought some stuff with them, and probably acquired some new furniture then. So it's how they would have lived through the 1940s – into the 50s actually.'

During the war it became increasingly difficult to buy new furniture as production was restricted and demand rose with losses in the heavy bombing raids of 1940–1. Shipping space for imported timber was strictly limited by the demands of war: ships ploughed across the Atlantic with material for war production or with cargoes of food for a hungry population that had imported a very high proportion of their food before the war. Britain depended on these maritime trade routes for vital supplies from all over the world, and shipping was at risk from German U-boats in the 'Battle of the Atlantic' submarine warfare that peaked between 1941 and 1943. There were the same restrictions for home-grown wood too: increasingly timber was required for service personnel's wartime accommodation, to make hundreds of thousands of bunks for air raid shelters, to build Bailey bridges and dozens more urgent wartime requirements. Plywood, the staple wood used for inexpensive furniture, was withdrawn in January 1941 since it was extensively used in aircraft production. Manufacture of new furniture gradually ground to a halt as firms used up their pre-war stocks of timber and were unable to obtain any more. Prices of second-hand goods soared and, if you already had the necessary furniture, this was not the time to think of replacing it.

It was a hard problem to solve: rationing, the solution for an equitable distribution of food and clothes, would not work for furniture. It wasn't as if everybody wanted to buy one table and two chairs every year and a bed every other year, say. If you had been bombed out, you would need to replace a whole houseful of furniture, whereas if you had had a home for several years, you could probably go without acquiring any more for some time. So rationing wasn't a practical option. In any case, who was going to make the furniture? Not only was timber required elsewhere – so were carpenters. Only men over forty and women were

Washing without an Acme is like cooking without a stove

The makers deeply regret the enforced shortage of Acme Wringers due to wartime restrictions. Many of our regular Dealers are at present without supplies but, when conditions allow, immediate steps will be taken to replace used-up stocks.

WRINGER — MANGLE — CLEANSER — ALL IN ONE!

12

allowed to work in the furniture industry from 1941; younger men were liable to be conscripted or drafted into other jobs considered vital to the war effort. Something had to be done to regulate the situation and the government considered an number of options – price controls, quota allocations and, for the first time, the introduction of purchase tax – before eventually introducing the utility scheme at the beginning of 1943.

This scheme prescribed not just the supply but the design too: what furniture could be made and to what specifications. It was stamped CC41 (originally meaning Civilian Clothing 1941 – the year the mark was introduced). Only twenty items of essential furniture could be produced; as Monica Felton described in *British Achievements of the War Years*, gone were 'such comfortable pieces of furniture as deep-sprung armchairs and the conventional three-piece suite of two armchairs and a settee – a sacrifice made necessary by the shortage of springs and other materials needed for upholstery'. The design was specified in a booklet produced by the Board of Trade with the help of 'one or two of the best available designers of furniture' including the distinguished Gordon Russell, who considered that 'to raise the whole standard of furniture for the mass of the people was not a bad war job'. The furniture was very plain and thus simple and quick to make – no unnecessary ornamentation at all was allowed, and though it looks refreshingly minimalist to our modern eyes, to the people of wartime Britain it looked rather drab and basic with no barley-turned legs or Grinling Gibbons-like swags. So much so that some keen do-it-yourselfers would get out their chisels and carve scrolls, half circles and other decorations in the wood.

A Utility Furniture exhibition was held in London October 1942, attracting over 30,000 visitors. It subsequently toured the country, showing people what they could expect. Though the *Architect's Journal* sneered that the furniture 'was very ugly to look at', the general public was more interested in its availability than anything else, and it was generally conceded that utility furniture was of good quality. Indeed, pieces are still be found in homes today, so well made was it. The Ministry of Information was particularly pleased with the introduction of utility furniture: 'There is no doubt that the success of the scheme has been remarkable, both in effecting big savings in labour, and in ensuring a distribution which is widely applauded for its fairness. More surprising is the fact that, as with utility clothing, the need for economy has been turned to definite and positive advantage by designers, and that there has been a real, and no doubt permanent, rise in the standard of public taste.' It instanced 'a table based on the design of an eighteenth-century card table, with a top which swings round and opens to double its original width, disclosing a sizeable storage space underneath for knives and forks, table linen and mats. There is an easy chair which unfolds into a single bed and which is

taken from a design originally produced by William Morris, one of the most remarkable of all English designers of furniture, at the end of the last century; and one of the chairs is a modification of the Windsor chair, which has been at home in British kitchens for many hundreds of years.'

But even utility furniture was available only to 'priority classes' with a permit and these were given only to people who had been bombed out or newlyweds setting up in their own homes, though there were a few concessions for those who had to move in with parents. Each item of furniture needed a certain number of units in addition to the purchase price (which was controlled by government) – a wardrobe took eight units, for example, and a kitchen chair one. Bed settees were available for fifteen units to those who lived in bedsitters, but to nobody else! No permit was needed for cots, playpens or high chairs, and towards the end of the war, those entitled to furniture were also allowed to obtain curtain material, which until then had meant the surrender of precious clothes coupons. In the first month after the scheme came into operation in January 1943, 18,500 'furniture permits' had been issued to those who were eligible.

'Kitchenette... conveniently arranged.' Lia's recreation
of the kitchen as it had been described in 1932.

1940s HOUSE

So the Hymers family was going to live in a house furnished not with utility furniture but the more bulky, decorative pieces of the pre-war years, and that is what Lia set out to source. First of all she needed to find the fixtures and fittings. A deep ceramic Belfast sink and wooden draining board for the kitchen, metal light switches with a bronze finish rather than plastic (and the house had originally been advertised as having '12 electric lighting points, 2 power points, switches, ceiling roses and pendants included in the price'), tiled fireplaces to replace those that had been removed, taps that were appropriate both to the period and the income of the family – as everything had to be. Again it was back to poring over archives of trade catalogues in the V&A, and here Lia found the Ideal Home exhibition catalogues from the 1930s particularly useful.

Then it was time to go on the road: the family was due to move in April so, in the cold, dark mornings of January and February, Lia and her assistant Nick travelled the country tracking down what would be needed to sustain the Hymers family during their 'war years'. She found the appropriate tiled fireplaces in Norfolk. In the Caledonian Road in London's Islington she unearthed the 1930s gas stove with its

The 'front reception' room. 'It was just perfect. Just how we imagined it only better' was the Hymers' verdict on the decoration and furniture in the 1940s house.

four legs and tiny oven that Lyn and Kirstie would have to bend down to peer into as they cooked casseroles and baked cakes. The coke-burning boiler that she snapped up for heating the water for the house came from Surrey. 'Even though it wasn't the easiest thing to light and it kept going out until the family got the hang of it, that boiler became the real heart of the home,' reported Lia. 'They kept food warm on the top and huddled round it to keep warm themselves.'

Having decorated, furnished and equipped the 1900 house, Lia noticed a difference. 'The stuff for the 1940s house was cheaper – it doesn't command the same collector's kudos, or prices, as Victorian furniture, but on the other hand because it's less valuable, there seems to be less of it around. People seem to dispose of things rather than selling them. That was a real problem when it came to rugs. They obviously wore out and people simply threw them out.' And generally 1930s furniture – at least that which would have been affordable to a family living in Braemar Gardens – was not of very high quality; most of it was machine-made, and veneered or lacquered so that quite cheap, insubstantial soft wood was used and not a great deal has survived.

There had been a reaction against Victorian and Edwardian 'clutter' and a 1930s manual recommended 'drawing rooms and sitting rooms are for amusement and comfort, and furniture should be well made, graceful and strong. Overcrowding is bad in taste, and too many ornaments and pictures provide a distracting and muddled effect.' So bearing this stricture in mind Lia started with the big things – beds, a sofa, a dining room table and chairs, wardrobes, dressing tables, chest of drawers, a kitchen cabinet – many of which she found in a huge antique and junk fair held on an ex-RAF airfield in Lincolnshire. 'We arrived before dawn,' she recalled, 'and had to find our way with torches, but we found some fantastic things. A wonderful "imitation vellum" chinoiserie-inspired standard lamp with tassels, for example, a cloverleaf-shaped footstool which was made out of golden syrup tins covered in cut moquette, dressing tables, a bakelite radio set… All sorts of things.'

Once the furniture was acquired, Lia started to equip the 1940s house with the things the family would use: the kitchen presented a particular problem. 'I looked at lots of cookery books to see what people would have used in the kitchen and talked to Marguerite Patten, the food expert who had worked for the Ministry of Food during the war, is an authority on wartime cooking and was advising the programme team about recipes for the family's meals. Then it was a question of balancing what a family would have really had in their kitchen in 1940 and what the Health and Safety experts would allow now. But I managed to get most of what I needed – pie dishes, pastry brushes, saucepans, Pyrex casseroles.' There wouldn't have been a fridge as only about 25 per cent of families had one in 1939; fresh food was kept in a cool larder. Adds Lia, 'I had to buy things like muslin jug and basin covers to keep

No television, no video, no computer games. Amusements for Ben and Thomas, 1940s style.

the food protected from flies in the larder – they were fringed with beads so the weight kept them from slipping off. Kitchen scales were a particular problem. I just had to get accurate ones. When food rationing was at its most stringent in 1942, and you would only have had two ounces of butter for each person to last a week, you can see how vital it was to be able to measure everything with complete accuracy. None of this guesstimating that we do when we cook today, a handful of this, and a slurp of that. You would have got through your rations in a single sitting!'

Lia was also fortunate that her grandfather, who had been a wartime illustrator for the Ministry of Information, had meticulous habits and kept a complete inventory of all the possessions that he had had in his South London home, which was very similar in size and scale to 17 Braemar Gardens. 'It was invaluable to me in working out what I should get for the Hymers family.'

It was not only dealers that Lia used to fit out the house: a number of private individuals responded to her request for household effects. 'It is absolutely amazing what people keep. I bought stuff from a lady in Cardiff who had all sorts of things – tablecloths, torches, handkerchiefs, letters and postcards, jigsaw puzzles, children's toys, a Winston Churchill commemorative handkerchief which had been sold to raise money for the war effort. And another woman who lives in Reading was able to let me have some wonderful 30s carpets, dressmaking paper patterns and knitting patterns, and she bottled fruit in kilner jars for the house too. All these things make such a difference. They really are about how people lived on a day-to-day basis.'

Books presented few problems: Lia had quite a collection herself and West Wickham is endowed with a very well-stocked second-hand bookshop where Lia was able to buy the sort of books she knew the Hymers would need. There were cookery books, books with household advice, and a few volumes of patriotic history.

'I felt that I had a responsibility to keep the Hymers entertained in the evening too with no television,' Lia pointed out, 'so I made sure that there were some stirring stories of Empire and adventure books and some thrillers and of course books to read aloud to the boys. And several board games – lotto, snakes and ladders, Monopoly for later in the war, and card games as well. Of course, Thomas is only seven and Ben is ten so they needed toys to play with. That presented another problem since a number of toys that children would have played with in 1940 are considered too dangerous now – flammable material or sharp edges, lead paint, that sort of thing. And children's toys of the period are collectibles and have become prohibitively expensive. I blew quite a chunk of my budget on some Brittains lead toy soldiers – I felt that if the boys were going to live through a wartime experience, they had to have some soldiers and a fort, and I bought two tiny – expensive – model Spitfires for the same reason. Then there was a leather football for Ben and we had to find a teddy bear for Thomas so that he wouldn't miss the one he was having to leave at home. Unfortunately Dinky cars are now such a collector's item that they were out of the question. I desperately wanted to get a Hornby train set for the boys and fortunately part way through their stay a West Wickham resident generously presented one to the boys at a beetle drive the family went to, so they could play with that while they were here, which was great for them.'

The house was finally ready in every detail, down to the 1930s teaset 'for best' in the glass-fronted cabinet in the living room; a walnut-cased clock on the mantelpiece with a bevelled mirror hung above; a crewel-embroidered fire screen in the hearth; a sewing kit stowed in an empty Meltis Newberry Fruits box in the dining room; down-and-feather-filled, satin-covered eiderdowns on the beds; brushes, combs, face creams, powder, cut-glass bowls for cotton wool and dishes for kirby grips on the dressing tables; a cut-throat razor and a badger-hair shaving brush for Michael in the bathroom; a Margaret Tarrant picture on the wall in the boys' room; a clothes mangle stowed in the garage. It was time to open the newly acquired, green-painted sunburst gates to the other residents of Braemar Gardens and hear their verdict on the 1940s house in their midst before the Hymers family moved in.

They approved wholeheartedly – but they didn't envy the family. 'It's going to be hard work,' said most of the women sagely. But the greatest compliment to Lia's painstaking research and magpie foraging came some weeks later when Lyn invited an elderly man she had met in the course of her 'war work' to the house. 'When he came into the sitting room, he just broke down,' she recalled. '"You'll have to excuse me," he said. "It is all just so right. I came here expecting to do what old codgers do and say, oh this isn't right, you've got that all wrong, but it's perfect." When I'd finished my tour of the house, he said, "To all intents and purposes, this is my mother's house. It's exactly how it was in the war, every little detail, it's all there." And he was so moved that tears kept rolling down his cheeks.'

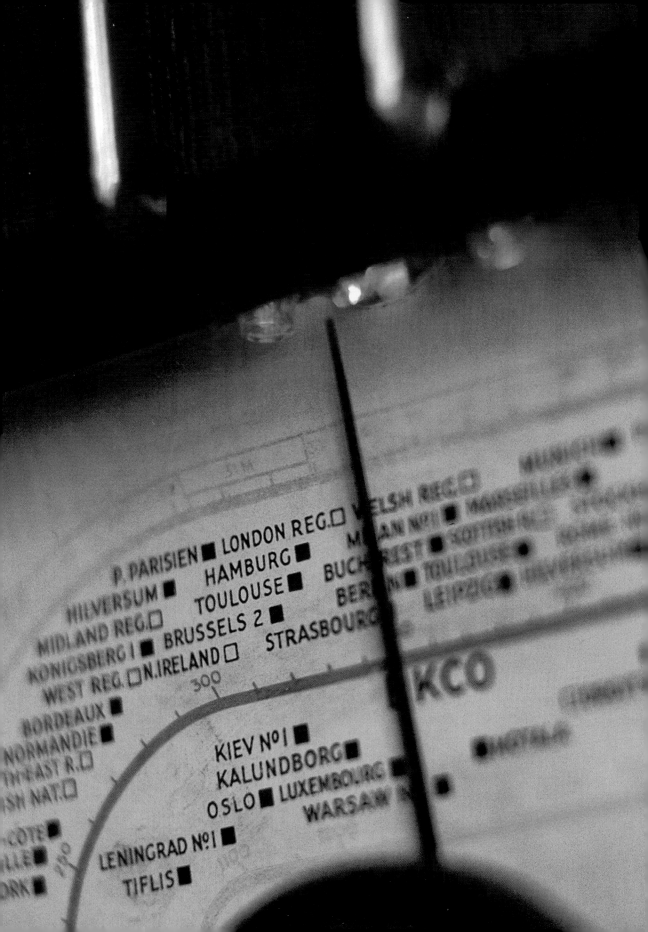

CHAPTER 3

'THIS COUNTRY IS AT WAR…'

'This morning the British Ambassador in Berlin handed the German government a final note stating that unless we heard from them by eleven o'clock that they were prepared at once to withdraw their troops from Poland a state of war would exist between us. I have to tell you now that no such undertaking has been received, and that consequently this country is at war with Germany.'

The first thing the Hymers did when the 'old-fashioned taxi' pulled up outside 17 Braemar Gardens, West Wickham, on Sunday 16 April 2000 and they got out, all dressed in 1940s clothes, was go into the front room and turn on the bakelite wireless. They listened to a recording of the clipped voice of the then Prime Minister, Neville Chamberlain, as he broadcast to the nation from the Cabinet Room at No. 10 Downing Street at 11.15 in the morning of Sunday 3 September 1939.

'I've heard it many times before,' Lyn said. 'Michael's got a recording at home, and it never fails to make me cry. But listening to it here in the 1940s house, I found it terribly moving. I kept thinking what it would have meant to the people who heard it in 1939. How anxious and uncertain they must have felt about what lay ahead. Many of the people listening would have later been killed or injured or lost loved ones. It's almost beyond the comprehension of a 2000 family. It was a very powerful moment.'

The announcement of war was for Chamberlain 'a bitter blow… that all my long struggle to win peace has failed'. A year before, on 30 September 1938, he had returned from meeting Hitler in Munich willing to be convinced that the German leader had

The bakelite wireless on which the Hymers heard Chamberlain's (above) broadcast to the nation.

1940s
HOUSE

no further territorial demands in Europe. His annexation of the Sudetenland, the *Anschluss* with Austria (the German annexation in March 1938) and his invasion of Czechoslovakia were the limit of his ambition to right what he saw as the wrongs of the Versailles Treaty, which in 1919 had pushed back the frontiers of Germany after its defeat in the First World War, and achieve *Lebensraum* (living space) for the German Reich. Standing at the foot of the steps of the plane at Heston aerodrome,

A reminder of the First World War as the nation prepares for the Second.

Chamberlain had assured his fellow countrymen and women: 'It's peace for our time… I advise you to go home to bed.'

But no one had been able to feel very reassured when it was obvious that, despite the talk of peace and an uneasy acceptance that 'selling the Czechs down the river' was a price worth paying for it, Britain was in fact preparing for war. 'How horrible, fantastic, incredible it is,' Chamberlain recorded in September 1938, 'that we should be digging trenches and trying on gas masks here because of a quarrel in a faraway country between people of whom we know nothing.'

In West Wickham a playing field and recreation ground were ploughed up and it was the same all over the country. Herbert Morrison, MP, who was the leader of the London County Council, ordered that trenches were to be dug on all LCC housing estates, and women residents pitched in with spades and shovels alongside the men. Even London's Hyde Park, home to the Great Exhibition in 1851, was scarred with 30- to 40-foot-long slits. At first the trenches were dug arrow straight, until the eminent scientist J. B. S. Haldane pointed out that this made them potential death traps – if even a small bomb landed at one end, the explosion would kill every single occupant. After this the trenches were constructed on a zigzag pattern (as they had been in Flanders during the First World War).

Although local authorities in heavily populated areas had been instructed by the Home Office to build sufficient trenches to accommodate 10 per cent of the population in their area, presumably, for those caught out of doors during a gas

attack or when an air-raid warning sounded, they never seemed to gain the public's confidence. Night-watchmen were posted to stop people falling in and in October a North London newspaper reported: 'Trenches for 100,000 people finished… and no one knows what they are for.' By the end of the year many of the trenches were filling up with water, and the earth banks were crumbling in.

Numerous brick shelters were built, but these were not popular: people only really felt safe underground. Cellars and basements were requisitioned and the Home Office ordered a survey of public buildings that could be adapted for bomb shelters; sandbags were issued and the authorities began to consider the full cost implications of providing their citizens with adequate protection from high-explosive bombs and incendiary devices dropped from the air. The West Wickham Labour Party was not sanguine when it met in March 1938, its members convinced that 'any future war would finish civilization as we knew it. It was impossible to defend oneself against air raids except at tremendous cost.' Meanwhile the local Peace Pledge Union refused to participate in 'preparations which they believe will hasten the destruction they are alleged to prevent'.

For hundreds of thousands of people, the spectre of war was one not of fearful speculation: it was still an all too recent memory. The guns had fallen silent on the Western Front just over twenty years before. And already it was predicted that this time would be much worse. Chamberlain's predecessor, Stanley Baldwin, speaking in 1935, had prophesied, 'There is one thing which differentiates modern war… and that is the increase in the horror of war, and the tacit assumption on the part of all nations that the civil community will no longer be immune from the horrors of warfare as they have been since the barbarous ages.'

In the 'war to end all wars', Britain had been strafed by zeppelins and later by twin-engined bombers. There had been no shelters at first and terrified Londoners had dived into Underground stations for safety. The total numbers of civilians killed in some 100 bombing raids in the First World War was just under 1,500. In the run-up to the Second World War the experts calculated – thankfully inaccurately as it turned out – that each ton of high explosives dropped would cause some fifty casualties, killed or seriously wounded. By these calculations, the 'knock-out blow' (which, it was anticipated, was what Hitler planned) would mean that 66,000 citizens would be killed in the first week of the war and another 134,000 would be seriously injured. And Pathé news footage of the civil war in Spain and the Italian invasion of Abyssinia, shown nightly in cinemas, graphically revealed how civilians were terrorized by the incessant air raids that were now a feature of modern warfare.

Chamberlain's broadcast made a tremendous impact. People were moved to record their reactions, such as one young Lancashire man: 'WAR! We couldn't believe it, though it seemed likely. Everything seemed more unreal; the wireless giving special announcements about the air raids and the closing of cinemas but the sun was still

Shops, offices and public buildings were sandbagged against bomb blast damage.

shining, and everything seemed so usual. I felt as though there should be *something obviously different* – bad storms or something like that.' A middle-aged teacher in a rural community 'held my head up high and kept back the tears at the thought of all that slaughter ahead. When "God Save the King" was played we stood.'

It seemed as if hostilities had started at once: as Chamberlain finished speaking, the air-raid sirens wailed, and ARP wardens wearing placards warning of a raid cycled round the streets, blowing whistles as they had been trained to do.

At 11.27 a.m., when the banshee wail of the siren rent the air, choral Eucharist was being celebrated at St Francis's Church just round the corner from Braemar Gardens. The congregation had remained in their pews as the choir boys filed into the cellar beneath the church, and from other churches in West Wickham worshippers instinctively hurried home. Once there, they would either stand foolhardily by the gates scanning the skies or, more practically, hurry to fill up baths with water in case of incendiary bombs, or nail blankets over their windows in case of gas attacks, as they had been instructed to do.

Most people seemed to think that this first air-raid warning of the war on that perfect, cloudless Sunday morning 'was a joke or some kind of hoax'. In fact it was the first phoney alert of what was to prove a phoney war – for a time. An unidentified aircraft had set the country at action stations. It turned out to be a French transport plane bringing a party of staff officers to London, though this was not revealed to the public for some time, nor was the fact that a technical hitch, which had reversed the normal radar images, had sent two squadrons of British fighter planes into the air to

engage in battle with each other over the Thames estuary. During the 'Battle of Barking Creek' two Hurricanes were shot down by Spitfires, and a Blenheim by the anti-aircraft batteries; one pilot was killed.

All that day volunteers were busy sandbagging buildings. An appeal went out from the matron of the Children's Heart Hospital in West Wickham for volunteers to fill the 30,000 sandbags needed to protect the building, and the local firemen responded, working all day in the warm sun to get the job under way. Barrage balloons were winched into the air. Walking in Battersea Park, in London, the artist Frances Faviell watched as 'Flossie and Blossom', Chelsea's two balloons, went up 'slowly and awkwardly like drunken fish'. And looking up the Thames towards Westminster, she counted 'over eighty members of this glittering silver barrage intended to protect us from low-flying enemy planes. But the scene was so peaceful, the gardens in the park so lovely, and the people walking by the river so unperturbed and ordinary with their perambulators and dogs, that it was impossible to realize that these silver roach in the sky were there because we were at war. War seemed too archaic and remote a word to contemplate.'

Thomas, carrying his gas-mask case, outside the sandbagged church hall in West Wickham.

1940s
HOUSE

That Sunday in April 2000 six decades later, the Hymers family were at the start of their 'wartime experience' that would take them from the outbreak of war in 1939 to VE day on 8 May 1945 – in nine weeks. As he had shut the door of their Victorian terraced house in Otley, Michael realized, 'This was it now. I couldn't turn back, there were too many people involved and the wheels had been set in motion, here we go for better or worse. I am generally looking forward to it, but I have some concerns about what lies ahead.'

It would be an experiment in trying to distil the essential features of the 'home front' into living history, to see how they would cope as a wartime family would have had to do with the privations and restrictions of war. How a modern family accustomed to takeaway curries and convenience foods, to throwing things away when they broke or were worn out – or they were just tired of them – to having a bottle of wine in the evening, crisps and sweets for the children, chocolate and cream cakes for Lyn, an endless supply of cigarettes for her and Kirstie, would manage as rationing tightened its grip. How would the years of the choices that come with affluence equip them for living in a 1940s house where there were few conveniences?

'It was separate beds for the duration'. Lyn and Michael's bedroom.

The Hymers already knew that the demands of war would make life progressively harder. How well would they be able to think themselves back into the war years? Would they develop the fortitude and ingenuity required to 'make do' on all fronts and deal with whatever surprises were in store? What might they learn from the experience? Would it give them new insights into what the Second World War generations had lived through, since neither Michael nor Lyn had been born until a few years after the end of the war? Would the experience change them? Would their weeks in the 1940s house bring this close and feisty family even closer together? Or would the strain lead to conflict?

The first practical thing to do was to explore their new home. Everyone was pleased with how bright it was. Michael, who has got 'lots of books with pictures of 30s semis in them' thoroughly approved of the decor, and Lyn and Kirstie thought it was 'beautiful'. For Lyn, 'The house exactly recreates how I imagine living in the 1940s to be, sitting in the living room in the evening, listening to the wireless, all the furniture, the decor, the things that we are going to use, our clothes. They really make me feel part of the 1940s already.'

Indeed, Lyn was all for ringing up the estate agent in Otley and putting their Victorian terraced house on the market and moving back in time permanently. She was, however, a little nonplussed to find that for the first time in their married life she and Michael were to sleep in single beds. Lia had explained that was a very fashionable furnishing conceit for the 1930s, influenced by Hollywood movies and evidence that a family could afford two beds and sets of bedding rather than one. Lyn grew pragmatic: it would lessen the impact of Michael's snoring, and with her 1940s curlers and kirby grips she wondered how seductive she would be – particularly as Michael had already pointed out how much older she looked in her 1940s clothes, with her 1940s haircut and make-up. 'No one is going to fancy their mother, are they?' insisted Lyn. And as Ben pointed out, 'Grampy and Granny can always push their beds together if they want to.'

Lyn and Kirstie were stoical about the kitchen: they had not expected a dishwasher, of course, or a fridge – but there was a reasonably capacious larder. Lyn was curious to see how effective it would prove at keeping food fresh, though she had realized some time ago that there were no out-of-town supermarkets for a weekly shop; in the wartime 1940s women shopped daily for their family meals. Lyn's heart did sink, though, when she realized what hard work washday for a family of five was going to be without a washing machine, or the possibility of a high-street launderette. Just the primitive electric boiler to heat the water up in, the dolly stick to agitate the clothes, and the mangle in the garage.

There were to be a couple of disappointments that first day: there were no gas masks, and no Anderson shelter. And there were the rabbits… The boys had been

thrilled when they discovered that while there might not be chickens or a neighbourhood pig being bred for bacon in the back garden, there was a rabbit. In fact there were five and one was very evidently pregnant. Ben and Thomas were delighted, and saw them as furry pets provided for them to play with, but Lyn realized straightaway why they were there. 'It's a rabbit-breeding station. These rabbits are being reared for the table. Talk about pets – we are expected to eat these animals!' (And make fur gloves and warm cravats from their skins.) The twenty-first-century sensibilities of Lyn and Kirstie were immediately roused: 'There is no way that we can make rabbit pie of animals we will grow fond of. And it will be traumatic for the boys. They just don't realize.'

In true Hymers fashion, a round-table conference was called of the adults, who decided that the rabbits would have to go. As Michael said: 'There's all the difference between going to the butcher's and buying a ready-skinned, ready-to-eat rabbit, and actually seeing one running round its pen and feeding it for eight to twelve weeks and then knocking it on the head and eating it.'

At first there was talk of taking the rabbits out into the countryside on a bus and letting them go in the wild, but would they survive? Finally it was agreed that they would have to be taken back to the West Wickham pet shop where they had been bought. Which is what happened, though Thomas was only consoled for the loss of his pets when his grandmother took him into the local butcher's the next day to show him dead rabbits hanging up, and pointed out that this would have been the destiny of 'Old Speckled' and 'Old Easter', as the boys had christened their 'pets', and their offspring. It would remain to be seen, as the war progressed and meat went on ration, whether the Hymers would think wistfully about the rabbit pie they had so humanely forsworn.

Michael was 'very disappointed' not to find an Anderson shelter in the garden. It had long been an ambition of his to have one of these corrugated iron shelters that would have served to protect the family in the event of an air raid. 'If we haven't got an Anderson shelter,' he decreed, 'we must decide which room we are going to use as an air-raid refuge.' Articles had started appearing in the newspapers after the Munich crisis pointing out that it was 'up to householders to take steps to ensure that their home is as safe as it can be should war break out and enemy aeroplanes zoom overhead'. The *Daily Mail* invented an imaginary family, the 'Carringtons', who sounded as if they lived in a house much like 17 Braemar Gardens – 'a trim semi-detached house with a brick-built garage of which they are very proud' – and advised 'Mr Carrington' to take stock of his home and think which would make the best refuge-room. Upstairs rooms were 'ruled out. They do not give sufficient protection against small incendiary bombs, which will cause a lot of trouble.' The 'room you call the breakfast room' was suggested: 'It is 10 feet by 10 feet and so will hold five people

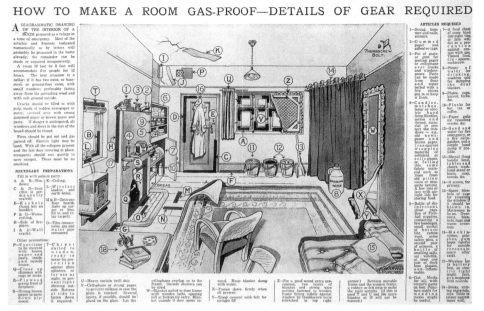

The pervasive enemy. The *Daily Telegraph* 17 March 1938 advises
readers about protecting a room against a poison-gas attack.

for a continuous period of twelve hours without ventilation. This is most important.
Although an air raid may be over in a few minutes, it might be necessary to stay in
your refuge-room for some time until any danger of a gas attack is over.'

So the choice of a refuge-room became an agenda item for family discussion.
With no cellar or basement, the recommended place, Michael favoured the dining
room (which was of similar dimensions to the more affluent Carringtons' breakfast
room): it was at the back of the house and 'a room facing the garden' was
recommended 'because the soft earth may allow the bomb to go in deep before
exploding and thus reduce the risk from the bomb's splinters'. It was already provided
with a table that could be jammed up against the wall for the family to squash under
for some minimal protection. But Lyn and Kirstie were reluctant to see the dining
room, which they thought was a particularly pretty room, with the furniture
disarranged, pictures taken down and probably a heavy rug or carpet hung over the
French windows and the door in case of a gas attack. They suggested that maybe
the family could shelter under the stairs, but there was not enough space there, nor
in the chimney breast as was possible in some houses.

Lyn and Kirstie opted for the garage. But would that be strong enough to withstand
a bomb blast? Perhaps, as Michael suggested, in 1939 several neighbours would have
got together, identified a suitable outhouse and strengthened and equipped that to
accommodate several families. Or maybe there had been a public shelter in West
Wickham? (In fact several had been built by 1939, and their whereabouts and capacity

were regularly advertised in the local press. There was a surface shelter that could accommodate 100 on the site of Yew Tree Cottage, which had been demolished to construct Glebe Way that ran through the North Downs.) But that was hardly an appealing prospect, dragging the family round the streets in the middle of the night to share an above-ground shelter that might not have been built to the proper specifications with a double-cavity wall, in which case it provided little protection.

The situation was at stalemate.

Hitler will send no warning – so always carry your gas mask

ISSUED BY THE MINISTRY OF HOME SECURITY

As for the other disappointment: Michael, the collector of 1940s memorabilia, had a gas mask he'd bought back home in Yorkshire, but there was no gas mask here in West Wickham, which surprised them all. Poison gas had been used to devastating effect in the trenches of the First World War, first by the Germans, then by both sides, and it was clear that the Italian campaign in Abyssinia in 1938 had deployed mustard gas, the most dreaded of all, which caused appalling and often fatal blisters. Hitherto, however, gas had not been used against civilians.

It was the issue of gas masks that really brought the threat of war home to people: 38 million were handed out to men, women and children during the Munich crisis in September 1938 – but, to the concern of parents, there were none yet suitable for babies.

The masks were both terrifying and reassuring; on the one hand they were an indication of the totality of the expected conflict. War was not going to be a matter of fighting in a foreign land, it was going to be a campaign in which civilians would be in the front line too – women and children affected by some of the same weapons of destruction as the fighting men. As the crime novelist, Margery Allingham, read in a handbook given to her by a policeman in her Essex village, there might be 'phosgene [that] filled your lungs with water and produced gangrene of the extremities', or mustard that 'had scarcely any odour but blinded you and ate your flesh away' or some nameless gas that 'smells of geraniums, one whiff and you're a gonner'. And they were frightening to look at too, instantly transforming the wearer into a pig-snouted alien, or an 'elephant foetus' in Allingham's opinion.

Householder at war: Michael Hymers outside 17 Braemar Gardens.

John Lewis reminded partners that 'those who come without their [gas mask] must not be surprised if they are dismissed as unsuitable for employment in time of war'. There was never any legal obligation to do so, but in the early days of the war men, women and children dutifully took their gas masks wherever they went. They carried the masks in buff-coloured cardboard boxes on a string over their shoulder – though soon enterprising retailers were selling fancy gas mask containers, and women's handbags with a special section for a gas mask went on sale.

The tops of pillar boxes were smeared with a special gas-sensitive paint that would change colour if liquid gas landed on it, and ARP wardens were issued with a larger version of the sort of wooden rattle beloved of football fans to clatter in the event of a gas attack.

But while the issue of gas masks was a chilling prediction, it was also reassuring evidence that the government was preparing for war and was making the organization of its citizens' safety a priority.

It had originally been intended to leave gas masks at 17 Braemar Gardens for the Hymers family, since they were such a potent symbol of the fears of the early days of the war – in fact authentic masks had been procured. The family would have been taught how to put the masks on, chin first, the women crushing their elaborately coiffeured 1940s hair as they fastened the straps around the backs of their heads. Indeed, the prospect of gas masks was the main reason why Michael had shaved his beard off: he thought it 'more authentic. I knew that a lot of men in the early part of the war shaved their beards off because they were concerned about getting an airtight fit round the gas mask. A beard would have made that difficult.' Not that beards were very usual among 1940s men (other than naval personnel and bohemians) anyway.

But in fact the Hymers were not allowed to go through the 'gas mask drills' that were a feature of every wartime British citizen's life, because of the asbestos content in the canisters of the masks. In 1940 there was ignorance of the dangers of inhaling asbestos; in 2000 the risk is recognized, and prohibited.

So potent was the gas mask as a symbol of civilian warfare that Michael in particular regretted that the family would not get the chance to grapple with this malodorous rubber contraption – even though, by our standards today, their 38 million wartime counterparts were courting danger by this very act of protection.

Although the fear of gas attacks (and grotesque rumours about impending science fiction horrors) never entirely went away, a gas attack on Britain was at least one of the anticipated terrors that thankfully never happened. As early as November 1939 people had grown careless about this danger, ignoring the slogan 'Take care of your gas mask and your gas mask will take care of you', 'forgetting' their masks when they went out. A survey conducted in November 1939 on Westminster Bridge revealed that only 24 per cent of men were carrying their gas mask and 30 per cent of women, while in Lancashire on the same date it was 6 per cent of men and 9 per cent of women. Rows of the familiar brown cardboard boxes soon lined the shelves of railway lost property depots. Ironically the novelist H. G. Wells, author of the prophetic *War of the Worlds*, was already observed not to be carrying his mask in the very first month of the war. And a 1942 film, *The Goose Steps Out*, starring the comedian Will Hay, showed a German spy being instructed during his training that in order to pass muster as an Englishman he must *never* be seen carrying a gas mask.

That first evening the family was plunged into the realities of how a 1940s family would have lived. Lyn had been instructed to cook rissoles for the family's evening meal. She was daunted: 'There was a magnificent joint of cold beef, it would have been perfect with salad. But no, I had to mince the meat in an old-fashioned mincer screwed to the kitchen table, then Kirstie made the breadcrumbs by pushing bread through the mincer, then I made the rissoles to a wartime recipe and fried them in

lard. It took me four hours and we were all exhausted when we'd finished eating. And then there was the washing-up to do, and the kitchen floor to mop and it was after eleven o'clock at night by the time we'd finished. It made me realize that we've got to get very organized.' But she felt a pang of remorse when she watched her grandsons wolf down the rissoles. 'Poor little mites, they were so thrilled – they never normally get home cooking, so I suppose it was worth it.'

As she got into bed that first night in the 1940s house, Lyn contemplated the weeks ahead: 'I'm sure we will suffer all sorts of hardships and things will be withdrawn that we are used to having around every day. But whatever happens to us it's not going to compare with the hardships and the pain people suffered during the war, and I want to do justice to that.'

In the single bedroom next door Kirstie was resolute: 'I'm here for a purpose. I am here for the experience of living in the 1940s, whatever happens, I am not going to give up. I am not going to say that I want to leave, no matter how bad it gets. I'll persevere and sort things out the best I can. There'll be nothing that will make me leave.'

Wartime resolve in the 1940s house. Lyn, Kirstie and Michael decide on action.

CHAPTER 4

'IF ONLY THEY'D TELL US WHAT TO DO'

When the Hymers family had a moment to start sifting through the pile of papers that were waiting for them at 17 Braemar Gardens, they found a government leaflet that had been issued in July 1939. Public Information Leaflet No. 1, 'Some Things You Should Know If War Should Come', was distributed to every home in the country and promised that 'further leaflets will be sent to you to give guidance on particular ways in which you can be prepared'. It was to be the first of an avalanche of instructions and advice emanating from official sources such as the Ministries of Information, Food, Home Security, Labour and National Service, and local authorities.

In wartime, posters seemed to be everywhere – one Mass Observation respondent reported that on his short walk from the office in 1941 he spotted forty-eight posters including those telling people:

- to eat National Wholemeal Bread
- not to waste food
- to keep your children in the country
- to know where your Rest Centre is
- how to behave in an air-raid shelter
- to look out in the blackout
- to look out for poison gas

- to carry a gas mask always
- to join the AFS [Auxiliary Fire Service]
- to fall in with the fire bomb fighters
- to register for Civil Defence Duties
- to help build a plane
- to recruit for the Air Training Corps
- to save for Victory

Michael ponders another sheath of official advice
the family have received from the 1940s house equivalent
of Churchill's (above) War Cabinet.

Newspapers, magazines and radio were endless founts of wisdom too, while there were always family, friends and neighbours who had had a good idea, had heard a rumour or remembered how it had been in the First World War.

In that first leaflet, householders were sternly instructed to 'read this and keep it carefully. You may need it' (in bold print) and it continued: 'The Government are taking all possible measures for the defence of the country, and have made plans for protecting you and helping you to protect yourselves, so far as it may be, in the event of war. You, in your turn, can help make those plans work if you understand them and act in accordance with them.' It went on to explain about air-raid warnings, gas masks, lighting restrictions, fire precautions, evacuation, identity labels and food, and concluded, 'Arrangements will be made for information and instructions to be issued to the public in case of emergency, both though the Press, and by means of Broadcast Announcements. Broadcasts may be made at special times, which will be announced beforehand, or during ordinary News Bulletins.'

It had long been recognized that unlike the First World War, which was essentially a soldiers' and sailors' (and in a few cases an airmen's) war, this new conflict was going to be a total war – or, in a phrase that sounded less menacing but indicated the dangers and sacrifices that would involve almost everyone in Britain to a greater or lesser extent, a 'people's war'. This would mean that civilians would have in effect to be 'conscripted' to the war effort. As Winston Churchill put it in 1940, it was 'a war of unknown warriors [in which] the whole of the warring nations are engaged, not only soldiers, but the entire population, men and women and children. The fronts are everywhere. The trenches are dug in towns and streets. Every village is fortified. Every road is barred. The front lines run through the factories. The workmen [and, he might have added, women] are soldiers with different weapons, but with the same courage.'

During the six years that the war lasted, the state took a more invasive role than at any time in history: civilians were required to register for identity cards, which had to be produced on demand. They were advised that 'in war you should carry about with

'Do not help the enemy in any way' government leaflets issued in 1940 instructing the British people what to do in case of invasion.

you your name and address clearly written. This should be on an envelope, card or luggage label, not on some odd piece of paper easily lost. In the case of children a label should be fastened, e.g. sewn, on to their clothes in such a way that it will not readily become detached.' One of the most poignant images of the war on the home front in Britain remains photographs of evacuees tagged with labels tied to their coats as they waited transportation to 'destination unknown' on the eve of the outbreak of war.

The imaginative might realize that this desire to label the nation's citizens was not only to make sure that they were where they should be, doing what they should be doing at the time that they should, but to provide identification in the event of one of the many terrible 'incidents' of aerial bombardment or gas attack that were expected. For the victims of these, swimming pools and warehouses had been requisitioned for temporary morgues and hundreds of thousands of emergency cardboard coffins stored.

Conscription (which during the First World War had not been brought in for two years – and then reluctantly) was reintroduced in May 1939 when the Military Training Act required men between twenty and twenty-one to undertake six months' military training. On the day war broke out the National Service (Armed Forces) Act made all men between eighteen and forty-one liable for conscription. Call-up took effect in stages, as the various age groups were called to the colours. Men in 'reserved occupations' escaped service in the Forces altogether, although they were liable to be directed into particular jobs. As the war progressed, regulations bit harder: in December 1941 conscription for women in certain categories was introduced. Food rationing took effect from January 1940, and clothes rationing was introduced in early June 1941. Limitations were put on what manufacturers could produce; raw materials were issued on a quota basis; production was 'zoned' to save on transport costs, so what was obtainable might depend on where you lived; permits had to be obtained for furniture; parts of the country were out of bounds – the beaches along the south coast after the fall of France in June 1940, when fears of a German invasion were very real, troops' training grounds and military equipment storage sites, particularly in the run-up to D-Day in June 1944.

Mail was censored: letters were opened and anything that might possibly be helpful to the enemy – details maybe of a soldier's whereabouts that might suggest a troop build-up in a certain area, or the location of factories involved in war production – was excised. For the same reason of security no weather forecasts were issued during the war. Blackout regulations were strictly enforced and heavy fines imposed for transgression; property could be requisitioned for military purposes or to house those made homeless by bombing – as indeed 17 Braemar Gardens was; householders deemed to have spare room could have evacuees or war workers billeted on them.

The long arm of the state reached into every cranny of life, it sometimes seemed. You could be fined for wasting food, as a woman in Barnet, Hertfordshire, was for

Kirstie *could* have been fined for wasting food.

feeding the birds in her garden in 1943. The width of lapels on men's suits was prescribed, as was whether their trousers could have turn-ups, if women could have embroidery on their blouses or lace on their collars.

Although there were always complaints about some piece of mindless bureaucracy or some unnecessarily petty and officious official, in general the population accepted that Britain was on a war footing: everything else was secondary to achieving victory, and people co-operated in the regulation and restrictions of their wartime lives. As early as 1939 there had been widespread popular support for food rationing, without which, it was realized, there was the danger of better-off being able to buy up scarce supplies. 'Fair Shares', by which sacrifices imposed by shortages would be spread, became the great wartime slogan. So successful was food rationing, a demand arose for the same principle to be applied elsewhere. When clothes rationing was mooted, Winston Churchill was concerned that this would prove a deprivation too far, but when in 1941 the President of the Board of Trade, Oliver Lyttleton, successfully pushed it through, Churchill admitted that he had been right.

As the clouds of war darkened over Europe British MPs were recalled from their holidays on 24 August 1939 to pass the Emergency Powers (Defence) Act by which the government was empowered to make such regulations as appeared necessary or expedient to secure public safety, the defence of the realm, the maintenance of public order, the efficient prosecution of the war, or the maintenance of supplies and services essential to the life of the community; in short, to act as it liked without reference to Parliament. The first hundred-odd new regulations under the Act were enacted five days later.

Later in the day that war was declared, the Prime Minister assembled his War Cabinet of nine. Churchill returned to the job he'd had in the Great War – First Lord at the Admiralty – and the signal was sent out to the fleet: 'Winston is back'. Anthony Eden was sent to the Dominions Office, while the 'men of Munich' – pro-appeasers to beyond the last minute, men like Lord Halifax – remained in government, but a number of new ministries for Economic Warfare, Food, Shipping and Information

were set up and the Home Office became part of a new Ministry of Home Security, responsible for coping with air raids and Civil Defence.

In May 1940 everything changed. Following the fiasco of the Norwegian campaign, Neville Chamberlain was forced to resign and was succeeded as Prime Minister by Winston Churchill. A coalition government was formed, containing members of all the major parties in Parliament. In charge was a War Cabinet of five members, with the leader of the Labour Party, Clement Attlee, serving as Deputy Prime Minister. The trade unionist Ernest Bevin became Minister of Labour and National Service, responsible for the mobilization of manpower on the home front. Herbert Morrison, once in charge of London County Council, was appointed Minister of Home Security. The deputy leader of the Labour Party, Arthur Greenwood, who in the debate before the declaration of war had been urged to 'speak for England', had a roving commission as Minister without Portfolio. Like his predecessor, Churchill found it hard to find the right man for the post of Minister of Information, the whole idea of such a ministry being regarded as un-English by the public and distrusted by the press. After a series of failures, which included the former Director-General of the BBC, Sir John (later Lord) Reith, Churchill finally

The enforcers: members of the 1940s house War Cabinet in session. From left:
Piers Brendon, Juliet Gardiner, Guy de la Bédoyère, Susan Jebb and Norman Longmate.

1940s HOUSE

appointed his close confidante Brendan Bracken. A flamboyant character, he rapidly proved equal to his novel and demanding job. Despite many minor ministerial changes and reorganizations it was what Churchill later described as 'this famous coalition' that was to see the war through to its triumphant conclusion – and dictate the conditions under which the British people were to endure it.

If the Hymers' experience of the home front was to have validity, they would not only have to understand how civilians' lives were directed during the Second World War, but have some direct experience of it too. The government leaflets they would find in the house, and which would arrive at various junctures, the announcements they would hear on the radio or read in the newspapers of the period that were delivered to them, were not items of nostalgia or idle curiosity: they demanded action, and many of the regulations were enforceable by law, with transgression punishable by fines or even imprisonment.

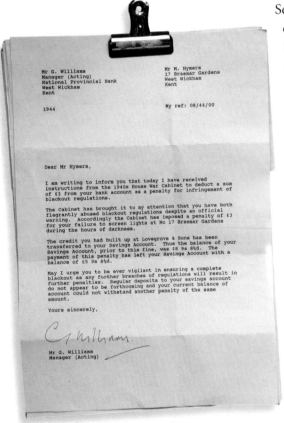

Letters between Michael and his 'bank manager' negotiating the family's wartime budget.

As the 1940s house was intended to be a microcosm of how life had been for millions between 1940 and 1945, a parallel 'War Cabinet' was appointed in effect to 'direct' the Hymers' wartime lives as the government had directed those of its citizens at the time. But this time the War Cabinet was not made up of elected politicians, or of businessmen co-opted for the duration, but of experts in aspects of the Second World War. They would translate the conditions at various stages of the war and communicate essential information and instructions to the Hymers family, informing them of any new edicts or changes of circumstance. The Cabinet would ensure that any regulations in force were strictly adhered to, and that any transgressions were punished as they would have been during the war.

There were five members of this 'War Cabinet'. Norman Longmate is not only the foremost social historian of the home front (and many other aspects of the Second World War too), but also has personal experience: thirteen years old when war broke out, he joined the Home Guard in 1943 and from 1944 to 1947 served in

the army both at home and overseas. Piers Brendon is a historian too, and has written widely on the social, cultural and political history of the nineteenth and twentieth centuries, including a biography of Winston Churchill. He is Keeper of the Churchill Archives at Cambridge, which holds around a million Churchill papers including the original, hand-corrected copies of Churchill's famous wartime speeches. Piers was born in 1940 and has some memories of his early childhood in Cornwall during the war. Susan Jebb is head of Nutrition and Health at the Medical Research Council's Human Nutrition Research in Cambridge: she devised and oversaw the health tests that the Hymers took at the beginning and end of their wartime experience. The fourth Cabinet member was the writer of this book: I (Juliet Gardiner) am also a historian, writing mainly on social and cultural aspects of the Second World War; my 'portfolio' was how the war affected the lives of women. The 'War Cabinet' meetings were chaired by Guy de la Bédoyère, a historian with a particular interest in air warfare who is also a qualified pilot, frequently taking off from Biggin Hill to overfly West Wickham.

The War Cabinet met regularly to discuss how best to make the Hymers' experience as authentic as possible – what issues they would have been confronting at various times. Also we monitored how they were coping with the various vicissitudes they were encountering, and whether they needed more information. We generally oversaw the experiment, often with the aid of videos transmitted from the house. We met where the real Wartime Cabinet had met, in the rabbit warren of rooms conveniently situated deep beneath Whitehall between the Houses of Parliament and 10 Downing Street. Here Churchill had announced in May 1940: 'This is the room from which I will direct the war.'

In addition to the Cabinet Room the underground passages (which have been restored and now form part of the Imperial War Museum and are open to the public) housed the offices of the Chiefs of Staff of the Army, Navy and Air Force as well as those of General 'Pug' Ismay, Churchill's Chief of Staff and overall strategic adviser (Churchill himself took the post of Minister of Defence). In addition there was a large map room, the hub of the operation, where the movement of troops and shipping convoys in all the theatres of war was plotted, as well as a blackboard used during the Battle of Britain to record a tally of enemy aircraft shot down each day. There was an annexe to the map room where thin threads of wool showed the movement of German troops in the Russian campaign, equipment for studying aerial photographs to determine bombing targets or estimate damage, and a device for 'scrambling' phone calls.

There was also a room equipped by the BBC so that Churchill could speak to the nation from his underground bunker, another for transatlantic phone calls to enable him to get in touch with President Roosevelt whenever necessary, a typing pool that

was kept busy twenty-four hours a day, and sleeping accommodation for staff who could snatch only a few hours' rest during the blitz when it was unwise to venture out as bombs hailed down. Churchill himself had a bedroom in this complex, although it was often hard to persuade him down from the roof of the building from where he liked to watch the raids in progress, or convince him that the morale of the nation was too important for him to risk his life by returning to his official residence during a particularly fierce raid.

Like the British public, the Hymers did not meet the War Cabinet, or have any direct communication with us. They simply received 'official' information and instructions delivered to the house. We explained our role in a printed notice the Hymers received a couple of days after they had moved into 17 Braemar Gardens:

> We write to inform you of our role within the '1940s House' project. Our purpose is twofold. First, it is our responsibility to establish those elements of home front living we feel it is important and feasible to authentically recreate and re-examine within the terms of the experiment. Our other role is to monitor your progress… As in wartime, we have also asked people within the area to observe your activities and report to us on a regular basis. Consistent with the terms of the Emergency Powers Act we will, if necessary, act upon 'information received'.
>
> To enable you to experience different phases of wartime living, we have decided to divide your time within the 1940s House into specific periods. It will be necessary to advance your experience on a number of occasions. This change will be signalled to you by a letter from the Cabinet.
>
> We are therefore writing to inform you that from Saturday events will be advanced to the year 1940. Relevant information about changes to your budget and local pricing will be made known to you separately.

The Hymers came to dislike the War Cabinet; they particularly resented what they considered to be our 'snooping', and often thought that we were harsh in what we demanded of them. They were sometimes thrown by some new instructions or regulations just as they thought they had begun to get their world in order. But they came to accept that is how it would have been in the war. That they would have had to learn to live with uncertainty and anxiety, and the knowledge that a settled life and the ability to plan ahead with confidence were cruelly snatched away from the whole country on the day that war was declared.

During wartime, it was essential to know what the population was thinking, how it was bearing up under the strains, its reactions to government initiatives, what it regarded as effective, what it would not condone. As the politicians well knew,

morale was to be a vital factor in winning the war. Hitler's strategy would be to break the British people's resolve to fight; their leaders would then have to sue for peace. But 'snooping' on people's lives was an accusation directed at an organization that was to become of great importance in the 'people's war'. Mass Observation had been set up in 1937 following an event that had revealed a surprising gap between official opinion and the views of the public.

On 10 December 1936 Edward VIII had abdicated the throne, declaring that he had 'found it impossible to carry the heavy burden of responsibility and to discharge my duties as King as I would wish to do without the help and support of the woman I love' and concluded, 'God bless you all. God save the King' (his younger brother, the shy, speech-impaired 'Bertie' who, as George VI, would be Britain's wartime king).

Lyn stands by the kitchen sink reading a leaflet from the ARP telling them how to protect their windows against bomb blasts.

Edward had fallen in love with a twice-divorced American socialite, Wallis Simpson, whom he wanted to marry. Her divorced status made this impossible in the eyes of the 'Establishment' – the Prime Minister Stanley Baldwin, the Cabinet and the Archbishop of Canterbury – since as King, Edward was head of the Church of England; nor would they countenance a morganatic marriage which would neither have made Mrs Simpson queen, nor any children the couple might have heirs to the throne. So Edward opted for love and a life in exile. Orchestrated by Lord Beaverbrook (who was to be appointed Minister of Aircraft Production by Churchill in 1940), the newspaper tycoon owner of the influential *Daily Express* and friend of Edward, the 'King's matter' had been hushed up in the British press and pages were torn out of foreign magazines before they went on sale.

The public were deemed to have no right to know, while rumours circulated furiously; the nation only learned authoritatively of the grave constitutional crisis and the likely loss of their popular monarch (who, some suspected, had too often voiced his sympathies for the poor and unemployed for the Conservative government to exert themselves unduly to retain his services) a few days before the instrument of abdication was signed. It was clear that the country was out of step with its leaders: 'Hands Off Our King' read placards, 'Abdication Means Revolution'. It didn't, of course, and throughout the war years George VI, who was crowned on 12 May 1937, and his queen, Elizabeth, became a respected and even loved royal couple. Meanwhile the pro-appeasement sentiments of the Duke and Duchess of Windsor (titles granted to them by George VI) seemed to have become pro-Nazi as pictures appeared in the press of the couple being warmly greeted by Hitler in Berlin a few months after the abdication.

But the gulf revealed between the 'Establishment' and the 'people', between the press and public opinion, was disturbing. A few days after the abdication, a letter from a schoolteacher was published in the *New Statesman* urging that the public reaction to the abdication provided 'material for an anthropological study of our own situation (in contrast to those of "primitive tribes") of which we stand in such desperate need'. Charles Madge, a poet, journalist and surrealist, replied that was already happening and, linking with a fellow journalist and anthropologist Tom Harrisson and Humphrey Jennings, who was working for John Grierson's documentary film unit, they formed Mass Observation to investigate the British way of life.

By the end of 1937 over 500 people had been recruited through appeals in the press as unpaid Observers. They were charged with keeping a detailed record of everything they did, from waking to bedtime, on the twelfth day of every month throughout the year. Mass Observation saw these 'day surveys' as an experiment in amassing data about the lives of 'ordinary' people as well as 'training' volunteers in the anthropological art of 'continuous observation'. These were not scientific surveys, like those produced by the

burgeoning statistic-gathering outfits: nor were they intended to be. Mass Observation recruited amateurs with no quantitative training, they sought a subjective view of life, recorded the correspondent's own agenda. 'They tell us not what society is like but what it looks like to them,' wrote Harrisson and Madge.

It was, of course, a political project, 'the challenge of the man in the street, of us against them; it was a populist demand, that democracy should mean what it says, rule by the people appraised of the facts'. The outbreak of war gave Mass Observation a focus since, as its historians Angus Calder and Dorothy Sheridan point out, 'All its findings had significance in relation to national morale.'

By 1940 Mass Observation had been (secretly) co-opted to work with the Ministry of Information (Madge was not happy with this, seeing the danger that MO would became an arm of the government's propaganda machine, and indeed it was at this time that the *Daily Express* dubbed some members of Mass Observation 'Cooper's Snoopers' after the Minister of Information, Duff Cooper). As part of the nexus of organizations that provided a 'war barometer' for the government, Mass Observation monitored wartime morale in a number of ways. There were diarists, there were paid panel members given specific information to collect and reports to write, and there were the regular Directives (questionnaires) issued to volunteers soliciting information on range of topics relevant to the specific period of the war when they were issued.

A typical Directive issued in June 1942 asked 'everyone' three questions including 'What do you believe about the news you are getting nowadays? Give your comments and criticism on BBC news bulletins and communiqués.' It then quizzed 'everyone who can possibly spare the time', 'How is the rising cost of living affecting you now? On which things do you economise, and which things have gone up in price that affect you most?'

Then there was: 'Apart from things such as windows that are always made of glass, give a rough inventory of all glass objects in your house. Describe your feelings about glass. Are there any objects for which glass is not essential which you feel ought to be made of glass? (e.g. windows, tumblers, water jugs, etc.) Are there any objects which are sometimes made of glass for which you feel any other material would be more appropriate?'

And: 'What are your own beliefs about "obscenity" and swearing? What words, if any, do you consider obscene? Do you use these words yourself? What are your feelings if you hear other people using them? (Don't be shy!)'

Also: 'What do you feel about: (a) the possibility, (b) the desirability of our invading the continent?

The Hymers, too, received Directives based on those of Mass Observation, soliciting information on how they were coping with their wartime situation, and all

the family filled in their answers. Air raids were top of everyone's list of a wartime inconvenience, as was the blackout, and as a housewife Lyn fervently added 'the ability to plan meals'. They all listed 'food shortages' as another 'inconvenience of wartime', but it was only the adults who regretted the lack of soap! Giving the odd contemporary reference, all missed pizzas, the boys wanted crisps again, while Kirstie pined for Mars Bars, Michael for Brylcreem and Lyn for washing soda, toothpaste, olive oil, chocolate (occasionally) – and of course cigarettes.

Throughout the war, Mass Observation produced literally hundreds of reports based on surveys, Directive responses and diaries, and also published a number of books. *War Begins at Home*, which came out in 1940, gave a vivid account of the 'phoney war', while *Living Through the blitz* reported on the social effects of air raids which proved extremely useful: the MO report from Coventry after the heavy raids there in November 1940 showed that though provision had been made for the victims' material needs, little thought had been given to the psychological trauma that bombing, bereavement and injury caused. It urged better rest centres, more support for voluntary social workers and the fullest possible factual information for the citizens of Coventry about what had happened to their city.

But as well as its wartime use, the material collected by the Mass Observation project has proved an invaluable source of wartime information and impressions ever since, and a small proportion of the miles of paper generated (now housed in the Mass Observation archive at the University of Sussex) has been published over the years in anthologies and in a few cases as edited diaries. Naomi Mitchison, who spent the war years on the family estate near the Mull of Kintyre in Scotland, was the author of one such diary. Another is *Nella Last's War*, which had been given to Lyn so that she could learn more about a housewife's experience in the Second World War.

Although Nella Last lived in Barrow-in-Furness and her two grown-up sons were in the forces, Lyn was able to identify with many of Mrs Last's feelings and frustrations. Sometimes, though, she grew irritated at her 'nerviness' when in Lyn's eyes she did not have too hard a war, with only 'my husband' at home, a car in the garage (unlike the Hymers) – even if lack of petrol prohibited its use for much of the war – and domestic help in the house, enabling her to undertake a full round of voluntary work with the local WVS and to make things for sale at the bazaars held to raise money for local charities. But Lyn used Nella Last as a benchmark on occasions to justify her actions or compare how she was feeling. It was all part of her commitment to the 1940s house project: to live the experience as authentically as possible, to find out everything she could about daily life in the period to ensure that she had no advantages that would not have been available to her wartime counterparts, that the family lived with the same restraints as they would have done – and understood as clearly as possible why they were doing so.

Information came from books the Hymers had brought with them, or had found in the house, from the Cabinet Directives and the various government and local authority leaflets that were posted through the letterbox on a regular basis. It came too from the newspapers of the period that were delivered, both the national press and the local paper, the *Beckenham Journal*, which kept the Hymers up to date with what was happening in the world at the particular period of the war that they had reached. But because it largely depended on imported raw materials, paper was in short supply: in 1938 newspapers and magazines had been using up 23,000 tons of newsprint a week; by 1943 this had fallen to 4,320 tons, though demand from the forces increased this slightly later. The 'quality press', *The Times*, the *Daily Telegraph* and the *Manchester Guardian*, managed to keep to six or eight pages by strictly limiting their circulation, while the popular press (newspapers such as the *Daily Mirror*, the *Daily Sketch*, *Reynolds News*, the *Daily Mail* and the *Daily Express*) fell to as little as four pages. No paper was allowed to increase its circulation, so papers soon sold out. It was the same with women's magazines, an invaluable source of information and advice – often contributed by readers – which both shrunk in size and, unable to increase their subscription list, soon disappeared from newsagents' shelves. The ever-popular *Housewife* was pocket-sized by 1940 and became a much-thumbed possession, to be passed around among friends and neighbours.

The radio (or wireless) was another essential source of information: wartime families frequently made it an evening ritual to sit round the bakelite set with a cup of watery cocoa or Horlicks, listening to the nine o'clock news. It was the same for the Hymers family. Every evening they would sit down to listen to a recording provided by the War Cabinet. Sometimes it was a news bulletin; on other occasions it might be a stirring speech by Winston Churchill, a message from the King, an address by the Queen to the 'women of Britain', or an information programme such as *The Kitchen Front*. Maybe there would be an extract from one of the popular comedy programmes that were designed to keep up wartime spirits and stiffen resolve – *ITMA* (*It's That Man Again* with Tommy Handley) or *Mr Cropper's Conscience* or *Hi Gang!* with Ben Lyon, his wife Bebe Daniels and Vic Oliver (who married Churchill's daughter, Sarah), providing insights into the preoccupations of the war years. Then there were extracts from the music hall and programmes such as *Workers' Playtime*, popular music and sketches broadcast to factories and offices to boost morale and production.

There was another source of information and advice that the Hymers came to value particularly: the people of West Wickham and the surrounding area who shared their wartime memories with the family attempting to relive some aspects of them. There was Mr and Mrs Tilling, who lived a few doors away. Peter Tilling had lived in Braemar Gardens all his life; he and his wife Nina were to prove a mine of information,

and became the neighbourly support so vital in wartime. There were local historians Joyce Walker and Patricia Donaldson; there were Jackie and Dean Whybra, members of a highly active 1940s society that puts on 'wartime events' in the area, who helped Lyn and Kirstie with suggestions about their clothes, hair and beauty routine. There were the West Wickhamites whom the Hymers met at the beetle drive that had been organized in the local hall, who shared wartime memories, hints and even their home movies, and many more knowledgeable and helpful people. The only thing Lyn missed was someone who 'had been a bit nearer the age that I am now during the war.

Everyone I meet was a child in wartime, and it seems to have been fun for them. I want to meet someone who had the responsibility of running a home and coping with rationing and all the endless chores and the worries of wartime living. But of course they'd be in their nineties now, so it's not very likely!' It was not until nearly the end of their stay that Lyn was to get her wish.

During the war, it seemed that many people were aware of the singular historic times through which they were living: they wanted to hold on to something permanent in that fragile, uncertain, disrupted world, to pass on their experiences to their children and grandchildren. Often they kept diaries, or wrote copious, descriptive letters with the instruction to the recipient to keep them. The Hymers were no exception: Ben wrote his name in a small black notebook and added his age, ten. 'Week one, day one,' it started. 'Today was a very exciting day. First we had a hair cut (short back and sides)… then we put our 1940s clothes on. To be a 1940s boy feels good because I feel important… I feel like Julian from the Famous Five [Enid Blyton's adventure series] and I would probably go round saying, "I say", "lashings of ginger beer", "by Jove", "golly, gosh", "old chap". But despite this promising start, Ben was so busy with his new life that by 'week two, day thirteen' he had lain down his quill.

Lyn however, persevered: she had started to keep a diary from the moment the Hymers knew that they had been chosen to be the 1940s family, and continued until she was back home in Otley again. No matter how tired she was, she would sit down last thing at night (which was sometimes in the early hours of the morning) and pen an entry, even if it was only to record that she was almost too exhausted to write. 'I wanted to do it for the boys. It's a unique experience and I don't ever want them, or us, to forget how it was.'

Ben's diary opened with a drawing of the family leaving Otley on that 'very exciting day'. Thomas also started a diary when he arrived at the 1940s house.

CHAPTER 5

'IS YOUR BLACKOUT REALLY BLACK?'

'**M**y husband has wanted to build an Anderson shelter all his adult life,' wrote Lyn in her diary. 'Some men aspire to scale Everest, fly to the moon, or become a millionaire, mine just wants an Anderson shelter. We all feel sorry for him, he must be bitterly disappointed.'

It was day three in the 1940s house and the family still could not resolve the problem of a refuge-room at 17 Braemar Gardens for protection in the event of an air raid, since there had been no Anderson shelter awaiting them on their arrival in West Wickham. No one much liked the idea of a Morrison shelter, a steel mesh 'cage' some 2 feet 9 inches high that could be fitted into the dining room since its reinforced steel top could be used as a table. Families crammed in here with their bedding for some measure of protection as the bombers flew overhead, but these were more often provided for houses that had neither basement nor cellar, and no garden that could accommodate an Anderson shelter. In any case, they came into use only in 1941, towards the end of the blitz (named after the new Minister of Home Security, Herbert Morrison), and at this stage the Hymers were still in the early days of the war. Lyn decided to visit some neighbours and see if she could find out what they had done about a shelter in the war.

She had just gone upstairs to 'take my pinny off and tidy myself up when the doorbell rang and I could hear screams of delight from the children. Our Anderson shelter had arrived! Michael was so pleased.'

Lyn and Michael put up the blackout in the living room at
17 Braemar Gardens.

The Anderson shelter, named after the then Home Secretary, Sir John Anderson, was a masterpiece of simple engineering. Soon after being made responsible for the country's air-raid precautions in November 1938, Anderson consulted an old friend, William Patterson, a Scottish engineer who within a couple of weeks came up with a prototype for a cheap, easy-to-erect domestic shelter. Originally intended to be installed inside houses, technical problems of anchorage meant that it became a garden shelter. Curved sheets of non-corroding corrugated steel were clamped together and bolted to stout rails. It might have been a simple construction, but erecting it was a significant task – as Michael found out.

Lyn was worried about him 'doing all that digging on his own. He's over fifty and overweight.' Eventually Michael accepted help from some neighbours to get the heavy and unwieldy shelter in place. In 1939 neighbours would have helped each other with their shelters or, if there were no able-bodied men in the vicinity, ARP wardens would lend a hand or maybe the Boy Scouts. In 2000, all the Hymers were getting tired and dispirited helping Michael with this back-breaking task, until two of their next-door neighbours put their heads over the fence and, in true wartime spirit, offered their muscle power too.

The defender: Thomas stands guard over the Anderson shelter as it awaits erection.

The official directions instructed householders to dig a hole 7 feet 6 inches long and 6 feet wide, to a depth of 4 feet. The 6-foot panels, bolted at the top to form an arch, were then pushed into the ground. There were flat steel plates at either end, one with a section that could be unbolted in an emergency; the other with a hole at ground level through which the occupants climbed into their shelter. Michael hung a sheet of sacking over the doorway; this would have been soaked in water and was believed to offer some protection against the poison gas that everyone feared.

Since Anderson shelters were 6 feet high, most people could stand up in the middle of them, and the standard length of 6 feet 6 inches allowed two people to lie down in comfort. The shelters were intended to accommodate six people sitting or standing; in the Hymers' case it was five when they were on their own, but seven if there was an air raid alert while their younger daughter Jodie and her husband were visiting Braemar Gardens. At such times it could get pretty uncomfortable, particularly if it was many hours before the 'All Clear' sounded – as it often was during the blitz from 1940 to 1941. Indeed, during the fifty-seven nights of bombing from September to November 1940, many Londoners in effect slept every night in their Anderson shelter, sometimes going in as soon as they'd grabbed something to eat after they got home from work, and not emerging until morning.

The shelters were dark, and ingenious methods were tried out for lighting them. Oil lamps were not recommended as the oil could easily be spilled by accident or in the event of an explosion nearby; and the fumes could build up dangerously in a confined space. The Hymers experimented with different places to put candles so the family could read, knit or play board games, or Lyn could write her diary or letters home. At the same time they were careful about the fire risks of lighted candles in a confined space with the straw-stuffed pallisters they used to try to sleep on. They also had to make sure that no light shone out of the doorway: blackout restrictions applied everywhere.

Heating an Anderson shelter in winter was a problem: 'Never have a coke or other brazier in your shelter. It gives off dangerous fumes.' 'Anything that burns uses up oxygen, without which you cannot breathe'. The solution was either the crush 'of people's bodies [which] provide a great deal of heat and the temperature of the shelter rises as soon as it is fully occupied' or a hot water bottle, or bricks warmed in the oven and placed in the bed or sleeping bag. Lyn was delighted to have been presented with a stone hot water bottle at the beetle drive the family attended and, had they needed the shelter in winter, would no doubt have found it very useful. It was also suggested that a flowerpot upturned over a candle 'will give off a great deal of heat'. While many had reason to be rather sceptical about that, they could see the sense of the suggestion that 'a balaclava helmet, such as every soldier is familiar with, will keep draughts off your head'.

Bringing your dog into the shelter was not recommended as it might get hysterical if there was a raid (dogs were not allowed in public shelters), and it should certainly be muzzled, if it hadn't been evacuated to the country – or already met its maker, which was the fate of 400,000 London pets, humanely gassed by the RSPCA in the first days of the war. Cats, on the other hand, were likely to precede their owners into the shelter in the event of an alert, and there were stories of caged birds and even goldfish that led peripatetic wartime lives in and out of shelters with their owners. Canaries (used to going down coal mines to test the gas) were found to be tough, while budgerigars gave up rather more easily, and fish, perhaps surprisingly, were found to be sensitive to shock.

When the shelter was erected, earth was then shovelled over the top to a depth of at least 15 inches for added protection (indeed, many thought this was the protection) and this provided additional growing space in the garden. A 1939 seed catalogue recommended collections for covering the mounds of air-raid shelters: berberis, cotoneaster, cydonia – though it was more likely to be nasturtiums, marigolds or sweet william, or vegetables: marrows, carrots perhaps, or radishes.

The main complaint about Anderson shelters was that they were damp, and they usually did have a few inches of water sloshing around the floor. Michael was aware of this problem and gave the matter some thought. For several days he collected buckets full of clinker from the boiler and spread this over the floor, When he had built up a satisfactory layer of damp insulation, he laid planks of wood over the ash, nailed them down and the Hymers were the fortunate tenants of a floored, snug and dry shelter.

But Michael was not satisfied to leave it there. Rather than making do with deckchairs and cushions for the boys, as Lyn suggested, he decided to build bunks. Another government leaflet showed the handyman how 'with a little trouble and at very little cost you can make your Anderson shelter a comfortable winter sleeping place for your family', and explained how 'four adults and four babies, or four adults and two older children, can find sleeping room in a standard Anderson shelter' using wood frames with wire netting or canvas stretched across them covered with sacking. Acting on this advice, Michael bought wood that Lyn thought they could ill afford from their budget, and constructed bunks for the boys to replace the collection of chairs they had rammed into the shelter. (One of these chairs was so uncomfortable that the family played musical chairs all night so no one would have to sit for more than fifteen minutes in extreme discomfort.)

These efforts were not entirely appreciated by Michael's fellow shelterers, however: apart from the extravagance, Lyn in particular felt that the loss of floor space was poor compensation for somewhere to stretch out particularly when Michael moved a bed in. It made

Ben Hymers' drawing of the blitz, sketched during long hours in the Anderson shelter.

reading or writing difficult if not impossible, since there was now nowhere to put a candle down safely, and suspending it from the beam might supply ambient light but it was worse than useless for close work. The same leaflet advised that 'by far the best bedding for any shelter is a properly made sleeping bag. Nothing else gives so much warmth.' It gave instructions how to fashion these from thick army blankets or similar, or 'parts of old blankets or even old woollen skirts', lined with muslin or cotton and stuffed with folded newspaper 'which should be changed every month'. Somehow neither Lyn nor Kirstie got round to this further improvement.

Families earning less than £250 a year were issued with a free Anderson shelter; those earning more than this had to buy their shelters at a cost of about £7 (plus the cost of erection and equipping) and by September 1940 nearly a quarter of a million Anderson shelters had been produced. As a middle-income family with an annual income of £360 a year, £7 was deducted from the Hymers' budget to pay for their Anderson shelter, and then as Lyn rarely tired of remarking, there was all that wood for the floor and the bunks. No doubt had the family been there longer Michael would have thought up further improvements to their garden bunker. Whether these would have included an effective deterrent to the toad that took up residence in the Anderson at one point, to the horror of Lyn and Kirstie (though as Ben pointed out, it could have been a rat), is not certain.

Michael sticks tape over the windows to prevent the glass shattering in the event of a bomb falling nearby.

Another leaflet, 'Your Home as an Air Raid Shelter', explained that 'When a high explosive bomb falls and explodes a number of things happen. Anything very close to the explosion is likely to be destroyed and any house which suffers a direct hit is almost sure to collapse. Other dangers of a less spectacular kind can cause far more casualties. Blast can shatter unprotected windows at considerable distances and fragments of glass can be deadly, while bomb splinters can fly and kill at a distance of over half a mile if there is nothing to stop them.'

Wartime householders collected these cigarette cards, which instructed them in air-raid precautions, including dealing with an incendiary bomb and using a stirrup pump.

So as well as building a shelter the Hymers needed to protect their 'wartime' house from the danger of flying glass. They did this by sticking tape in a criss-cross pattern over all the windows 'at intervals which leave no more than 6 inches of glass clear', giving a crude mullioned effect which also looked consistent with the period. There was plenty of advice on how best to do this in leaflets, in newspapers and even from enterprising tobacco manufacturers who before the war had aimed to increase brand loyalty by including a card in every packet. These collectable series had depicted sportsmen and women, stars of stage and screen, footballers, household hints and gardening tips. Now their subject matter was securing the safety of your home in wartime, and a series of fifty cards with air-raid precautions was produced with an album to stick them in for future reference. There were suggestions for making your home safe against gas, servicing your gas mask, anti-bomb blast measures and how to set up a stirrup pump in a bucket in the hall and on every landing so that any incendiary bombs could be extinguished before they caused a fire. An alternative was to place a bucket of sand at strategic points around the home into which such devices, having been scooped up with a long-handled shovel, could be dropped and rendered harmless.

There were also several cards with suggestions about how to black out your home, and that is one of the first tasks the Hymers faced in the 1940s house. 'Tuesday 18 April', reads Lyn's diary, the third day: 'A letter arrives from the ARP warden who is coming to check our blackout on Saturday. What blackout? I haven't even had time to explore the depths of my knicker drawer, let alone make blackout.'

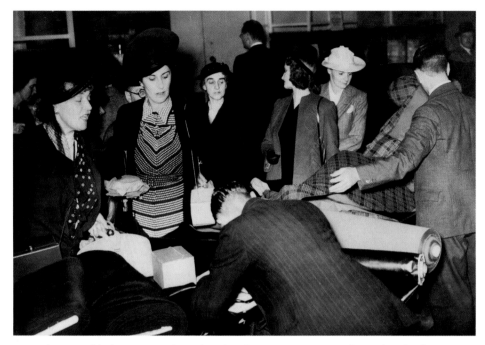

A run on blackout material in a London department store at the outbreak of war.

The blackout was designed to give the enemy no help in locating targets for aerial bombing, and made the most immediate and dramatic impact on the eve of the outbreak of the Second World War. It 'transformed conditions more thoroughly than any other single feature of the war', in the opinion of one of the official historians of the war. There had been blackout 'rehearsals' – Bromley held one between 12.30 and 4 a.m. on the night of 9–10 August 1939 when all 'lights [were] to be Extinguished or Screened' – but the totality of the blackout and its unthought-of consequences had come as a shock to most people when it was enforced at sunset on 1 September 1939. This gave a foretaste of the stringent regulations that would govern other aspects of daily life as the war progressed. All illuminated signs were to be turned off; there were to be no lighted windows in public buildings, schools, hospitals, factories, commercial premises, and of course private houses and flats too. Darkness was to be all-enveloping for five long years until restrictions were partially lifted in the 'dim out' (or officially 'half lighting') allowed from 17 September 1944 until the end of the war.

The Hymers had been provided with a copy of Public Information Leaflet No. 2, which had been distributed in July 1939 giving advice to householders about the most effective form of blackout: 'The most convenient way of shutting in the light is to use close fitting blinds,' it recommended. 'These can be of any thick, dark-

coloured material such as dark blue, black or dark green glazed Holland, Lancaster or Italian cloth. If you can't manage this, you could obscure your windows by fixing up sheets of black or dark brown paper mounted on battens.' A West Wickham shop announced on 2 September that it had 'a plentiful supply of ARP paper now in stock'. The 45-inch-wide type cost 3d a yard; the 30-inch-wide, 2d.

In 1939 the government had had the foresight to make available plenty of bales of blackout material for shops to order. It cost about 2s a yard and was made of cotton or sateen. But there was such a rush on dark-coloured material on the eve of war that many shops that had under-ordered ran out, and householders had to improvise hanging heavy blankets or old quilts at the windows, or – a popular early wartime trick – painting light bulbs blue, shading them with cardboard, or even taking them out altogether. Most people however found the effect of this so intolerably gloomy that they preferred to cover their windows instead; meanwhile many country dwellers never blacked out upstairs windows but went to bed by flickering candlelight.

Michael fits blackout over the front door.

The Hymers used a variety of devices: for the living room, Kirstie hand-sewed curtains to hang in front of the existing floral print cretonne ones, and did the same for the bedroom windows, the kitchen and dining room. Michael made a wooden frame, stretched some fabric over it and painted it all with an evil-smelling mixture he'd found the recipe for in the supplied government leaflet: '1lb of concentrated size, 3 lbs lamp black in powder form, ½ gill of gold size. The size and lamp black should be thoroughly mixed and 2½ gallons of boiling water added. This quantity will cover about 80 square yards of material.' He used these in the bathroom and on the landing and hall. Finally the Hymers covered the top lights of all the windows with stiff black paper held in place with drawing pins and did the same to the lavatory.

'It makes the house so gloomy,' complained Lyn, 'and it makes the family gloomy too' – which was a common wartime perception. Norman Longmate reports a Cornish housewife thinking that the blackout was sufficient to make life intolerable 'even without a war to go with it'. At first the boys found that the blackout confused their sense of time: 'I kept waking up and it was still dark, so I thought, "Oh well, I'd better go back to sleep again,"' said Ben, 'then I realized that it was the blackout.' Kirstie decided that even before she could make herself a cup of tea in the morning, she had to take down the blackout to let the light flood into the house – and she often flung open all the windows too as if to further banish the gloom.

Putting up the blackout was a nightly chore: it had to be done according to the time of year, thirty or forty-five minutes after sunset, blackout time was noted in the newspapers and on the radio. It would take between five and ten minutes every evening to black out all the windows at 17 Braemar Gardens and, if the family returned home after dark, they had to remember not to turn the light on in a room before the blackout was in place. The paper was apt to tear with constant removal, so after a bit the Hymers left some windows covered all the time. And even when they went out into the garden after dark – if there was an air raid for example – they had to turn the light out first to prevent light flooding out.

'Is your blackout really black? Can it be detected?' trilled the topical ditty that ended the popular weekly wireless programme *Mr Cropper's Conscience*. Mr Cropper 'was fat and fifty, amiable and kind, tender-hearted, shrewd and thrifty, all those things combined'. He was also 'rather selfish now and then' but was kept on the straight and narrow by his conscience, which often sounded remarkably like the Ministry of Food, or Fuel, or Home Security.

Like thousands upon thousands of their wartime counterparts, the Hymers sometimes broke the lighting regulations. During the war an ARP warden wrote to the local West Wickham paper complaining that 'four days after lighting restrictions were announced many houses were still showing light, and what's more, the inhabitants do not seem to realize its seriousness'. He identified three classes of offenders: those who were using blackout 'of insufficient opacity with the result that light shines through'; those who don't pay sufficient attention to how well their curtains or blinds fit – not properly pressed into the corners of windows or not meeting properly in the middle; or 'light shown on opening the front door… the light must be switched

---

IS YOUR BLACKOUT REALLY BLACK?

'Don't keeping lying on your back
Go out and inspect it
Don't keep stewing in your bath
When your lights are showing.
Walk along the garden path
And you'll see them glowing
Is your blackout really black?
Have you drawn that curtain?
Here's the warden on the track.
It's better to be certain.
Is your blackout really black?

off before the door is opened'. He suggested that 'when it is really dark outside [householders should] go outside each night and see that their house is showing no light', and that 'in any room which is seldom used and has not been properly protected, take the electric light bulbs out of the fittings'. Sometimes people forgot to cover up small bathroom windows, while there were those who seemed to be under the impression that German bombers (or maybe the ARP wardens) could see only the front of houses, and though they were assiduous in blacking out those windows that faced the street, the light shone out at the back. Whatever the cause, the result was likely to be the same: 'Put that light out!' a passing ARP warden or policeman would yell if even a chink of light was showing. Neighbours, concerned that light showing from one house would act as a beacon for the bombers thus endangering the whole area, would denounce transgressors to the authorities and the arm of the law would be round in a trice.

Before the visit of their 'ARP warden', the family worked against the clock to get all the blackout in place. The judge of its efficacy was Patricia Knowlden, who had passed the warden's exam in 1941 when she was only fourteen (she had been helping her ARP warden father deliver leaflets since he had joined in 1938); she had been West Wickham's youngest ARP warden when she was allowed to join officially and receive her uniform in 1944 at the age of seventeen. After she and the family trooped outside to see if any light was showing, she pronounced herself satisfied – departing with the instruction, 'Keep it dark!' However, busy one evening a week or so later, the Hymers forgot to draw the blackout curtains in the living room. Their misdemeanour was captured on CCT cameras (the modern electronic equivalent of the snooping neighbour); the War Cabinet saw the evidence and, considering it a flagrant breach of regulations, imposed an exemplary fine of £3, docking the money from Michael's £7 10s a week wages (in 1940 including overtime).

The Hymers were in good company: the regulation of lighting 'criminalized' 925,000 people during the war – approximately one person in every fifty (though no doubt some offended more than once) was deemed culpable of infringing blackout regulations. In 1940 alone, the peak year for such activity, there were 300,000 prosecutions.

None of the Hymers was pleased to have this swingeing penalty imposed on them, but Lyn was very distressed – and made not a little angry – by the fine. It was not so much the pecuniary implications, but what appeared to be hostility from the faceless War Cabinet. It was one of the moments of the wartime experience that made her feel particularly isolated: marooned in a time warp that no one else was sharing, living by regulations that did not intrude on their neighbours' lives, far away from home, unable to communicate with family and friends by phone, coping with shortages in the midst of plenty. It was sometimes as if the present had been

Safety for sixpence: Woolworths' luminous flowers for blackout nights.

reeled back for the Hymers while all around them it lapped at their daily lives. There were television aerials and satellite dishes on every house, cars in every drive, advertisement hoardings for the consumer society on every corner, empty crisp packets, burger boxes and drinks cans casually littering the pavements. It was not that the Hymers would have had it different – they had signed up for a wartime life and they were determined to experience it in as many aspects as possible – but there were times, and this was one of them, when Lyn realized that one of the benefits of the war could not be recreated outside the five of them. This was the camaraderie of a shared experience, of all being in it together, of a unity born out of adversity.

It would have been useless to blackout homes, factories, shops, pubs, cinemas and the like while leaving street lights to snake a path for the bombers, and it was the lack of street lighting that added an immediate and intense hazard to the war as people stumbled along pavements, banged into walls, fell off kerb stones and were unable to find their own front doors. Kerbs, sharp corners and steps were painted white, and three white circles were painted round the trunks of any tree where pedestrians might collide with it, and similar treatment was accorded to phone boxes and pillar boxes. In cities and towns, trolley buses were a particular threat to life, known as the 'silent peril' as they glided noiselessly along their tracks in urban streets. Traffic lights were covered and only a small cross-shaped slit indicated whether it was

safe to proceed or not. Cars had to have their bumpers and running boards painted white and at first had to muffle their headlights with a sock or cardboard shield, but as road deaths mounted a speed limit of 20 m.p.h. was introduced and specially designed metal covers were fitted over headlights which let out slivers of light pointing downwards. Dashboards could not be illuminated and drivers had to judge their speed by the sound of the engine.

A cyclist was fined £1 on 26 September 1939 on the outskirts of West Wickham for riding his bike with a light that was 'very bright, throwing a beam of 20 to 25 yards'. When apprehended by the police, the young man explained that he had stuck a single sheet of tissue paper over the glass 'and thought that that was all right'. The Chairman of the Magistrates' Bench didn't think so at all, and warned that 'if there were any more cases of that kind they would have to deal with them more severely'.

Advice for getting around in the blackout was plentiful, from carrying a white Pekinese or wearing a white gardenia (as a seventeen-year-old, West Wickham-born Marjorie Moyce had tried that but didn't find it very effective) to splashing luminous paint on your door bell or knocker. Connie Winter (who was then Connie Manser) remembers in the winter running all the way to West Wickham station to catch a train to her London office by following the white line down the centre of the road. 'I often used to run into the paper boy following it the other way.'

By December 1939 the regulations were relaxed slightly to permit 'diffused ' street lighting which bathed a small circle of pavement in dim light. Rather than further relax blackout restrictions, the government reduced the hours when they were in force: in November 1939 each night's blackout was reduced by an hour so it ran from half an hour after sunset to half an hour before sunrise, and this was extended by fifteen minutes each end of the day in the summer months. In February 1940 summer time superseded Greenwich Mean Time all year round for the remainder of the war, and in 1941 double summer time – two hours ahead – was introduced; from 1942 until the end of the war it was progressively lighter up to nearly midnight from April until mid-August. Although this was a help for farmers turning increasingly marginal land over to crops to feed the nation, and made life seem a little less oppressive at home, it was not much welcomed by mothers trying to persuade children that it really was bedtime despite the fact that it was still broad daylight outside, nor illicit lovers seeking some privacy.

But the night remained a treacherous time to venture out. In September 1939 those killed in road accidents in the blackout rose by nearly 100 per cent and that excluded those who had fallen off railway station platforms, down steps or into canals or emergency water containers in the pitch dark. An advertisement appeared in the local West Wickham paper warning 'Wait – you can see the car when the driver can't see you!' and offered 'four simple rules for getting home safely in the blackout'.

Nevertheless, in the first week of the war there were a number of fatal accidents attributable to the blackout in Beckenham area: a couple were killed and eight others injured when two cars collided; a motorist saw 'a light coloured object' in front of him in the blackout, and 'on feeling a bump, he braked, got out and found a woman [who subsequently died from her injuries] lying in the road'; a cyclist 'who had been riding a bike for more than twenty years' was knocked off his machine and killed; an octogenarian tripped over a kerb in the dark and died of his injuries; a pedestrian 'appeared to lose his bearings in the blackout although he had made the same journey from West Wickham to Beckenham many times' and was hit by a bus as he tried to cross the road; and a young mother, getting up in the night to attend to her crying baby, refrained from switching the light on in accordance with blackout regulations, fell down the stairs and was found dead by her husband who had also been wakened by the baby.

Indeed, in January 1940 a Gallup poll showed that pretty well one person in every five had sustained injury during the blackout. These were often not serious – falling down a kerb, crashing into a wall or a fellow pedestrian, tripping over a pile of sandbags – but painful and a sufficient deterrent, coupled with transport difficulties, to keep most people at home in the evenings. Cinemas and sports stadiums had been closed on the outbreak of war but, when it was realized that this could be deleterious to morale and that the heavy air raids expected had not materialized, most had opened again by December. The blackout limited social lives, threw people back into the bosom of their families for a quiet evening's reading, listening to the wireless or playing board games – adverts started to appear in the local paper asking for people wanting to swap jigsaw puzzles. A popular song of the period captured the mood: 'There's no place like home,/But we see too much of it now'.

After 13 September 1939 pedestrians were permitted to carry a small torch provided that it was shrouded in tissue paper and the light shone down on to the pavement. But, predictably, such was the demand for the number 8 batteries required the most popular type that they remained in short supply for most of the war.

It was the ARP wardens and the police who enforced blackout regulations and, in the early days of the war with no air raids to take precautions against, they were vigilant – even officious – about using what powers they had. Many were the ARP wardens who reprimanded anyone in the street whom they saw lighting a cigarette, since strictly speaking even that tiny glow was a contravention of blackout regulations. Michael Hymers, elaborately correct after his blackout fine, patiently constructed a cover for his cigar, so that he could smoke in the garden since Lyn and Kirstie had banned him from doing so in the house.

Air-raid wardens were members of the Civil Defence Service, whose task was to counter the threat of air raids. They included some full-time, paid staff and a huge

body of volunteers organized by local authorities under the aegis of the Minister of Home Security. 'The general idea of an air-raid warden is that he should be a responsible member of the public chosen to be a leader and adviser of his neighbours in a small area, a street or a small group of streets, in which he is known and respected,' explained an official circular issued in March 1937. Men had to be over thirty (or over twenty-five 'if not available for more active service'); women over twenty-five. The coverage was local, roughly every square mile in cities and towns containing ten air-raid warden posts, sandbagged concrete boxes. Each post had responsibility for around 500 people and the vast majority of wardens – around 90 per cent – were part-timers, some only available in the evening.

At the head of the pyramid was a chief warden, often a retired soldier; next would come district wardens, and then post wardens in charge of some half a dozen sectors. Each sector was headed by a senior warden who would probably have another six wardens with him. At first Beckenham Council had decreed a quota: only one in six wardens could be a woman – but, given the realities of war, it soon relaxed this edict and announced that 'any ladies will be acceptable provided they are suitable for the work'. Wardens checked into the posts when coming on and going off duty and patrolled their own sectors when there was an alert. There was a telephone line linking each post to the central Control, and West Wickham residents were urged in September 1939 to keep the lines free 'by refraining from long conversations on the telephone'.

The point about this web was that as the wardens patrolled their patch, they knew the streets intimately, where everyone slept at night, who was away, and so on. If there was an 'incident' they could direct the rescue services to where there were likely to be people in need of rescue, buried in rubble or trapped beneath fallen timbers. The warden's duty was to report incidents to the Control Centre, call out and direct the

Reporting for duty: ARP wardens at Springfield, Essex.

appropriate services, comfort the victims until help arrived, identify poison gas, look in at public shelters, investigate UXBs (unexploded bombs), administer first aid, direct those bombed out to rest centres and those wounded who could get there to first-aid posts, and even deal with minor fires until help arrived.

The shoulders on which these onerous, responsible and sometimes harrowing duties fell were often somewhat frail, since most younger, able-bodied men had been called up for military service, or were in reserved occupations that might mean very long hours and hard physical work, often away from home. While full-time ARP wardens were paid £3 a week for men and £2 for women, with skilled rescue workers paid more in line with the wages in the construction industry, at first the part-time volunteers were not paid anything, though they were not supposed to work more than forty-eight hours a week! During the blitz most far exceeded that, and by then it had been agreed they would be paid for time spent on air-raid call-out. Initially, since they were essentially supposed to be civilians engaged in civil defence, ARP wardens did not have a uniform, but instead wore a badge, an arm band in some areas and a 'tin hat' (actually a steel helmet) coloured or marked to identify which branch of the CD they were in. But by 1942, in recognition that it was useful to be able to identify those officially dealing with an incident, they were issued with blue uniforms.

Robert Edom who, as a boy, lived a few streets from Braemar Gardens in West Wickham, remembers when his father was appointed street warden and 'took charge of the official street stirrup pump and two buckets, one of sand and one of water. These were kept in a state of instant readiness on our front doorstep and a white post was nailed to our front gate to indicate their location. I was very proud of this… Father was issued with a tin hat too with a "W" painted on it, but it made his bald head sore so he tended to wear his trilby hat instead. We never did use the stirrup pump on national service but it did come in handy for watering the carrots during dry spells.'

Would Michael have been one of those to volunteer as an ARP warden? The rush prior to the start of the war had not been overwhelming, though the aftermath of the Munich crisis had seen marked improvement. A report appeared in the *Beckenham Journal*, the West Wickham local paper, the day before war broke out reporting that that there were 'several thousand [local] volunteers' for ARP duties, 'which should have great effect for the public good in the event of the worst happening'. These citizens were already hard at work filling thousands of sandbags – even the mayor helped out there – and making sure that the trenches that had been dug for temporary shelter in case of air raids were serviceable. But the paper cautioned that while in 1938 the borough had 1,000 wardens in place out of the 1,200 it required, that figure had fallen by the outbreak of war. The relocation of many large firms into the country, taking their employees with them, as well as conscription, had deprived

this commuter belt of many of its most able-bodied volunteers, 'many who were trained are not now available'. So 'still more wardens are wanted, men between the ages of thirty and sixty-eight and women between twenty-five and fifty-eight. They are urgently needed for day, night or whole-time service in the borough.' Training would be given with 'bus fares recoverable at the termination of the training'.

During the blitz the demands on the ARP, as on the other Civil Defence services, were enormous. On New Year's Eve 1940 Herbert Morrison announced the introduction of compulsory fire watching, and regulations followed requiring that all men aged between eighteen and sixty not in the services or already doing Civil Defence duties, or working as policemen or seamen, 'or the blind or insane', to register to undertake up to forty-eight hours' firewatching a month. This law proved hard to enforce – indeed there was not a full complement of firewatchers to protect the Houses of Commons when they caught fire in May 1941, and many works premises were destroyed because there was no one watching out for incendiary bombs falling on them. Women formed informal firewatching teams too, usually centred on their street or church, and from 1943 women aged between twenty and forty-five were made liable for firewatching – now renamed 'Fire Guards'.

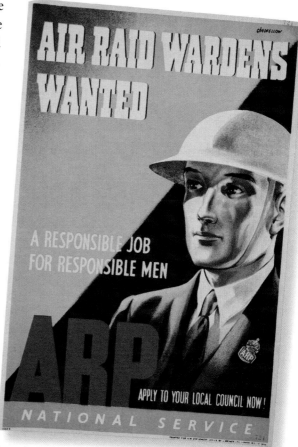

Given that fact that Michael was in a 'reserved occupation' making aircraft parts in a factory away from home, this was probably what he would have done rather than become an ARP warden. While it is possible that Lyn or Kirstie would have been part-time ARP wardens, or taken some other Civil Defence role such as shelter marshals, ambulance attendants, workers in a first-aid post or a control centre, with their family responsibilities it is more likely that they would have been firewatchers too, and perhaps taken up some voluntary work. It was something the War Cabinet would have to consider.

CHAPTER 6

SPITFIRE SUMMER

On 7 May 1940 the House of Commons was debating the fiasco in Norway, where Allied troops had withdrawn in the face of the German advance. The ex-Colonial Minister and veteran Conservative politician Leo Amery turned on the Prime Minister Neville Chamberlain. He quoted the words used by the seventeenth-century republican leader, Oliver Cromwell, to the Long Parliament when he thought it was no longer fit to conduct the affairs of the nation: 'You have sat too long here for any good you have been doing. In the name of God, go!'

Though Chamberlain won the vote that night, it was by a greatly reduced majority and it was clear that he could no longer count on the support of many in his own party, particularly those who filed through the lobbies in 'khaki, Navy blue and Air Force blue' uniform. The Labour leaders, Attlee and Greenwood, had conveyed news from their party conference meeting in Bournemouth that Labour would serve in a wartime coalition led by anyone but Chamberlain. But without Labour in government, the close co-operation of the trade unions, who were to be essential partners in the great push for increased war production, could not be guaranteed.

On the evening of 10 May, Chamberlain resigned and the maverick politician Winston Churchill was summoned to Buckingham Palace and charged with forming a new government. On 13 May, Churchill addressed the House for the first time as Prime Minister: 'I have nothing to offer,' he told the hushed members, 'but blood, toil, tears and sweat.' He spelled out his war aims: 'Victory – victory at all costs, victory

> Michael realizes his lifetime ambition to sit in a Spitfire as he talks to the plane's modern-day pilot Lee Proudfoot.

in spite of all terror, victory however long and hard the road may be… Come, then, let us go forward with our united strength.'

But privately he admitted, 'I just hope to God it's not too late.' The situation was increasingly grim: though the war at sea had raged ferociously since September 1939, on the home front it had been a 'phoney war', or 'bore war' as Churchill had called it when people began to question why they were bothering with the blackout every night, had mislaid their gas masks, and over half the children who had been evacuated to the country on the outbreak of war had returned to the cities by spring 1940. Food rationing had been introduced in January 1940, and there were shortages, but quite a range of unrationed food was still available – though more expensive – and in these early years the shortage of material goods was neither as acute nor as extensive as it was to become later, when essential possessions broke or wore out and were found to be literally irreplaceable.

On 9 April 1940 the German armies had occupied Denmark and Norway; the campaign to defend Norway had been chaotic and had been a key factor in Chamberlain's downfall. On the same day that Churchill took office, Hitler's armies invaded Holland; within four days it had surrendered, and Belgium fell on 28 May. French forces marching to the aid of Belgium were cut off by German tanks advancing over the Ardennes, while the 'impregnable' French Maginot line had proved to be an ineffective deterrent against German attack. By 22 May the Germans were nearly at the coast and the British Expeditionary Force was forced to evacuate at Dunkirk. Between 26 May and 3 June a total of 338,226 British, French and other Allied troops were ferried over the English Channel to safety in a seaborne flotilla that included Royal Navy ships, merchant vessels and a motley crew of tugs, lifeboats, pleasure steamers, barges and even rowing boats, between 850 and 950 craft in total. The troops were forced, however, to abandon most of their heavy weapons and equipment.

The railway line from the coast to London ran past the playing fields of Ron Cox's West Wickham school, and on the morning of 4 June 1940 the rumour spread through the school that carriages loaded with evacuated soldiers were stopping at the signals. The boys crowded into the school tuck shop to buy cakes and biscuits, which they took up the embankment to the carriages. Within minutes whole boxes of tuck together with jugs of lemonade were being handed to the dirty, bedraggled troops. It was the same all along the line: housewives and members of the voluntary services would hurry up to the waiting trains to press cups of tea, sandwiches and cake on the soldiers. It was a heroes' welcome, but without a victory.

On 2 June the Allies withdrew from Norway and twelve days later the Germans entered Paris. The French government signed an armistice with Germany on 22 June and with the other Axis power, Italy, on 24 June.

'All Behind you, Winston'. Low's 1940 cartoon of Churchill's 'people's army' of politicians. Shoulder to shoulder with the Prime Minister march Attlee and Bevin. The phalanx includes Morrison, Chamberlain, Halifax, Eden and Amery.

'Very well, alone!' ran the caption to Low's famous cartoon of a defiant Britain (though not entirely alone since she was supported by Empire troops), and the Bromley ARP wardens' service rolled off an alarming notice announcing 'THE GERMANS ARE AT BOULOGNE'. It continued, 'Do you realize that this means that they are less than thirty miles from our coast, and that we may have Air Raids at any moment? Have YOU taken all possible precautions?' It instructed all those who were 'NOT doing something' to enrol for a series of lectures for wardens – which 'is FREE'. Or, 'if the Wardens' Service does not interest you, why not take up First Aid, volunteer for the AFS, the Anti-Parachute Force, or give a home to Refugees? ENGLAND EXPECTS EVERYONE TO DO THEIR DUTY! Are you SURE you are doing yours in the hour of need?'

By 1 July 1940 more than half of all British men between twenty and twenty-five were in the services. That meant that more than a fifth of the entire male population between sixteen and forty was in uniform. But that left quite a proportion who were not – and the threat of invasion meant that as many bodies as possible were urgently required for Civil Defence. In October 1939 Churchill had suggested that there were thousands of middle-aged men who were not eligible for military service but were anxious to 'do their bit' for the war effort, and had suggested to Sir John Anderson that a 'Home Guard' of half a million civilians should be formed. On 14 May as German troops swarmed into Holland, Anthony Eden, Secretary of State for War in Churchill's new cabinet, broadcast an appeal for 'large numbers of men… between the ages of seventeen and sixty-five to come forward now and offer their services in order to make assurance [that an invasion would be repelled] doubly sure. The name of the new force which is now to be raised will be the Local Defence Volunteers. The name describes its duties in three words. You will not be paid, but you will receive free uniforms and you will be armed. In order to volunteer, what you have to do is to give your name at the local police station.'

As the minister finished speaking men were already pulling on their jackets and making for their nearest police station. They were in no doubt that they were needed: Hitler's troops were nearing the French coast and suddenly the English Channel seemed very narrow indeed. Next morning long queues of men eager to volunteer had formed and Bromley Police Station was so besieged that a West Wickham man was obliged to return home and try again later. Within twenty-four hours of the broadcast around 25,000 men had signed up; by the end of May the figure had reached nearly 400,000 and the flow showed no sign of drying up. By 17 May more than 1,000 LDVs were on duty at 10.30 p.m., standing on the white cliffs of Dover scanning the Channel for an invasion force. 'My expectations [which had been for a maximum of 15,000] have been far exceeded,' admitted Eden.

'England expects everyone to do their duty.'
Propaganda was a powerful force on the home front.

1940s
HOUSE

The Home Guard (as the LDV had been renamed at Churchill's suggestion on 23 July) were supposed to be able to fire a rifle: many could not, though the old soldiers of the First World War who joined up in their thousands (one volunteer from Perthshire had first seen action in the Egyptian Campaign of 1884–5) certainly could. But there were rarely sufficient Lee Enfields to go round: one between ten was not uncommon in the early days and ammunition was frequently so scarce that it could not be 'wasted' in practice and the 'uniform' for many months consisted of an armband marked 'HG'. It may be easy now to smile at this 'Dad's Army' with their ill-fitting khaki overalls (when they finally arrived), drilling on the village green or suburban playing field, empowered to challenge every car or pedestrian abroad at night to identify themselves, combing cornfields for reported parachute landings. The fear of German airborne troops floating down in parachutes and gliders, as they had so chillingly done in Holland, was very real. It was bound up too with the fear of 'fifth columnists', traitors who would help the invaders, and the rumour machine that suggested that they would come in disguise – as nuns maybe – and thus be hard to detect. Even the normally steady *Times* carried an editorial on 11 May 1940 telling its readers that enemy parachutists 'might speak English quite well. Some might be sent over in civilian clothes to act as spies. The general public must be alert.'

But equipment grew more plentiful and sophisticated as the war progressed: 'First came the khaki forage caps,' noted Robert Edom, for whom watching the Home Guard training in a West Wickham field that the local children used for a playground 'when it wasn't being used for goat grazing' added some interest to those deadly dull Sundays when 'buying a stick of liquorice… promised to bring down the wrath of God'. Then along came the haversacks, 'useful for keeping elevenses in. They were filled with dummy wooden rifles and a tin filled with small bits of metal which when shaken vigorously sounded vaguely like a machine gun.'

The mayor of Deptford, as a member of the LDV, receives musketry instruction from a regular soldier.

Later in the war, the Home Guard began to be better equipped with firearms used by the army, including Bren guns, Browning Automatic Rifles – already familiar from films about American gangsters – and 'Tommy guns' known officially as Thompson sub-machine guns. It also received some weapons specifically designed for it like the Northover Projectors, which resembled a drainpipe mounted on two legs and were designed to fire glass bottles filled with highly flammable phosphorous gas, and more systematic training was gradually introduced. The local Home Guard practised grenade throwing at West Wickham Park Sports Club and received instruction and training at the Wheatsheaf pub. Peter Tilling's father, who had represented Britain in the International Rifle Shooting championship in 1939, was one of those who trained the West Wickham Home Guard, while his mother baked rock cakes for their canteen. Soon the demand for those competent with rifles was so acute that the thirteen-year-old Peter, a keen shot like his father, found himself teaching men four times his age and more, how to fire.

Members of what George Orwell (himself an eager recruit) called a 'People's Army officered by Blimps' proved themselves all over Britain to be conscientious and resourceful in guarding key installations, keeping a vigil along Britain's coastline, manning roadblocks, defending aerodromes, protecting factories, demonstrating the value of local knowledge in manoeuvres and generally releasing regular soldiers for training and for more urgent tasks. By June 1941 one in every five adult males who was not in the armed forces or engaged in essential police or civil defence work was a member of the Home Guard, and that did not include the thousands of women engaged in unofficial support capacities. When the King, George VI, inspected the 4,400 men of the West Wickham Home Guard as they paraded around the Cricket Club on 10 August 1940, they all marched in step, stiff as ramrods as the King took the salute on the pavilion steps.

West Wickham was situated in the outer line of defence around London which consisted of anti-tank lines with deep trenches, barriers, pillboxes and roadblocks. When Churchill guaranteed, 'We shall defend our island, whatever the cost may be, we shall fight on the beaches, we shall fight on the landing grounds, we shall fight in the fields and in the streets, we shall fight in the hills; we shall never surrender' – this is what he had in mind. The town was made ready: trenches and tank traps were dug in woods and playing fields (one was scheduled to cut right through West Wickham's football pitch but at the last minute it was diverted through the grounds of one of the town's large houses thanks to the public-spiritedness of its owner). Concrete blocks were set up to delay enemy tanks, sometimes with slots for metal hoops, so that, given the order that the Germans had landed, these could be inserted to provide what was hoped was an impenetrable obstacle. Poles and barricades were dug into the ground to prevent enemy troop carriers and gliders from landing, while

drums of oil and creosote were concealed by the side of main roads to form 'flame traps' for enemy transport and so impede advancing troops.

To confuse fifth columnists and thwart the invader, signposts were removed and railway station names painted over. Dr Ron Cox, a local historian, recalls that his uncle was obliged to paint out 'West Wickham' on the advertising sign that hung beneath the crossbar of his firm's delivery bicycles, while the local paper drew attention to a notice in a West Wickham estate agent's which had been amended to read 'Live in healthy [blank].' Church bells were silenced and permitted to ring only to warn of an invasion. 'Shadow larders' were set up with stocks of food that would have allowed about 9 pounds a head of tinned meat, soup, stew or beans, tinned milk, emergency biscuits, sugar, margarine and tea. These were then distributed to forty-four local food minders who stored them in their homes ready to dole them out to the 200 or so households for whom they were responsible.

'Wars are not won by evacuations,' Churchill had told Parliament on 4 June 1940 as the Dunkirk exercise drew to a close, anxious that the nation's relief might sap its pugilistic resolve. 'But,' he added, 'there was a victory inside this deliverance, which should be noted. It was gained by the Air Force.' It was believed they had inflicted heavy losses on the Luftwaffe.

A church in Gravesend, Kent, with its sign conscripted to confound the enemy in the summer of 1940.

The RAF was soon to be in the front line of the war again in a way that had a dramatic effect on the life of West Wickham that summer. 'Sealion' was the German code name for the invasion of Britain. Hitler was unable to understand why, after the fall of France, Britain would not sue for peace and on 16 July 1940 issued Directive No. 16 on preparations 'for a landing operation against England'. But first the RAF would have to be eliminated so that it would be unable to foil a German cross-Channel attack. It took the Luftwaffe precisely six minutes to cross the Channel to Dover; in five more the planes were directly over the airfields of Fighter Command 11 Group. This covered the south-east, including the triangle of airports – Biggin Hill, Croydon and Kenley – that surrounded West Wickham and, as the Fighter Command stations nearest to northern France, were probably the hardest pressed of all. In mid-June 1940 the 'Battle of Britain', the term coined by Churchill for the German High Command's attempt to gain air supremacy over southern England

A paper seller displays the score in the battle for Britain on 15 September 1940.

in advance of the planned invasion, began. Throughout that perfect, hot summer the skies over West Wickham were scarred by the vapour trails of planes and the scream of dogfights between the British Hurricanes, Spitfires and Blenheims rising to engage the apparently superior German force of Messerschmitts, Junkers, Heinkels and Dorniers in battle.

Ron Cox was sitting his General School Certificate that June as the planes wove about the sky, zooming down and letting rip bursts of machine-gun fire: 'It was like watching a war film.' On the day he was due to take his French exam, a master strode into the hall and instructed the candidates as they prepared to turn over their question papers: 'Don't waste time looking out of the windows. If you hear anything falling, you can get under the desk, but under no circumstances are you to talk.' Later, Robert Edom remembers looking out of the window of his dining room in West Wickham and seeing a Focke-Wulf 190, which came into service in July 1941, flying down his avenue at rooftop height. As a nine-year-old boy, he was 'proud that not only did I identify the plane without recourse to my aircraft recognition book but I actually saw the helmeted head of the pilot'. Peter Tilling, who lived in Braemar Gardens during the war and still does today, was thirteen when the Battle of Britain started. He found it 'quite exciting really. Sometimes you could actually see the tracer bullets hit the aircraft. They really didn't seem very far away at all and a few times we had airmen coming down with parachutes and I used to get on my bike and go off to find them. There was one plane that crashed a few roads away, and I got on my bike and cycled over and picked up a parachute harness as it burned. It was what all boys did at the time, collect souvenirs of the conflict.'

The roof of West Wickham Post Office housed a lookout post for the Royal Observer Corps, one of a network that covered the whole of south-east England to alert Fighter Command of any approaching aircraft, especially those too low to be picked up by British radar. It was manned by volunteers who included the manager of the Westminster Bank in the High Street, a local greengrocer, businessmen and a one-time Wimbledon tennis umpire.

Throughout June and July the Luftwaffe concentrated their attacks on shipping in the Channel supplemented by raids on south-coast ports. The tactic was never as

successful as Hitler and the Commander-in-Chief of the Luftwaffe, Goering, had anticipated: though some 30,000 tons of shipping were destroyed, that was a small part of almost 1 million tons that ploughed across the Channel weekly. So on 12 August the tactics were changed and the Luftwaffe, ordered to destroy the British Air Force in as short a time as possible, launched a series of concerted attacks on British airfields, knowing that these were targets the RAF was bound to defend. They flew night sorties as well to stretch British fighter capabilities. Biggin Hill was attacked six times in three days at the end of August. This was a much more successful strategy, but it would have probably been even more so if the Luftwaffe had concentrated on putting the British radar chain, the 'eyes' of Fighter Command, out of action.

The pilots who flew in the Battle of Britain became known as 'the few' after Churchill's historic tribute to them on 20 August 1940: 'The gratitude of every home in our island, in our Empire, and indeed throughout the world… goes out to the British airmen who, undaunted by odds, unwearied in their constant challenge and mortal danger, are turning the tide of the world war by their prowess and their devotion. Never in the field of human conflict, was so much owed by so many to so few.' The Battle of Britain cost the Luftwaffe approximately 1,294 aircraft and the RAF around 788. In August 1940, the deadliest month of the Battle, 230 RAF pilots were killed: their average age was twenty-four.

Spitfire summer. Michael, Lyn, Ben and Kirstie scan the skies at Biggin Hill.

Michael Hymers' admiration for the Battle of Britain pilots – and his interest in the planes they flew, particularly Spitfires – meant that he was very eager to visit Biggin Hill aerodrome, which was less than three miles from his 1940 home.

Biggin Hill, or 'Biggin the Bump' as it is known for its commanding position on the North Downs, was part of the inner patrol zone of the London Air Defence Area in the First World War. No. 141 Squadron Royal Flying Corps was posted there with its Bristol fighters, each of which sported a bright red cockerel painted on the fuselage, and the airfield was able to claim at least one German Gotha bomber shot down.

On the outbreak of the Second World War No. 601 Squadron was based at Biggin Hill, equipped with wooden-framed Hurricanes and the more recently introduced metal-framed Spitfires. During the 'phoney war' No. 79 Squadron was the first to claim a 'kill' when a Dornier DO 17 was shot down on 21 November 1939 – the first of thousands. Hurricane patrols flew from Biggin Hill during the Dunkirk evacuation, but by the start of the Battle of Britain Biggin Hill had become a Spitfire station.

Between 18 August 1940 and 7 January 1941 Biggin Hill aerodrome was attacked twelve times. The most serious being two attacks on the night of 30 August when a small formation of low-level bombers dropped 1,000 pounds of bombs, reducing the aerodrome to a shambles with workshops, stores, barracks, WAAF quarters and a hangar wrecked. Thirty-nine personnel were killed and a further thirty badly injured. In two raids on 1 September a runway was seriously damaged, as was the sector operations room, the teleprinter network was wrecked by a 500-pound bomb. Three members of the WAAF were awarded the Military Medal for their refusal to leave their posts until the very last minute. Despite the heavy damage sustained, Biggin Hill remained operational throughout the entire Battle of Britain, though for one week the damage was so severe that only one squadron could operate from it.

Having surveyed a Spitfire on the runway at Biggin Hill, Thomas gets a chance to sit in the cockpit.

The German offensive against Russia released Fighter Command from a purely defensive role and it began launching attacks on occupied Europe which were given code names like 'circuses', 'rhubarb' and 'rodeos'. In the

Remembering 'the few'. Thomas and Ben at Biggin Hill.

summer of 1941 the arrival of Spitfire VBs contributed to the station's success and during 'Operation Jubilee', the combined raid on Dieppe in August 1942 (a disastrous rehearsal for D-Day) the Biggin Wing claimed fifteen enemy aircraft for six RAF pilots lost. The intense frontline fighting from Biggin Hill and its sector stations Lympne, Hawkinge, Gravesend and West Malling meant that periodically squadrons had to be withdrawn and rested in quieter sectors, and they were replaced by other brave conscripts to the RAF and volunteers required to bring the squadrons up to strength – men from Poland, Holland and Belgium as well as Britain.

Biggin Hill was to become a household name in 1943 when the station and its sector airfields were the first to claim 1,000 enemy aircraft destroyed. The official veil of secrecy that shrouded the operational details of RAF Fighter Command at the time was drawn aside to give publicity to Biggin Hill's claim, and over 1,000 guests were invited to one of the most spectacular parties of the Second World War. Three lobsters labelled 'Hitler', 'Mussolini' and 'Goering' adorned the top table, and fifty London taxi drivers insisted on driving the pilots up to the London hotel where the celebration was being held, free of charge.

It had been a tradition during the war to have an 'open day' at Biggin Hill on Empire Day, and this has continued after the war to commemorate the Battle of Britain. In June 2000 during the sixtieth anniversary of 'Spitfire Summer', to their great delight the Hymers family were picked up in a 1940 taxi and driven to Biggin Hill Open Day. It was a memorable day: they watched the pilots 'scramble' and saw

the Spitfires and Hurricanes taxi along the runway and take off in formation. Michael, Ben and Thomas watched enthralled as the small, light, highly manoeuvrable planes darted and wheeled overhead. But their biggest thrill came when the planes 'pancaked' and Michael and the boys were invited in turn to sit in the cockpit of a Spitfire with one of the pilots, Lee Proudfoot.

'It was brilliant,' enthused Ben. 'It was a real Spitfire. It was the bit I enjoyed best of everything that happened in the 1940s house.' Michael was awestruck to realize that he was sitting in one of the planes he had read so much about, pored over pictures of, could quote facts about the dimensions, speeds, fuel consumption of – and indeed was modelling in balsa wood in the garage of 17 Braemar Gardens. 'For as long as I can remember I have wanted to get close up to a Spitfire. I'd never even seen one on the ground before. I first became interested in Spitfires as a teenager when I used to watch old war films and see them in combat. I just thought that it was a perfectly shaped plane.

Then once when I was on holiday in Weymouth I heard this amazing sound of an engine, long before the plane came into view, and I realized that it was a Spitfire when I saw the wing shape. I though the arc of the wing was quite beautiful.

But I never thought that I'd actually have the opportunity to sit in the cockpit and fiddle with the controls. Lee was telling me that it is the best plane he's ever flown, it's a perfectly balanced machine. It was his dream to fly a Spitfire ever since he started to train to be a pilot, and I am sure that there are hundreds of pilots who would give anything to try out a Spitfire. It must be an amazing feeling. I would love to fly one myself. If I could fly, that is!'

But Michael found it a sobering moment too: 'I kept remembering how many of the young men – many scarcely more than boys – who had sat in the cockpit just like I was doing, hadn't come back. They'd been shot down, or baled out over the sea or over enemy territory. It really made me realize the dangers they faced, the sacrifices they made to keep England free.'

Standing there looking at her husband, and delighting that his life's ambition was being realized, Lyn quietly resolved that she would never complain about the lack of cooking equipment in the 1940s house again. She fervently hoped that she would have been in the front line offering her 'Saucepans for Spitfires' as the newly appointed Minister of Aircraft Production, Lord Beaverbrook, had urged in 1940. And Kirstie felt a pang as she watched Ben, thrilled to be in the cockpit, fiddling with the controls, making aircraft noises. She thought of the 'actual pilots who had flown these Spitfires during the war, so many had been killed fighting for their country. They were so heroic – and so tragic too.' And she reflected that if her ten-year-old son had been that age in 1940 it would only have been six more years before he could have joined the RAF and soon have been flying dangerous missions in defence of his country.

CHAPTER 7

INTO THE SHELTER

'I was sitting in the dining room in my nightie and dressing gown, writing my diary,' said Lyn. 'It was teeming with rain outside, and I was thinking thank goodness I'm in the house, in front of a coal fire, safe and warm, when the air-raid siren went off. It was totally unexpected. We'd had a few daytime raids already, but this was completely different. Michael and the children were in bed, and Kirstie was making her way upstairs. It was very dark and very eerie, There was no thought in my mind that it wasn't real, that we were play acting – I just leapt up and did what had to be done.

'It really shook me. I was on autopilot. Without a thought Kirstie ran upstairs for the children, and I went to get some provisions. I scooped up some warm clothes and the emergency basket we kept ready by the back door for such an occasion. All it had in it were the bare essentials – candles, matches, a torch, a bottle of water, a game for the boys, writing paper and a pen – so I grabbed the stone hot water bottle that I'd been given and I got some blankets and slipped through the mud to the Anderson shelter and flung them on the children's bunks and lit a candle on the table. It was still pouring with rain and I had to make several trips so I tucked my nightie into my knickers. One time I was in such a hurry that I hadn't fastened the suitcase properly and it sprung open and all the dry clothes fell out into the mud.

'Then Kirstie passed Ben and Thomas down to me – they'd just woken up, and we had to reassure them. That must have been the most important thing in the blitz, to try to reassure the children, though heaven knows it must have been difficult with bombs falling all round.

Ben and Thomas peer out from the Anderson shelter
their grandfather built in the garden.

'The whole thing went like clockwork. We hadn't had any prior discussion, it just seemed that we knew instinctively what to do. We slipped into a lifesaving routine. We did it for real, we went into the shelter for real. The panic and the fear were there. Once we were all in the shelter safely, we sat shaking, but then these feelings went and I was back in 2000, but for those few minutes I had been reliving history. I really felt that I knew what it must have felt like to get your family into the shelter when the siren sounded. The feeling stayed with me for days and I kept shivering when I thought of families huddling together in the shelter. not knowing whether they would live or die. It made all our hardships seem pretty trivial by comparison.'

A speaker had been set up in the hall at 17 Braemar Gardens to relay the high single note of an air-raid alert followed after an indeterminate interval – sometimes an hour or so, on other occasions the best part of the night – by the welcome note of the 'All Clear'. The Hymers family had been in their 1940s home for a fortnight and their wartime calendar had advanced to the late summer of 1940. In June that year the first bombs to fall in the London area fell on a ploughed field in nearby Addington. West Wickham was bombed for the first time on 31 August when a house in The Avenue, the other side of the station from Braemar Gardens, received a direct hit and collapsed on to the house next door, rendering it uninhabitable. No one was hurt, but the Thompson family whose house had been badly damaged was severely shocked. Subsequently their daughter grew so used to getting messages saying, 'Don't go home, there's a land mine in your garden' or 'There's a UXB [unexploded bomb] near where you live' that she 'went so far as to carry my toothbrush around with me', as she told Joyce Walker, who wrote the history of West Wickham during the war.

There had been air-raid alerts throughout August as the Luftwaffe attacked airfields in a concerted attempt to wipe out the RAF bases. A hundred German planes attacked Biggin Hill and dropped 200 bombs on 18 August. The record books of local schools after term had restarted make distressing reading as they register the days that the school was closed because of air-raid alerts, or when children had to troop out of the classroom into the shelter several times during a normal school day; and there were days when many failed to turn up for lessons after a night disturbed by air-raid alerts.

Saturday 7 September 1940 was a particularly beautiful day in a summer of near perfect weather. West Wickham residents were taking tea in their gardens, mowing the lawn or dozing in the sun, when suddenly at 4.15 p.m. the skies started to fill with the drone of squadron after squadron of German bombers – 300 in all, supported by 600 fighters – making for London. Goering had arrived on the Channel coast to personally direct the Luftwaffe's

Having been given the 'All Clear' signa emerges from Anderson shelter the m after another raid.

change of tactics: it was now aiming to lure out Fighter Command with a massive, concentrated attack on London. In effect, it was the abandonment of Operation Sealion, the invasion that had seemed so imminent, though it was not to be formally postponed by Hitler – in effect cancelled – until 17 September.

Bombs – over 300 tons of high explosive and many thousands of incendiaries – rained down on the docks and the surrounding East End (West Ham, Poplar, Bermondsey, Stepney) all night, until 4.30 the next

morning. The long-feared nightmare of the blitz had begun. For fifty-seven consecutive nights (bar one when the weather was too bad for the bombers), and often by day as well, the capital suffered a devastating assault from the air. That first night the fires conflated as members of the AFS, many of whom had never fought a fire before, worked alongside the regular fire service to quell the flames that threatened to engulf the city. The fierce red column of smoke that rose from the blaze could be seen from West Wickham 12 miles away, and two crews of AFS men with their pumps were sent to West Ham round 7.30 that evening and from there were ordered to the waterfront at North Woolwich.

As Bert Purkiss, one of those who went from West Wickham to help out the hard-pressed London firemen, remembered: 'Fires were everywhere – in peacetime a major fire was judged to be a "thirty-pump affair". At midnight on 7 September there were nine huge conflagrations rated at "100 pumps each" and as the night wore on, row after row of dockers' cottages were alight as firemen could do little more than stand and watch as their heavy canvas hoses ran dry, and many were trapped by the sheets of flames. The water mains had been damaged and the Thames was at low tide, so for several hours all that could be done was rescue pets and valuables for the people before the flames crept along the streets to their houses.'

Many had worked continuously for forty hours to try to control the inferno, as blazing timbers crashed down and burning rubber belched out clouds of black smoke. The tea and sugar stored in the dockside warehouses gave off a sickly stench as it burned, while

While families waited inside their shelters, outside firemen would have been fighting fires across London.

boiling paint soared into the air, coating hoses and nozzles with sticky varnish. Buildings collapsed, the intense heat blistered the paint on the fireboats in the Thames and the air was so full of burning matter and sparks that it was painful to breathe.

By September the blitz had extended beyond the East End with its docks, warehouses and row upon row of back-to-back houses, to the rest of London, and in late November it spread across the country. The raids on the capital, though lighter after mid-November for a time, continued with dreary and terrifying regularity, including the 'great fire raid' of 29 December 1940 when a strong westerly wind fanned the flames and a low tide meant that the Thames could not be pumped and the mains were nearly dry – but now London was only one target among many others.

On 14 November the Luftwaffe turned its attention to the Midlands city of Coventry – 449 bombers struck, more than on any previous night in London: 554 people were killed, 865 were seriously injured and the city centre including the fine medieval cathedral was razed. A new word entered the language: 'coventration'. Then it was the turn of Southampton to experience 'episodic blitzing' – erratic raids, following no discernible pattern, where a town or city might just be beginning to

King George VI visits victims of a bombing raid.

recover from a night's devastation when another raid would come and then another a few days or weeks later. In less than a fortnight of raids, 481 people were killed in Southampton; then Portsmouth was bombed from December to April. Bristol had twenty-six raids from November, through December into April, while Plymouth was attacked in November and then consistently throughout the spring of 1941.

From February to May, German air power was directed against ports around the south-west and west coast from Plymouth to Cardiff, Swansea, Merseyside and Clydeside. The aim was to destroy the Royal Navy's bases and knock out the docks unloading war matériel and supplies from the US, brought by the convoys that the infamous U-boats had not been able to stop. The Germans turning inland again, Manchester and its industrial belt of Bolton and Stockport was blitzed on the two nights preceding Christmas Eve 1940 and again in January 1941, while Birmingham suffered seventy-three separate raids from November to May. There were major attacks on Tyneside, Cardiff, Sheffield, Nottingham, Newcastle and Belfast, and on Hull from March to May 1941 when, out of the city's housing stock of 93,000, only 6,000 homes escaped damage. Later, in 1942, came the so-called 'Baedeker raids' when historic towns that had featured in the German guidebook series – such places as Bath, Canterbury, York, Norwich and Exeter – were bombed. Many other places throughout Britain from Aberdeen to Falmouth suffered air raids between 7 September 1940 and 16 May 1941.

In March 1941 the bombers returned to London, which endured heavy and almost continuous raids until mid-May. Indeed, the night of 10 May 1941, the last night of the blitz, was the worst: it was a clear night with a 'bomber's moon' and again the Thames was at a low ebb. Fires raged from Hammersmith in the west to Romford in the east. There were 2,200 fires in all, including a major conflagration at the Elephant and Castle, and that night Westminster Abbey, the Law Courts, the War Office in Whitehall, the Royal Mint, the House of Commons and the Tower of London were hit. A quarter of a million books went up in flames at the British Museum – as did £100,000 worth of gin in the City Road. In the single raid, 1,436 people were killed and 1,792 were seriously injured.

The next morning it was not possible to see the early summer sun for the pall of smoke that hung over the city. A third of the streets were impassable; 155,000 families were without gas, water or electricity; all main line stations but one were closed for weeks. It was eleven days before the last fire was finally put out – scraps of charred paper blew in the wind as far as 30 miles from the capital. The garden of the Westminster bank in West Wickham High Street was littered with burned fragments of bibles and prayer books that had blown from a City church.

It could have been the end, but then almost as suddenly as they had come Goering's planes wheeled east to bomb Russia in support of the attack Hitler had – fatally – launched on the Soviet Union in June 1941. There were still raids on London

and provincial targets (Hull in particular) during June and July, but essentially the blitz was over – for the time being.

London had suffered seventy-one major attacks between September 1939 and May 1941: 18,291 tons of high explosives were dropped, resulting in 19,877 civilian deaths and 25,578 serious casualties – something under half the total for the country: 41,987 dead and 49,405 seriously injured. Around one and a quarter million houses had been destroyed or seriously damaged, a high percentage of the total housing stock.

But it was not only the cities and large towns that felt the effect of the blitz, though these received the most frequent and most concentrated attacks. Flying home, having missed their targets or failed to drop all their bombs, the German planes would strafe and bomb trains, rail lines, bridges, suburbs, villages, hamlets, even isolated farms – and West Wickham stood squarely on the bombers' 'way home'.

In the early hours of 8 September 1940 bombs fell in West Wickham as the raids on the East End were at last coming to an end. A wardens' post was demolished, though fortunately the seven wardens on duty escaped with only minor injuries which did not inhibit them from going to rescue a woman who had been trapped underneath the wreckage of a bombed house nearby and whose frantic cries for help they had heard. Friday, 13 September, was an ominous day: bombs fell on the High Street and several other locations in West Wickham, and two members of the Evans family were killed when a bomb fell on their home in Station Road, while another family had to be dug out of their Anderson shelter after part of their house, which had been damaged in the attack, collapsed.

Marjorie Moyce was a teenager when war broke out; she lost several old school friends when bombs fell on Pickhurst Avenue in May 1941, killing ten people. She remembered that after she had joined the Land Army and would come home for a visit, she would 'notice piles of plaster in the gutters where people had swept out their ceilings that had come down in a raid'. One day, as she approached her own home, she realized with a sinking heart that the piles were getting bigger. Full of apprehension, she rounded the corner. But all was well.

That night, Peter Tilling was with his parents and some neighbours in the shelter that his father had built when a stick of bombs came down and one fell in the space between 16 and 18 Braemar Gardens, right opposite to where the Hymers were to live in their '1940s house'.

He remembered: 'We all came out of the shelter to look – both houses had been blown down and it looked as if four more were on fire. It was the blackout, of course, and there was light pouring from these houses exactly as if they were burning. But it turned out that the plaster falling from the ceiling had knocked all the light switches on so that's why the houses looked as if they were ablaze. Fortunately there was no one living there at the time – which is why the blackout wasn't in place,

Peter Tilling, who still lives in the street today, stands outside the remains of 16 and 18 Braemar Gardens after an air raid in May 1941.

I suppose. My father and my older brother were both in the Civil Defence and they rushed over to turn the lights off. Then incendiary bombs started falling too. Luckily they did not hit any houses, they just fell in the middle of the road. So everyone lugged out whatever sandbags they could find to put them out, and got out the stirrup pump and soon we'd dealt with them all.'

The Tillings had just got back in the shelter when a large bomb fell in Ravenswood Avenue, which backs on to Braemar Gardens: 'That was a quite a large bomb, which must only been about 35 yards from the shelter, and it really shook us all. We really did feel it that time.' Mr Tilling did a paper round during the war and vividly remembers not being certain every morning as he set off with his sack of newspapers 'if there would still be a letterbox to push it through'.

In October and November West Wickham suffered more heavy raids and losses of life and property, as did most of the suburbs and towns that ringed London. In October a Messerschmitt was shot down by RAF fighters and its pilot baled out, slightly wounded, and was marched to the police station.

On 7 October a bomb fell close to St Francis's Church, blowing out the east window and destroying the organ and one of the walls, leaving an enormous crater almost as wide as the road. A piece of concrete fell through the roof of the Plaza Cinema, slightly injuring two soldiers, and the film show had to be brought to an end as light was flooding in though a jagged hole in the roof.

Later that month a 500-pound bomb demolished shops in the High Street, including Woolworth's, and an ARP officer who was in an adjacent flat at the time had to crawl through debris and perilously hanging wreckage to report the incident. In November a children's home was hit and the cook and a maid were killed. Staff had to distract the children as stretcher cases were carried past the window. After that sobering incident, the children were evacuated to Herefordshire for the rest of the war.

In January incendiary bombs fell on St John's Church, and glanced off the roof on to the lead guttering and organ chamber: the timbers were already alight before a fireman saw the flames and single-handedly climbed up the wall to extinguish the fire and save the church. On 16 April 1941, as London experienced one of the worst raids of the war, more than twenty large bombs fell on West Wickham: six Canadian soldiers were killed in one incident and soon the High Street was ablaze after hundreds of incendiary bombs had fallen. With great courage, householders followed the example of the weary ARP workers in shovelling the bombs out of the windows and rendering them harmless by covering them with earth from the garden. Two 500-pound bombs fell in Grosvenor Gardens, and a warden narrowly missed death when a huge lump of clay from a bomb crater, weighing over a ton, crashed through the roof of his house as he was taking his son to a shelter. The centre of Bromley, the nearest sizeable town, was destroyed that night.

Nearly a month later, on the worst night of the London blitz, 10 May 1940, eight people were killed in West Wickham in one incident and a fourteen-year-old boy was thrown up into a tree by the force of the blast and paralysed from the waist down. Several huge craters appeared in the roads and a gas main was fractured, sending flames shooting into the night sky that could be extinguished only by plugging the main with wet clay from the craters.

On such occasions the emergency services were stretched to their limits: wardens were fully occupied dealing with air-raid incidents, alerting the appropriate rescue services, giving help where they could, touring the public shelters, baling out water from Anderson shelters, informing and calming the public during and after a raid and fulfilling their traditional role of enforcing blackout regulations in the town – though meeting much less resistance than they had before the blitz started. They were no longer resented as 'little 'itlers' for their supposed dictatorial attitude, nor criticized as being 'parasites and slackers' as they had been in the House of Commons during the 'phoney war', after which their numbers had been cut and some paid wardens dismissed. Most members of the public now saw the sense of the ARP wardens' vigilance, welcomed their ubiquitous presence in the streets and respected their diligence and often bravery in the face of the unexpected.

Michael and Ben consult advice from the Ministry of Information about air-raid precautions.

More even than the explosions, it was fire that was to prove the greatest hazard of the blitz. By 1940 the structure of the service that had to deal with these nightly conflagrations consisted the regular firemen, numbering about 6,000 (often ex-soldiers imbued with military discipline and a certain contempt for their colleagues in the Auxiliary Fire Service), the AFS with some 60,000 full-time volunteers and hundreds and thousands of part-timers, who had 'for reasons of patriotism, a fondness for bonfires or some other motive', according to Constantine FitzGibbon who wrote a

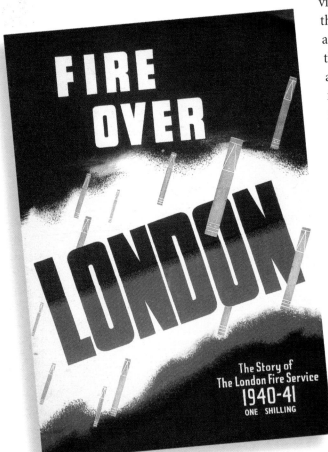

The Story of
The London Fire Service
1940-41
ONE SHILLING

vivid account of the London blitz, joined the AFS in the early stages of the war, and in 1940 had decided to stay with the fire fighters rather than enrol in the army, navy or air force. Some, who had inclined to pacifism before the war, but no longer regarded this as a tenable option when they saw the dangers their fellow citizens faced, also joined the AFS.

The attitude of the regular service to their wartime colleagues was often far from welcoming. FitzGibbon calls it 'shabby' and recalls conversations with London AFS members who reported that the regular firemen would not let them use their showers when they all returned filthy from attending the same fire. No attempts were made to provide them with canteens: 'in general they were treated with the rough contempt that boys of eight receive from their seniors aged eleven'. Indeed the writer, Henry Green, whose novel *Caught* captures the relationship between the AFS and the Fire Service painfully and vividly, felt so bitter about the situation that when his book was published in 1943, its foreword read: 'This book is about the Auxiliary Fire Service which saved London in her night blitzes, and bears no relation, or resemblance, to the National Fire Service, or any individual of that Service, which took over when raids on London had ended.' This wording has not been revised in subsequent editions.

But as Angus Calder has pointed out, pay for regular firemen was very low and resources and equipment often inadequate; it was not surprising that there was some suspicion of the 'amateurs' who flooded the service prepared to work for only meagre compensation for loss of income, long hours, no guaranteed sick pay or injury compensation, and a call on equipment that was often inadequate for the regular service's needs. In West Wickham, however, Bert Purkiss insisted, there were no such tensions: 'We all knew we had a job to do and we just got on with it. We worked as a team,' he said.

There were women members of both the AFS (5,000 had volunteered) and the Fire Service; their contribution was to staff control centres, work as telephonists, help in mobile canteens and as drivers and motorbike despatch riders.

Despite the goodwill of the fire fighters and their selfless response to calls for assistance, the organization was not satisfactory: at the outbreak of war there had been 1,666 local authorities organizing fire brigades in Britain and few had more than twenty full-time firemen. Long after the outbreak of war, many remained ill-equipped – some authorities had no towing vehicles so pumps had to be pushed to

Lyn, Thomas and Ben eat supper in the shelter.

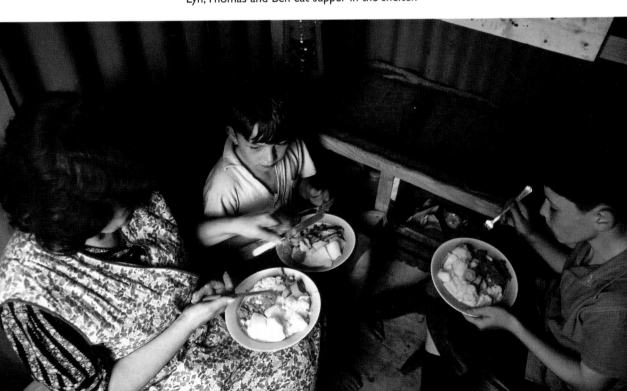

1940s HOUSE

the scene of a fire – and though most boroughs responded with alacrity to a call for help, others refused, sent only poorly trained auxiliaries or charged for assistance. But it was not until May 1941 as the aerial bombardment came to an end – for the time being – that it was announced that in recognition of the need for a more unified, directed service, the AFS and the Fire Service were to be merged into a National Fire Service under a Chief of Fire Staff. The mass of local authorities fused into fewer than fifty 'fire forces' operating under a central control, and many AFS men were appointed to senior positions over the heads of regular firemen.

As a service on the edge of Greater London, the calls on the West Wickham fire services were considerable: they had been there on that first terrible night of 7 September 1940, and on many nights during the blitz had responded to the call to send men and machines. But it wasn't only London that needed their services. Just before Christmas 1940, at twenty minutes' notice, the West Wickham station officer took thirty-two of his men to Manchester by bus to fight a blaze that threatened to engulf the city. The cathedral had been damaged and, in those days before fire watching had been made compulsory, there were locked commercial buildings with no one to put out the incendiary bombs that were raining down. From that night, West Wickham firemen worked for thirty-six hours continually against fires that, along with high explosive bombs, killed about 1,000 people and demolished or rendered uninhabitable 75,000 houses. But, not wanting to miss the festivities with their families, the smoke-blackened and exhausted men declined the offer of rest and set off to travel home on Christmas Day, only to find that transport cafes on their route declined to serve food and drink to these dirty and dishevelled heroes.

The crews also responded to calls from Plymouth in April 1941 when that West Country naval town was under intense and repeated attack.

ARP workers demonstrating the use of a stirrup pump to render incendiary bombs harmless.

One of the members of the West Wickham AFS at this time was Reg Long, who had volunteered in 1937. When the Hymers moved into Braemar Gardens, Reg was living at Glebe Court, an old people's home where Lyn and Kirstie were later to work as WVS volunteers, and he told Lyn about this time in the AFS. He recalled the sheer exhaustion, forty-eight hours on followed by twenty-four hours off – 'We just snatched sleep when and where we could. I learned to sleep on a scaffold tower.' He also recounted how he had been called out to an incident and found his own wife and small daughter had been trapped in the refuge-room under the stairs that he had reinforced when his house had been badly damaged in a raid. Reg remembered two of the most heart-rending incidents of the war in West Wickham. In the first incident on 19 March 1941 five AFS members had been on their way to Silvertown in East London to fight a blaze when, as they were driving along Plaistow Road in West Ham, a land mine had exploded, killing all five men. They now lie buried together in St John's churchyard.

The family emerge. Lyn helps Thomas out of the Anderson shelter.

Recalling the second incident, Reg still shook with emotion, sixty years later. On the night of 19–20 April 1941 he had been on leave when the AFS responded to another call to the East End. Their assembly point this time was the Old Palace School in Poplar, and as they were assembling to receive their instructions the building received a direct hit. Thirty-four AFS men were killed, including twenty-one from Beckenham, ten of whom were attached to West Wickham station. Thirteen members of the London Fire Brigade were also killed. One of the men who died was Reg's 'old school pal', and Reg told Lyn how he had taken a cake down to the station that his wife had baked for their anniversary the next morning, and heard the news when he arrived. He then had the terrible task of breaking the news to the wife of one of the other men, who had turned up at the station seeking news of her husband.

8 September 1940: the morning after an air raid in Mornington Crescent, north London.

KENTISH TI

HEROES OF THE A.F.S.

FIVE YOUNG MEN KILLED ON SERVICE.

A COMMUNITY MOURNS.

BISHOP OF CROYDON AT GRAVESIDE.

Gerald FitzGerald.   Stanley Short.   Frederick Moore.   Charles Drew.   Leslie Palmer.

A community mourns: the *Kentish Times* report of the deaths of five AFS men stationed at Coney Hall, West Wickham on their way to fight a blaze in the East End of London in March 1941.

'Valiant Fire Fighters Who Died in the Cause' ran the headline of the *Beckenham and Penge Advertiser*. A week after the disaster, the High Street was closed to traffic and the Union Jack flew at half-mast as the mile-long funeral cortège piled with wreaths for the AFS men wound its way to Elmer's End cemetery. The townspeople lined the route to pay 'tribute, honour, respect and gratitude to the Beckenham AFS', and Bert Purkiss served as a pall bearer for his friend Ken Bowles who had perished. 'We remember proudly the heroic men martyred in the cause of liberty', the inscription on their final resting place read. A plaque was subsequently placed on Beckenham fire station and Mr Purkiss was very moved when he discovered that a number of post-war flats built by the council bore the names of his comrades who had died.

'I'm glad that the AFS is being brought to the fore now,' mused Reg. 'There were thousands who were very brave, of course. We weren't the only ones by any means, but on Remembrance Day all the forces are represented at the Cenotaph – the army, the navy, the air force, even cadets who weren't born when the war was on – but the Civil Defence services are not there. And we were part of the war too.'

'That's why it's so important that I can hear about the war from you,' Lyn reassured him. 'It's by telling your story and others like you doing the same, that we *will* remember.'

CHAPTER 8

THE KITCHEN FRONT

'Medals for Housewives' proclaimed a Ministry of Food leaflet, and continued, 'The British Housewife is helping make a second front – the Kitchen Front – against Hitler.'

'The kitchen front' was indeed an essential operation – and sometimes it seemed to be its very own battleground. Food shortages, rationing, points, food substitutes, shopping, queuing: all these quickly became one of the main preoccupations of Britain's women in wartime when feeding the family called on all the stamina and ingenuity they could muster – often on top of working long hours outside the home, too.

But if the resources of women in the war were stretched to the limit how was Lyn, the self-confessed queen of the takeaway curry and the order-in pizza and the aficionado of pre-cooked supermarket meals, going to manage? And what about Kirstie, who admitted that like her mum, she didn't really cook much? And the boys, pizza fans both and unable to survive (or so they thought) without a twenty-first-century child's regular fuelling with crisps and fizzy drinks?

Lyn was conscripted into the kitchen front from day one of the Hymers' 'war'. A list of suggested menus had been drawn up for the family's meals for the first week, and that first Sunday evening at 17 Braemar Gardens Lyn found herself labouring to produce that dish of rissoles. At home in Otley she would have passed round a plate of sandwiches made from the leftovers of the lunchtime joint, or a salad, as the family watched television and enjoyed a glass of wine.

Lyn and Kirstie Hymers on their daily trip to West Wickham High Street to buy the day's provisions.

When she got round to checking out the kitchen larder, Lyn found that it was reasonably generously stocked with the sort of food that a thrifty household in 1939 would have laid in. Housewives had been encouraged to stock up prudently. The government had suggested that 'as an ordinary householder [you] will be doing a good service if you can manage to get in some extra stores of food that will keep. These will be a stand-by against an emergency… For those who have the means, a suitable amount of foodstuffs to lay by would be the quantity that they ordinarily use in one week. The following are suggested as articles of food suitable for a householder's storage: Meat and fish in cans or glass jars; flour; suet; canned or dried milk; sugar; tea; cocoa; plain biscuits… You may find it helpful to label the food with the date of purchase.' (And, it was suggested, initial it with a dab of white paint so it could be seen in the blackout.) But Lyn knew, as her wartime counterparts had suspected, that it would not be like that for much longer and that she should use these provisions sparingly and save them for the occasional wartime treat.

Looking round the kitchen that first afternoon, Lyn and Kirstie – and Michael too – realized that their wartime re-education programme was going to have to be pretty thoroughgoing. There was no easy click-the-switch hot-water system: just a solid-fuel boiler to heat water for washing and washing up. The Hymers looked at it warily, wondering how long they would be able to get the coke, coal or anthracite they felt sure it would consume voraciously, and how easy it would be to light – and keep alight. Of course, there was no washing machine, they hadn't expected that, but Lyn looked doubtfully at the primitive tub with an electric element for heating the water and envisaged long, steamy, backbreaking washdays. A dishwasher was positively science fiction, or at least a Hollywood dream, and no doubt most 1939 housewives would have regarded such an appliance as an unnecessary luxury. No washing-up liquid stood on the small wooden draining board of the deep ceramic Belfast sink, just a block of green kitchen soap. Kitchen roll was there none – just an assortment of rags for doing the dishes and mopping up spills.

There was no fridge and summer was coming. How effective would the larder be in that small kitchen? How would the family keep the food cool? Would the milk go off? The butter turn rancid? A mop and some brushes hung in the cupboard with a dustpan and an assortment of dusters but a thorough search revealed no vacuum cleaner, just a carpet sweeper. It was going to be hard work to keep the house clean and the family fed – there was no doubt in Lyn's mind about that.

In the first months of the war, food prices shot up alarmingly: by February 1940 they had risen by 14 per cent and the price of many other essential consumer goods had seen a similar or greater increase – clothing had risen by 25 per cent – and candles, which in 1939 cost 10d a packet, were 1s 6d by early 1940. This bore

particularly hard on the wives and families of servicemen, whose pay was low. At the start of the war a private was paid 2s a day, of which a proportion went to their families plus a government grant of 25s for a wife and two children – often a lot lower than a man's peacetime wages. It was not until 1943 that a serviceman's wife was given a War Service Grant of £3 a week.

In his first wartime budget in September 1939 the Chancellor of the Exchequer, Sir John Simon, announced a steep rise in the standard rate of income tax, from 5s 3d to 7s 6d in the pound. 'Now You Know There's a War' ran the *Daily Mirror*'s headline, and it was estimated that the war was costing £6 million a day by May 1940. Afraid that a further rise in the cost of staple foodstuffs would result in increased wage demands that would further fuel the inflation that was such a concerning aspect of a war economy, the government agreed in effect to subsidize the price of some foods and peg profits on essential consumer durables. Neither tactic was very effective, and it was clear that the answer was rationing.

Housework 1940s style. Lyn empties the carpet sweeper while
Michael gets in some coal.

Rationing had been introduced at the end of the First World War and ration books had been printed in 1938 after the Munich crisis, but the government seemed reluctant to introduce this regulatory measure. The National Register had been compiled by the end of September 1939 and it was clear that there were already beginning to be shortages in the shops of butter, bacon and sugar in particular. As a government leaflet reminded the public, 'You know that our country is dependent to a very large extent on supplies of food from overseas. More than 20 million tons are brought into our ports from all parts of the world.' Some 70 per cent of cheese and sugar, nearly 80 per cent of fruit, 90 per cent of cereals and fats and around half of all meat were imported on the eve of the war. Only potatoes and fresh milk were produced entirely at home. Pressure on shipping space and maritime losses meant that this would get steadily – if not dramatically – worse.

It was not that there was public resistance to the measure. No one liked shortages but they were prepared to accept them if they were fair and the better off were seen to be sharing the privations of the less well off. It was clear that not everyone was observing the government's stricture that 'to try to buy extra quantities of food when an emergency is upon us, would be unfair to others'. An East End grocer told Mass Observation: '[The shortages] are bringing all the rich people from the West End to take poor people's food. They come in their cars from all districts and buy… night lights and candles, tinned goods, corned beef and that sort of thing… They go mad on sugar. I've been rationing sugar for the last three or four days. A good shopkeeper keeps some back for his regular customers.'

The *Daily Express* ran a vigorous anti-rationing campaign but by November surveys revealed that it had again misjudged the mood of the nation: over 50 per cent of those questioned thought that rationing was both 'necessary' and 'fair'.

Rationing, the government explained, would 'prevent waste of food, increase our war effort, divide supplies equally. There will be ample supplies for our 44½ million people, but we must divide them fairly, everyone being treated alike' – and would prevent uncertainty: 'Your ration book assures you of your fair share. Rationing means there will be no uncertainty – and no queues' – though it was not to turn out quite like that.

Ration books were issued in October 1939; 23 November was the last day that the public could register at the shop where they intended to buy their food when rationing was introduced. From that date shopkeepers generally operated their own informal system, rationing butter (which was in particularly short supply), bacon and sugar, though rationing was not officially introduced until 8 January 1940 when each person was entitled to 4 ounces of bacon or ham, 4 ounces of butter and 12 ounces of sugar a week. Other commodities would follow as the demands of war grew more acute. At the end of January the bacon allowance was raised to 8 ounces,

'What's on ration today?' Lyn and Kirstie peer anxiously into the shop window.

which was actually higher than pre-war consumption. In fact, the rations allowed in 1940 not infrequently promised a more plentiful diet for poor families than they had been able to afford before hostilities broke out. As had been pointed out in a book published in 1936, *Food, Health and Income*, 'for a large part of the population, foodstuffs have in fact always been rationed by price' and it was estimated that only about 50 per cent of the population could afford 'a diet completely adequate for health according to modern standards' prior to the Second World War.

The Hymers would have to register with a West Wickham shop where Lyn and Kirstie could exchange their coupons for the family's food. The original idea had been to rent space in a local delicatessen, but gradually the owner of the shop, Nigel Lovegrove, grew so interested in the project that it was decided he would convert part of his shop and travel back in time with the Hymers, becoming a 1940s grocer for the duration – though 'the day the 1930s suit and apron arrived, I began to wonder what I had let myself in for'. Lia Cramer, the art director, found authentic 1930s equipment, scales, metal scoops and bins for dry goods for the shop within a shop. She supplied provisions and toiletries, tinned and dry goods, all of which were repackaged with replica 1940s labels, and the sugar was packed into authentic blue paper bags.

It was Nigel Lovegrove's responsibility to provide fresh fruit and vegetables appropriate to the period – no bananas, occasionally an orange that would usually be saved 'for children only', and certainly no out-of-season delicacies like raspberries or foreign exotica such as aubergines or passion fruit. In fact Mr Lovegrove's shop does not normally stock fruit and vegetables so, armed with information about what would have been appropriate at any particular time, he would have to send his daughter to the supermarket or cash-and-carry to keep his valued customers as content as possible. He also stocked bread, the National Loaf that was specially made by Loafer's Bakery in

the town. This was made with 'national flour', 85 per cent of extraction flour (that is, using nearly all the wheat including the husk; from 1 August 1943 calcium was also added), and it was not popular. Most people were used to white bread and though every effort was made, the National Loaf still turned out a dirty beige colour and many – including the Hymers when they tried it – echoed A. P. Herbert's (unscanned) verse which was a clear riposte to the jingle issued by the Ministry of Food.

It was a learning curve for Mr Lovegrove. He had not realized how complicated the rationing system and then the points system was and how frequently it changed; he was soon full of admiration for wartime shopkeepers who had had to come to grips with all the vagaries. Lyn and Kirstie had done their homework, so when they came into the shop their questions sometimes stumped him. He found himself avidly reading books on the home front, on wartime shopping and rationing at home in the evenings so that he could answer the Hymers' questions with confidence. Those of his customers who remembered the war were a great help too, and were very impressed by the authenticity of the 'shop', though wartime shopping with its shortages and uncertainties was not something anyone wanted to recreate. They pointed out that queuing was one of the most onerous features of the war, particularly for women who were also engaged in war work outside the home, and on one occasion Mr Lovegrove's regulars obligingly formed a queue for over an hour so that Lyn and Kirstie could have that frustrating experience too.

> **MINISTRY OF FOOD JINGLE**
>
> Pat-a-loaf, pat-a loaf
> Baker's man,
> Bake me some Wheatmeal
> As fast as you can:
> It builds up my health
> And it tastes so good,
> I find that I like
> Eating just what I should.
>
> **A.P. HERBERT'S VERSE**
>
> So I will bow to dear brown bread,
> Because, as my wise rulers say,
> We shall save tonnage this way.
> But let this point be understood –
> No man can tell me it is good.

Mr Lovegrove was informed when rationing allowances decreased or increased, and when there were particular shortages, price rises or other changes, and with the help of his daughter he created a database of prices and availability. When the Hymers made their purchases, no actual money changed hands; Mr Lovegrove entered the details into a ledger and each week informed the Hymers' 'bank manager' how much they had spent at his shop that week so that Lyn could work out the family's housekeeping budget.

He had to deal with the coupons and make sure that he had removed the correct number for the goods he had parted with, and he also had to deal with the Hymers' complaints. 'It was tough,' he admitted, and it was tough in wartime with customers blaming the face across the counter for government edicts. 'The hardest thing was when I had to tell them there was a real shortage of cigarettes.' Both Lyn and Kirstie

being heavy smokers, Lyn in particular, they found the dwindling packets of Capstans and Woodbines on the shelves at times made them very edgy – 'nervy' as it would have been in wartime parlance. 'More than once Lyn threatened to "chop my legs off" if I couldn't come up with the goods. They were also pretty put out when matches were in short supply.' (They could have followed the advice to split all matches in two with a razor blade.) Mr Lovegrove noted that they also took soap rationing 'very hard' – indeed, some of his customers suggested that the Hymers were having it a little too hard, that grocers, mindful that after the war shoppers would be able to take their trade where they liked, would always keep 'a little something under the counter' for their loyal customers. Most customers agreed that there had been a pretty active black market in the area and that 'you didn't go without if you had the money'.

Lyn soon found that though the shortage of butter was acute, at first the family was beginning to stockpile sugar since no one had a particularly sweet tooth. There were two alternatives: they could either barter it with neighbours who craved sugar, which was illegal but happened. Or, in the national interest, they could decline to take their full ration of that (or any other rationed commodity) and use the money – for food cost money as well as coupons – to do what the government suggested and invest the shillings and pence in National Savings for the war effort. Kirstie started to bake more. 'We found that we needed to bake scones, tarts, pies and puddings, which we never usually have at home, just to keep us from being hungry. And we gave the boys a jam tart and a glass of milk when they came in from school and that kept them going until dinnertime. So soon though we didn't have to watch the sugar, we certainly used up most of our rations.'

In addition to registering with a grocer, the Hymers had to find a butcher in West Wickham. Meat went on ration in March 1941 and here the system was slightly different: the amount was expressed in money rather than coupons. Everyone over six was allowed 1 shilling's worth of meat with the under-sixes getting 11d worth. The idea was that you could choose to buy a small amount of an expensive cut or a larger amount of a cheaper cut. Averaged out, it meant that each person was getting about 2 ounces of meat a day – and Britain in 1940 was a meat-eating nation. In her book *Eat Well in Wartime*, Leonora Eyles tried to be reassuring: 'A good many people in wartime will be forced to adopt a largely vegetarian diet, and it may reassure them to know that it can be both pleasant and healthy. Hitler, Mussolini – and our George Bernard Shaw – are vegetarians and whatever else one may think of them they are all men of strength and energy… a diet without meat need not be weakening.'

Housewives had to take their meat allocation every week and could not save it up for a special occasion. Offal was never rationed and there was great competition for kidneys, heart and liver. Recipes for cooking a sheep's head 'strongly

recommended 'by the Ministry of Food' as cheap and nourishing', making a hash of a calf's head, pig's feet in jelly or melts and skirt pudding appeared in women's magazines, and those who had always balked at the thought of brains or tripe steeled themselves to have a go. But no matter how difficult they were finding it to manage on their rations, Lyn never asked Michael Ashenden at Larratt's, the butcher in the High Street, for offal, preferring to try to think up yet another way to stretch the mince or stewing steak or scrag end of mutton she was able to buy. And she turned away at the sight of the rabbits hanging in the shop too.

Fish was never rationed either, but it was a scarce treat with the south and west coast mined and barbed-wired against invasion and the danger to trawlers from 'tip and run' raids in the North Sea. By 1941 the price of fish had increased seventeen-fold and some very strange varieties started to appear on fishmongers' slabs with names like ling and saith and, later, whalemeat (which was supposed to taste like steak after a great deal of elaborate preparation). The Ministry of Food was there with patriotic encouragement:

> When fisher-folk are brave enough
> To face mines and the foe for you
> You surely can be bold enough
> To try fish of a kind that's new.

Salt cod was much recommended, but not much appreciated since it tasted like boiled flannel – and anyway fish was out for the Hymers since Thomas had a fish allergy.

As the war progressed, shortages increased and rationing became more draconian: by June 1940 the bacon or ham ration had fallen to 4 ounces a week; you were allowed only 2 ounces of tea, which first went on ration in July 1940. Conversely, meat rose to an allowance of 2s 2d in September 1940, due mainly to the amount of slaughter caused by the switch to arable land, but was back to 1s by March 1941. As late as three weeks after VE Day, May 1945, the meat ration was still 1s 2d and nearly half of this had to be taken in the form of corned beef. The cheese ration was a terrible privation: in May 1941 it was 1 ounce per person per week, and though it fluctuated throughout the war, it was rarely more than 4 ounces. The butter ration also fluctuated, but again was usually 4 ounces, while cooking fats or margarine hovered between 2 and 3 ounces.

Preserves (jam, treacle or marmalade) were usually around 8 ounces a month, but in summer months an equivalent weight could be taken in the form of sugar to make the most of homegrown fruits for jam. Milk was restricted to 2 pints in November 1941 for those who were not priority consumers (children or expectant or nursing

mothers), and though this varied slightly over the war years, it was the average, though supplemented by a tin of powdered milk every eight weeks. Children under five were allowed seven pints of fresh milk.

The shortage of eggs was acute (unless you kept chickens in the back garden), but it was not possible to deal with this in quite the same way as other things, since hens 'cannot be relied upon to produce a steady stream of eggs to supply a general ration as we understand it' as a Ministry of Food booklet explained. So rather than a weekly or monthly ration as with other foods, eggs were 'allocated' when there were enough to go round. Those in 'non-priority classes' – those who were not expectant or nursing mothers, children between six and eighteen months and invalids – received an 'allocation' of twenty-nine eggs in the whole of 1942 – only slightly more than one egg a fortnight per person – and thirty in 1943. But this also underlined an important principle: the supply of eggs could not be guaranteed so they should not be rationed: rationing was not only a system of limitations, it was also a guarantee of availability. The government, realizing that it was in fact a form of contract with the people to supply their needs at a minimum level, refused to ration any product unless they could promise that the ration, no matter how meagre, would be there when the housewife took her coupons to the shops.

The famous dried eggs, which of course took up much less shipping space than the shell variety, were introduced in 'compensation' and a tin or packet (the equivalent of twelve shell eggs) was allowed every two months. Again the Ministry of Food and women's magazines were endlessly inventive with recipes for dried egg omelettes and the like, but few people took to these – though they were usually prepared to follow instructions for making cakes and puddings with eggs in their powdered form.

In December 1941 a 'points system' was introduced to enable consumers to choose between a range of goods not covered by rationing: tinned meat, fish

Michael Ashenden serves his 1940s customers.

and beans. It was later extended to cover cereal, dried fruit and pulses, biscuits, some sorts of preserves, suet, jellies and tinned sweet puddings each with a different points 'price'. Each ration book holder was allocated sixteen points for four weeks and this gradually rose towards the end of the war. This system was welcomed too: there had long been criticism about the unfair distribution of unrationed food, and it was comforting to know that the wealthy were now no longer in a position to corner the market in tinned salmon or sliced peaches.

'It's quite tough to get the hang of it,' said Kirstie, 'understanding the amount of points you have and keeping a running total and thinking ahead about saving some. Rationing is a pain to live with sometimes, but I can see why it was done. I think it was a fair system to stop those with the money buying the goods off the shelf and other people who didn't have so much money being left with nothing.'

Lyn found it hard too: 'I just haven't got to grips with the points system yet,' she admitted a few days after the family had been informed about this new initiative. 'I'm tending to be frugal because I don't really understand the system, and I think it's better to start off that way and then treat yourself if you find you've got points left over. I have only spent eight so far and that was to buy Weetabix for the boys and then some tinned peaches for them as a treat. But I'm sure I'll come to grips with it soon and it'll be second nature to me, just as it was for a wartime housewife. It's a challenge and I'll just have to rise to it like they did.'

The family found it hard to exist on the butter and margarine they were allowed. Kirstie used it in baking and then it was needed for the boy's 'pack-ups'. That meant that 'sadly butter in mashed potatoes is a thing of the past and potatoes can be horribly lumpy and tasteless without butter or milk, and we have to be careful with milk too. We are only allowed two pints a day and I think that's the rationing that I find hardest.' Two old-fashioned, wide-necked bottles of milk with cardboard tops were delivered every morning by Mr Tibbs, the milkman. One

Lyn and Kirstie carry their shopping (and gas masks) home from West Wickham High Street.

HOW TO DRY APPLES

We may be short of apples later in the year – through bringing munitions in the ships from Canada. so here is a way of preserving the present supply – it can be used for windfalls or blemished fruit.

Wipe the apples, remove the cores and peel thinly … Slice into rings about ¼" thick. Steep the rings for 10 minutes in water containing 1½oz salt to the gallon.

Thread the rings onto sticks or spread on slatted trays or cake racks covered with muslin. Dry in a very cool oven (leaving the door open to let the heat escape) or over a hot cylinder or on the rack of a stove until they resemble chamois leather … the process usually takes about 4 hours. Cool for 12 hours then pack in paper bags, jars or tins and store in a cool place.

Ministry of Food, Food Facts, No. 13

morning there had been a panic when Mr Tibbs had been late and Lyn was afraid that stringent milk rationing had been introduced and she hadn't realized. She sent Michael to scour the copy of *The Times* that had just been delivered, but there was no mention of milk rationing there. Then to their relief they heard the clink of bottles on the doorstep.

The Hymers missed milk in tea too, but that wasn't so much of problem as there wasn't much tea anyway with 2 ounces per person per week, and Camp coffee was scarce too. 'At home we make lots of pots of tea and then throw half of them away when they get stewed,' said Lyn. 'But here every time we make a pot of tea everybody drinks it before it gets cold. We take much less milk in tea and of course it's a lot weaker. No "one for the pot" any more.

'I don't like frying with lard, though I know wartime housewives used to make things like Spam fritters a lot, and Kirstie is starting to bake with lard. Actually I found a recipe for dripping pastry in a wartime recipe book and we are beginning to prefer that to pastry made with margarine. As for jam, I thought 8 ounces of jam per person per month would be excessive. At home a jar of jam can languish in the cupboard untouched for months, but because of the unavailability of butter now we tend to eat jam on bread, or if there's no milk for the boys' breakfast cereal, they'll have bread and jam instead, and at lunchtime if the cheese has run out, then we'll have jam sandwiches. The boys might even take it in their pack-ups, so suddenly jam has begun to be of a bit of a staple fare for us in the 1940s house.

Ben enjoying his reward for catching one of the adults swearing.

'We really miss cheese: we are big cheese eaters at home. I know the boys would like to take cheese sandwiches to school for their lunch and though I don't eat much myself I do like it in sauces, and I would like to make cauliflower cheese, macaroni cheese, dishes like that. But there often isn't enough cheese – or milk for that matter – so what I do now is pour a tin of tomato soup over the vegetables and bake them in the oven with a few herbs out of the garden instead.

'I tend to save my meat coupons up for the weekend so that we can have a joint of whatever is on offer. But that doesn't always work very well. There may only be a boiling fowl, and you waste so much fuel trying to get it tender, or render it down for stock, that I prefer to make vegetable soup.'

Sweets were on points from 1942 and the Hymers rationed these out to the children and used them as prizes for the board games they played in the evening, or for a penalty if an adult swore. Lyn was astonished at herself: 'We played Lotto the other night and I won, but I was told that I had to give the winegum to one of the children and I felt really disappointed. It's amazing – at Christmas at home I sat and devoured a whole box of chocolates and here I am in the 1940s getting excited about a single winegum.'

In fact rationing had wrought a considerable change in family relations. 'There's a pecking order now with food,' explained Lyn. 'The children are fed first and then Michael as the breadwinner, then Kirstie as my daughter, and last of all me. If milk is short, it's the grown-ups who go without of course, and I will often have dry bread to save on butter or margarine. It is a totally alien concept to me; in 2000 we all have what we want to eat and I admit that I am very extravagant with food and waste a lot. But not now, here in wartime conditions, there is definitely a hierarchy, and women come last – or they put themselves last.'

'My mother cooks and I bake.' Lyn and Kirstie at work in the kitchen.

CHAPTER 9

DIG (AND COOK) FOR VICTORY

'I'm Marguerite Patten,' said the charming, white-haired woman as she opened the front door of 17 Braemar Gardens. The Hymers had just piled out of the 1930s taxi to start their wartime experience, and the distinguished cookery expert was on hand to welcome them.

'I know,' gasped Lyn. 'We've got some of your books.' Which, it turned out, was just as well. The food shortages and lack of cold storage meant that Lyn and Kirstie had to do what most wartime housewives did, shop every day. The amount that a family of five ate meant that every weekday morning the two women set off for the shops with a wicker basket apiece and an idea in their head of what they would like to cook for that evening's meal, but with no assurance whatsoever that they would be able to get the necessary ingredients.

'You can't have any hard and fast rules about what you're going to eat. It depends entirely on what's in the shops. It's a challenge to make something nice to eat out of whatever you can get,' explained Lyn. Again it was a steep learning curve, but this time there was plenty of help. The Hymers would have found modern recipe books useless with their reliance on ingredients that were almost unknown in Britain fifty years ago: pasta, polenta, garlic, coriander. And pre-war cookery books were of limited value too since many of the ingredients they called for – eggs, cream, veal, raisins, onions – were in very short supply if they could be found at all. But since the 'kitchen front' was such a vital part of the war effort, the government mobilized its resources to stiffen the troops and provide them with new maps for this unknown terrain.

Michael working up a sweat as he follows the Ministry of Agriculture's advice to 'Do it now. Dig for Victory'.

Before the war Marguerite Patten had been a home economist in the electrical industry and an important part of her job had been giving cookery demonstrations of recipes for delicious meals based on lavish ingredients – and often plenty of time. The outbreak of war put a stop to that, and her efforts from then on were devoted to suggestions for keeping a wartime family well fed.

In April 1940 Lord Woolton, a former businessman, who as Sir Fred Marquis had run Lewis's – a large chain of department stores with branches in Liverpool and Glasgow – and before that had been a social worker in the slums, was put in charge of the Ministry of Food. It was a massive enterprise –'the greatest shop the world has ever known' was how Woolton described it. The sole importer of basic foodstuffs, the sole buyer of domestic fat, stock and milk, the ministry in effect controlled the manufacture and distribution of virtually all foods. By 1943 it employed 50,000 civil servants and one of these was Marguerite Patten who had joined in 1942, one of the hundreds of cookery demonstrators who took their skills to the nation at large. 'I was based in Cambridge and my very first cookery demonstration was held in the market square there' – where she and her team were in competition with fruit and vegetable stallholders shouting their wares.

Planning the family's meals depended on what Mr Lovegrove had in stock.

Marguerite gave demonstrations in centres set up by the Food Division of the Ministry, in markets, canteens, the outpatients departments of hospitals and mother and baby clinics, and set up counters in shops. Equipped with a portable stove, she showed people how they could make their rations go further and how to cook nutritious meals from very limited ingredients. This advice was not always welcome: the public seemed surprisingly insouciant about what was good for their health, and when a Wartime Social Survey polled 8,000 workers in 1942 they found that most were not much concerned with what was good for them; the foods they considered essential to their well-being were 'the items from their traditional diet they missed most' – that is, meat, the health-giving properties of lentils being disregarded almost entirely. And of course some housewives thought they knew perfectly well how to cook and considered a slip of a girl telling them how to make jam an impertinence, but most welcomed the advice and suggestions in those difficult days.

In 1943 Marguerite Patten took charge of the Ministry of Food Bureau in Harrods department store in London, and demonstrated recipes daily, often to women who were having to cook for themselves for the first time – cooks and kitchen maids having joined up or gone to work in a munitions factory.

If wartime housewives welcomed Miss Patten's recipes, so did the 1940s family. One day a notice appeared in Braemar Gardens announcing a cookery demonstration in St Mark's Hall, at the top of the road, at 3 p.m. on 24 May. Lyn and Kirstie were delighted and determined to go along to see if they could pick up any hints for planning their meals. 'It wasn't so much the quantity of food available on ration that was the problem,' Lyn complained, 'it was the sheer monotony. The choice was so limited that we seemed to be eating sausages [which were not often available to wartime housewives and contained high percentage of cereal or oatmeal] or vegetable pies for every meal.'

But then a letter came saying that as she was in the area Marguerite Patten would very much like to come to have tea with the Hymers after her demonstration to see how they were getting on in the 1940s house. Michael was thrilled to hear this, though he would be at work. 'Marguerite Patten represents everything about the home front to me. How women made do with what they had, and how they kept everything going under extreme difficulties and shortages. I think she's a wonderful woman.'

But the news threw Kirstie into a panic: 'I was the one responsible for doing the baking. Mum cooked the meals we ate, and I made the cakes and tarts and pies and puddings. I was quite pleased how I was getting on. I don't usually cook much at home, certainly I don't make cakes and pastry, but we need filling up here, and I had got into the habit of making puddings for most meals. I'd made a treacle sponge that had turned out really well: the boys thought it was delicious and kept saying, "I wish you'd cook this at home, Mum," but it's something else altogether to cook for

a wartime cookery expert like Marguerite Patten. I was really nervous. I got myself into a complete state looking through all the recipes I could find. So many of them called for ingredients that I knew we wouldn't be able to get, so I came out in a nervous rash about it all.'

In the event both occasions were a great success. 'I only wish this had happened five weeks earlier,' sighed Lyn, who'd gone to the demonstration with her new friend Nina Tilling. 'I could have made real use of the recipes.'

Marguerite Patten demonstrated some ingenious wartime delicacies – mock crab made with margarine, dried egg, an ounce of cheese, a little salad dressing, vinegar and salt and pepper. Spread on toast, or as a topping for mashed potato, it was very tasty. Then the audience was invited to guess what constituted the mock banana that was passed round, but no one recognized that it was parsnips with a drop of milk and a touch of banana essence. Corned beef hash, which was a wartime standard since corned beef was increasingly part of the meat ration, was pronounced a success, and so were the Spam fritters laid appetizingly on a bed of shredded lettuce, and the oatmeal sausages, and a mock apricot tart made with grated carrot, some plum jam and a little almond flavouring. The audience considered that Marguerite's recipe for mock cream made from margarine, sugar, dried milk powder and a tablespoon of milk, though not quite like the fresh dairy version, would improve a fruit pie no end. And they were surprised to learn that the crumble that is such a kitchen standby today for apples, plums or gooseberries, had been a wartime invention, an attempt to circumvent the shortage of ingredients for making pastry.

Then it was time to go to 17 Braemar Gardens where Kirstie was waiting anxiously. 'I'd been baking all day and I was terrified that I'd burn something, because unlike today when you'd just throw it away and start again, if I burned the scones, say, as I had the other day, I wouldn't have the ingredients to make another batch, I'd just have to scrape the burnt bits off and we'd eat what was left!'

The dining room table was set with the best china, a Clarice Cliff-inspired tea service normally kept in the glass-fronted cabinet in the front room for special occasions, and there were roses from the garden in a vase. Marguerite had brought a jar of parsley honey for the Hymers. 'You need 5 ounces of parsley, which is quite lot because parsley weighs very light, so throw the stalks in too. You chop it all up – stalks included – and boil it up with a pint and a half of water until it reduces to a pint. Then you strain it, add a pound of sugar and boil it again for about twenty minutes. Add half a teaspoon of vinegar, pour it into pots and cover with greaseproof paper. By the next day it will have set and looks and tastes like heather honey.'

The distinguished visitor pronounced the meal 'delicious' and, as she sampled Kirstie's orange and sultana loaf, eggless chocolate cake and sausagemeat and apple tartlets (a last-minute innovation), a slow smile of satisfaction spread over Kirstie's

face. 'I had been cooking all day, and it was hard work, but in the end it was more rewarding than just going down to the supermarket to get things as I would have done at home.' And Marguerite stressed that cooking with national flour and dried eggs and with such limited supplies of milk and fats had been a tremendous challenge for wartime cooks too.

Then the women swapped 'wartime' culinary experiences and Kirstie and Lyn quizzed Marguerite about what she could suggest for the pack-ups the boys took to school and Michael took to work. 'How about mashed pilchards and shredded carrot? Minced fried bacon rind and toasted oatmeal? Grated cheese and diced beetroot? Vegetable extract with mustard and cress? Fish paste and chopped parsley?' The Hymers looked thoughtful.

In demonstrating recipes during the war, Marguerite Patten had found the Ministry of Food advertisements an invaluable resource, and a number of these had been provided in the 1940s house for inspiration and information. 'Food Facts' were published in the national and regional newspapers and were topical, taking advantage of what food was currently plentiful or in season. Housewives were asked, 'Are you collecting these useful advertisements? Start now and pin them up in your kitchen.' Food Facts covered a number of topics on the kitchen front in addition to instructions about new rationing regulations and details of the points system that the Ministry of Food also announced in press adverts.

Many started with an exhortation along the lines of 'If you eat more than you need, you are wasting food as surely as if you had thrown it away. So eat what you need, but no more. Buy wisely and cater strictly. For your health's sake, as well as your country's, remember that "Enough is as good as a feast." Save food! Save money! Save cargo space for munitions!' The problem, as the Hymers found out, was that it was often not possible to eat enough on rations, let alone overeat, and the family often felt hungry. Neighbours who lived through the war assured Lyn they had indeed gone hungry. 'I think that I felt hungry most of the time,' reflected Nina Tilling.

A clear plate means A clear conscience

Don't take more than you can eat

There were ingenious recipes: vegetable hotpot, bottling rhubarb without sugar, vegetable stock when there were no bones to be had, potato pastry, corned beef mould, prune roly-poly and innumerable recipes for soup that pointed out that 'there's nothing so cheery for you as soup' and that 'soup is easy to digest when you are tired' – which most of the population were most of the time, during the war. Food Facts recommended keeping a stock pot on the go all the time to top up with whatever vegetables – parsnips or cabbage usually – were available and could be tossed in, and suggested that dumplings (which Lyn became a dab hand at making out of flour, baking powder and a few herbs from the garden) would bulk out the soup and make it a more substantial meal.

There were recipes for salted cod, which was 9d a pound, and advice to fishmongers about how to de-salt it 'so your customers will like it a lot' (though most didn't), for dried apple rings, rosehip syrup for children, for adding oatmeal, which was cheap ('threepence halfpenny per lb. or less'), to 'almost every kind of dish to make it go further and increase its food value'. And of course there was the recipe for the most famous wartime dish of all, the Minister of Food's eponymous 'Woolton Pie' (though it had in fact been devised by an under-chef at the Savoy Hotel). This was a vegetable pie (which could be varied depending what was in season), thickened with the ubiquitous oatmeal, covered with potato pastry, or mashed potato and topped with cheese if you had any left.

There were homely chats – 'the grocer/the butcher/the greengrocer says' – which explained to their imaginary customers why there weren't any onions, or why there was more corned beef on offer now, or why some people seemed to be getting more than their fair share. Then there was a cast of characters who made an appearance

in 1942 such as Mrs Merry, Mrs Goodchild, Mrs Simple, Mrs Candid, Mrs Harass, Mrs Faraway and Mrs Doubtful, who needed putting straight since they seemed to have 'got their facts wrong'. 'Cows aren't fifth columnist,' Mrs Doubtful was told sternly when she worried about lack of milk 'for Dad's duodenal'. 'Think again,' Mrs Goodchild was reprimanded when she wondered why 'my Johnny has to miss his orange juice' because he was over six; Mrs Harass was 'just plain wrong' when she complained that 'a boiled carrot is just a boiled carrot, and no news to anyone'. Mrs Faraway was reminded that it had been just as bad in the First World War when she regretted the lack of eggs, and predictably poor Mrs Simple was patronized when she asked if she should take 'that bit extra the butcher had offered her'. Whereas Miss Lightfoot, who 'works in a factory all day… doing her bit… but even in wartime conditions is seldom tired, never ill, never nervy' on account of eating potatoes and carrots every single day.

Indeed, Dr Carrot and Potato Pete were cartoon characters who made regular appearances in the Ministry of Food propaganda, urging their own consumption. 'Call me often enough and you'll keep well,' promised Dr Carrot, who looked fit and fresh and was supposed to contain sugar, but few were convinced – though they did believe that eating carrots helped you to see in the dark, as the famous Battle of Britain pilot 'Cat's-eyes Cunningham' attested (ignoring the contribution of radar).

There was a 'Food Facts Quiz' published at Christmas and families were encouraged to sit round the fire at the festive season quizzing each other with such teasers as 'Which is the correct way of mixing milk powder?' 'How much is fresh salted-cod per pound?' 'Which vitamins does cod liver oil contain?' and 'What is (or are) Rose Hips? A dress design? An authoress? An eastern dance? Pods of wild roses rich in vitamin C?'

Fuel consumption was obviously of concern to the Ministry of Food too, since coal and gas were essential for the war effort, and housewives were urged to save fuel with as much ingenuity as they could. The concept of cooking vegetables *al dente* was not one that was familiar to the average 1940s housewife: boiled tended to mean for some time. So the ministry had double the incentive in recommending steaming: it conserved vitamins and

---

LET'S TALK ABOUT XMAS FOOD

A recipe for Christmas pudding without eggs.

Mix together 1 cupful of flour, 1 cupful of breadcrumbs, 1 cupful of sugar, half a cupful of suet, 1 cupful of mixed dried fruit, and, if you like, 1 teaspoon of mixed sweet spice. Then add 1 cupful of grated potato, 1 cupful of grated raw carrot and finally a level teaspoon of bicarbonate of soda dissolved in 2 tablespoonfuls of hot milk. Mix all together (no further moisture is necessary) turn into a well-greased pudding basin. Boil or steam for 4 hours.

A Christmassy sparkle is easy to give sprigs of holly or evergreen for use on puddings and cakes. Dip your greenery in a strong solution of Epsom salts. When dry it will be beautifully frosted.

Ministry of Food advert. November 1942

saved fuel. For those who did not have a steamer or double saucepan it was suggested that holes could be punched in an old saucepan lid or sandwich tin and that could be inverted over a saucepan for vegetables or a pudding, with the saucepan's lid or an inverted pudding basin on top. Or you could hang a muslin bag of peas or diced parsnips in with the potatoes as they cooked. 'Shred greens and cabbages, break cauliflowers into sprigs, cut carrots and swedes into pieces before cooking: they take much less time to cook this way and it saves fuel,' the ministry instructed – one might think unnecessarily. And *never* peel potatoes.

Casseroles, or 'one-pot meals', were much recommended. 'Better pot-luck with Churchill today than humble pie under Hitler tomorrow,' warned a poster. 'Never turn the oven on to cook just one thing,' housewives were sternly instructed, and slow-cooking casseroles could be a particular boon to women who were out at work all day. It was suggested that a sheet of tin should be put on top of the cooker so that one gas ring could cook two saucepans; pressure cookers were recommended too as saving fuel as well as time – and a Ministry of Food pamphlet, *Food Without Fuel*, suggested using a hay box. After a stew was heated up, it could be transferred to a sturdy box stuffed with straw or newspaper where it would continue to cook all day in the conserved heat; but few people seem to have taken this route to fuel conservation.

> ## FOOD FACTS
>
> Those who have the will to win
> Cook potatoes in their skin
> Knowing that the sight of peelings
> Deeply hurts Lord Woolton's
> feelings.
>
> **Ministry of Food, Food Facts**

Lyn's concern about keeping milk fresh without a fridge was addressed too: she could fill a pudding basin with cold water and stand the milk bottle in this water. 'Saturate a flowerpot under the cold water tap. Put this over the milk bottle and stand in the larder or coolest part of the house.' The flowerpot cooler method could be used for butter or small cuts of meat too, or if she couldn't lay hands on a flowerpot, Lyn could soak a piece a muslin in cold water and drape that over the milk or butter in a dish of cold water.

Most Food Facts included a reminder to 'Listen to *The Kitchen Front* at 8.15 every morning'. There was no need to say which station, since on 1 September 1939 the regional and national networks were merged: henceforth, until the introduction of the Forces Programme in February 1940, there was only one network to listen to: the Home Service. At first this consisted of little other than news bulletins interspersed with tunes from Sandy Macpherson at his organ, and soon people were writing in to say that they would rather face the German guns than be forced to listen to any more of Macpherson's tunes. By October the BBC, aware of its importance for morale, increased the range of its programmes, though there was

still only one channel. After Lord Woolton took up his post as Minister of Food in April 1940 and introduced his inspired Kitchen Front campaign, the BBC translated this into a regular programme, which was first transmitted on 25 June 1940 and continued on an almost daily basis throughout the war years.

Marguerite Patten was one of the regular contributors to the popular and useful five-minute slot introduced by Freddie Grisewood (known as 'ricepud'), as was the cookery writer Ambrose Heath. Recipes were tested in the Ministry of Food's kitchens in Portman Square where Eileen Blair, George Orwell's wife, was one of those responsible. Lord Woolton made regular broadcasts on the programme and his warm Mancunian voice carried both authority and understanding. *The Kitchen Front* read out recipes, gave information, strictures like 'It's not funny to get more than your share', encouragement – and humour. 'Grandma Buggins' (played by the actress Mabel Constandurous) was a stock character, meeting the culinary efforts of her long-suffering 'daughter' with a sniff and the comment 'Another disguise for parsnips, I suppose.' 'Gert and Daisy' (Elsie and Doris Waters, in real life sisters of Jack Warner, later to play the title role in *Dixon of Dock Green*), a couple of Cockney 'chars' whose husbands, Bert and Wally, were away in the forces, often appeared – sometimes with Lord Woolton – and dictated a recipe. At Christmas 1941 it was for 'murkey', stuffed mutton in place of unobtainable turkey. 'How do you do that?' Gert asked. 'Use your imagination,' Daisy replied. 'Do you get that at the butcher's too?' shot back Gert. It seemed a fair question sometimes.

Listeners sent in recipes: 'Here's one for "Fighter's Pie". That sounds to me a grand name,' enthused Freddie Grisewood, 'almost as good as a wartime pudding I heard of called "Skinflint's Joy". Do you know, I think we could do with a few more names like these, if you would care to send them in' – which listeners did, and sometimes the dishes made according to the previous day's recipe arrived at Broadcasting House too.

Listeners also wrote in with questions: a housewife who was working in a munitions factory and had no time to get to the shops was told of a scheme operated by the WVS in Hounslow where thirty volunteers did

---

FOOD FACTS

*'I used to think one didn't oughter
Make a soup from vegetable water
But this, my dear – this IS a snorter!'*

The soup-pot need not use up hours of fuel. Put all your root vegetables (except turnips), bacon rinds, etc. in a large pot with plenty of water. Cook slowly for half an hour. Boil vigorously for a minute or two then put straight into the hay box or the oven when baking is done to use up the last of the heat. The soup-pot should be brought to the boil every day … don't disturb the fat on the top of the stock for this preserves the flavour, but remove before use. When you want to make soup you just take some of this stock, add what flavourings or vegetables you fancy and in a very short time your soup will be ready.

Ministry of Food, Food Facts

the shopping – free of charge – for women working in the war industries, and then let themselves into the workers' homes and packed the provisions away. 'Why not start one in your area?' suggested Grisewood. Another frequent problem addressed was what to do about the evening meal in the event of air raid.

Perhaps the most popular performer on *The Kitchen Front* was the 'Radio Doctor', 'the doctor with the greatest number of patients in the world', who pulled in between 6 and 14 million listeners with his advocacy of 'that humble black worker' (the prune) to 'keep you regular', his frank talk about bowels and bellies and his robust common sense about health and eating – 'Don't give Father extra butter, Mother, that's your ration.' The doctor was Charles Hill, Secretary to the British Medical Association who, after the war, as Lord Hill of Luton, was appointed Chairman of the Independent Television Authority, and then the BBC.

It wasn't just the kitchen that was conscripted into the home front, the garden was too. At the outbreak of war many farms had been given over to pasture, and cattle were fed almost wholly on imported foodstuffs. The pasture urgently needed to be turned over to crops of corn, potatoes and fodder for cattle. A massive ploughing campaign began. Farmers were offered a £2 incentive for every acre they ploughed up that had been grass for the past seven years, providing that they did so by December 1939. Working round the clock, many farmers ploughed by night – with wavy furrows as a result: the target was to get an additional 2 million acres under the plough by 30 April 1940. But as a Ministry of Agriculture poster pointed out: 'Women! Farmers can't grow all your vegetables. You must grow your own. It's up to you to provide the vegetables that are vital to your children's health – especially in winter. If you don't, they may go short. Grow all you can. Turn your garden over to vegetables.

DIG FOR VICTORY LEAFLET NUMBER 20

Get the older children to help you. If you haven't a garden ask your local council for an allotment. DO IT NOW. DIG FOR VICTORY.'

The 'Dig for Victory' campaign was the most famous of the war (previously the message had been 'Grow More Food' until a London evening paper came up with this much more compelling slogan). The first 'Dig for Victory' leaflet – there were to be twenty-five in all, and an estimated 10 million leaflets about growing food were in circulation in 1942 alone – was issued in February 1941 showing a boot pushing a spade in the soil. (The foot belonged to Mr McKie of Acton, London.) Each leaflet advised on some aspect of gardening – pruning fruit trees, potato blight, saving seeds.

City flat dwellers did their bit by planting tomatoes and herbs in window boxes, redcurrants and raspberries in tubs on balconies, while others rented allotments – it was estimated that by 1943 there were 1.4 million allotments in cultivation including those on railway embankments, grass verges, on Hampstead Heath, Hyde Park, the moat of the Tower of London, tennis courts, golf courses and other public open spaces, even flower tubs in Piccadilly Circus. In West Wickham four acres of Langley Park Golf Course were dug up, and 'plotters', as allotment holders were known, moved to cultivate part of Wickham Park Sports Club, recreation grounds and numerous other vacant spaces in the town. Indeed, a survey indicated that over half of all manual workers kept either an allotment or a productive garden, and the Hymers with their 70-foot garden were very well placed to 'Dig for Victory'.

'Dig for Victory': tending allotments under the shadow of the Albert Memorial in Kensington Gardens, London.

Moving into Braemar Gardens in April, the Hymers would be too late to get spring crops in, so the horticulturist Dennis Cornish had come up from his nursery at Stoke Gabriel in Devon in February and got their 1940s garden under way. He had been a gardener all his life, starting at the age of six, when he used to help his grandfather on his allotment. Now, as well as running his nursery, he has own television programme, *Dig It with Den*, and grew the plants for a 'wartime garden' at the Chelsea Flower Show.

Dennis Cornish ruthlessly dug perennials out of the herbaceous borders of 17 Braemar Gardens. Knowing that children were going to move in, he was careful to leave them some lawn to kick a ball around, but he increased the growing space, planting a selection of vegetables that should crop when the Hymers were in residence.

'I only used varieties that would have been available in 1940 – though many of these are still around today,' he said. He put in peas, the sugar snap variety that crop early; they are sweet, which was important since sugar would be rationed. There was an early cropping variety of broad beans, too, and a very reliable and prolific variety of French bean, called 'The Prince'. Dennis made a wigwam of hazel sticks for the runner beans. 'I planted "Painted Lady" there,' he said. 'It's beginning to be popular again as it has very exotic flowers, a pretty pink and white. Then I put in globe beetroots for salads. They're good because they're full of vitamins. Purple sprouting broccoli is another winner. It's cut and comes again, and it's coming back into favour these days too.'

Dennis also planted spring cabbage – 'That's a useful vegetable because you can use all the outer leaves as well as the heart.' He gave the Hymers a tip: 'Chop the cabbage off about a foot from the ground, make an x-shaped cut with a knife in the stalk and then it'll produce another crop. It's a very nutritious vegetable, is cabbage.'

Lettuces were planted too, again an early cropping variety. Dennis edged the borders with parsley 'to add flavour, and Lyn can cut bunches and hang them up to dry to use in casseroles and things'. Dennis put in onions too. There was an acute shortage of onions, particularly after the beginning of July 1940 when the Germans occupied the Channel Islands, which exported ample supplies in peacetime, gardeners found that crop after crop was destroyed by a particularly virulent variety of blight. Indeed, onions were so highly prized that, as Norman Longmate recorded, in February 1941 a raffle of a pound and a half of onions raised £4 3s 3d (not much less than Michael earned in a week in the 1940s house). They were very popular prizes at dances and

HOME-GROWN FOOD

NOVEMBER TO DECEMBER ISSUE

WHAT TO GROW BY THE MINISTRY OF AGRICULTURE
HOW TO COOK IT BY FREDDIE GRISEWOOD
(Of the B.B.C. Kitchen Front)

The Minister of Agriculture, the Rt. Hon. R. S. HUDSON, M.P., sends this special message to you :—

"Your family—especially the children—must eat vegetables to keep them fit. Green vegetables are vital to their winter health. It is up to you—women as well as men—to see they get them. Don't rely on others. Our farmers are doing their utmost to give you milk, bread, potatoes and other vital food. That is their main job, but you can make sure of getting enough vegetables too by growing your own. If you have a garden, turn it over to vegetables. If you have no garden, ask your local Council for an allotment."

The Hymers' garden also supplied them with a steady supply of flowers for the table.

social events and would not been looked at askance if given as a present. And he planted spring onions, shallots and leeks too.

Then of course there were the real-life equivalents of Dr Carrot and Potato Pete. The potatoes were Arran Pilot, which gives a good yield early, and the carrots were the cylindrical early ones – with very pretty frond tops. 'A vegetable garden can look almost as pretty as a flower garden,' Dennis insisted, 'what with carrot tops, runner bean and broccoli flowers and herbs like tarragon and dill and chives.'

Like onions, carrots are vulnerable to disease and, with no pesticides available in wartime and an increasing resistance to using them in 2000, Dennis's tips to the Hymers came in very useful. 'I crush up mothballs and sprinkle them round the carrots. What it does is to mask the scent of the carrot so carrot flies aren't attracted to it. I also tear up rhubarb leaves and leave them soaking in a bucket, which produces a noxious substance that can be sprayed on cabbages. I suggested that they should keep a galvanized metal bucket of water in the shed and put any spare shavings of carbolic soap in that to use as an anti-pest spray. It'll stop whitefly on the cabbages and blackfly too. And I've planted mint between the rows of cabbages and the Brussels sprouts. Cabbage white butterflies don't like the smell of mint, so they don't lay their eggs on the leaves. They're a real pest – even though they look so pretty.'

Dennis was in many ways nostalgic for the lore of wartime gardening: 'That's what gardens are supposed to be, an outdoor larder, soil and vegetables and plants. I've no time for all this decking and water features lark. What's natural about that? What does that produce that's any good to anybody?'

The Hymers could have cultivated the top of their Anderson shelter once Michael had finished building it and covering it with the requisite 15 inches of soil. They could have had a harvest of marrows to stuff and make 'pigs in clover' (another favourite of the Ministry of Food since the stuffing could include a generous measure of oatmeal or stale breadcrumbs that might otherwise have been wasted) or a splendid crop of rhubarb for puddings or to bottle (in the war they might have nipped out and shovelled up the deposits of the horse belonging to Mr Tibbs the milkman to make a rich manure for their crop). Or they could have grown rhubarb inside the shelter as some people did, or mushrooms since these flourish in the dark and damp and would have been delicious with the one weekly rasher of bacon that the family tended to save for a Sunday treat. But apart from a few carrots and some parsley they didn't: they extended the lawn up there, stuck up a flag, and periodically Michael would haul the lawn mower up and perilously perch on top as he tried to mow it.

Lord Woolton's propaganda urged:

Dig! Dig! Dig!
And your muscles will grow big.
Keep on pushing in the spade!
Never mind the worms
Just ignore their squirms,
And when your back aches, laugh with glee
And keep on diggin'
Till we give our foes a wiggin'
Dig! Dig! Dig! to Victory.

But patriotic and willing though the Hymers were, none of them was naturally green-fingered. Back home in Otley, Lyn and Michael have only a postage-stamp-sized back yard, more suitable for a deckchair and a couple of pots of geraniums, Lyn insisted, rather than a bed of veg. Spring 2000 was unseasonably cold and wet for most of the time, so many of the vegetables were later than Dennis had anticipated. The Hymers were grateful for their own leeks, carrots and potatoes and, later, lettuces to supplement their rations. But they nearly blew it with the peas, since they did not realize that they were sugar snaps that had been planted and they kept waiting for the pods to swell with green peas. In an effort to correct this regrettable lack of horticultural nous in the next generation, Dennis Cornish planted radishes for Ben

and Thomas to tend and showed the boys how to grow mustard and cress on sheets of blotting paper. Which was a start.

The Hymers didn't keep rabbits: indeed, they sent back the ones that had been waiting for them. Nor did they invest in a few chickens or bantams to provide eggs for the table and Sunday lunch when their laying days were over. In 1939 some 5 million hens were kept in back yards; by 1945 there were 11 million, housed in rickety boxes with wire netting stretched over the front, scratching about in the dust in many cases. To obtain chicken meal householders had to surrender their ration of shell egg. The meal would be mixed with household waste, lawn clippings and so on, and a small dose of cod liver oil for vitamins. It was a tough life – for the chicken. Wartime shortages meant that there was no space for passengers, and it was recommended that those chickens that declined to lay or that went broody should have their necks wrung, though many families found it hard to bring themselves to do that.

They could have kept a pig. Pigs were very popular in wartime. 'You can use every bit of a pig except its squeal' was a popular saying. Its body provided pork or ham or bacon, its head brawn, its innards sausages, faggots, lard and pâté, and even its trotters and tail could be pickled or boiled. By 1940, 70 per cent of imports of bacon, ham and other bits of pig had ceased and it was time to keep a pig for victory. In 1940 Lord Woolton launched an anti-waste campaign and anyone who threw away what could be consumed could be – and occasionally was – prosecuted. That year too the Small Pig Keepers' Council was set up to encourage people to keep a pig. Middle Whites were considered a good breed for householders: they were quiet and not too large, usually around 13 to 15 stones when fully grown, and that was a lot of meat.

'Sow for Victory'. Thomas with mustard and cress the boys had grown.

During the First World War pig clubs had been set up, and now these began to be revived either in the form of a few neighbours banding together to keep a pig, or a factory or other workplace buying several (famously the dustmen of Tottenham in north-east London bought a hundred pigs and attached a special bin to the back of each dust cart for potato peelings and the like to feed their animals). Members of neighbourhood pig clubs would contribute scraps for its food, take turns to boil up the scraps for an hour to destroy any bacteria, pay towards the insurance premium and help with mucking out.

By 1942 there were 4,000 pig clubs; so much of the imported meal that registered pig clubs were allowed was going to them rather than pig farmers that the pork products available to the rest of the population was reduced. The government curbed their activities by halving the meal allowance and insisting that pig owners either had to forfeit a year's bacon rations, or give the Ministry of Food half the pig when it was killed. Pigs were supposed to be slaughtered by a professional abattoir worker and the ministry trained instructors to visit pig clubs to teach them how to dismember their prized carcass – which was sometimes kept in the bath at a member's home – and salt the meat to preserve it (though pigs were usually killed between November and February to lessen the risk of the meat going off).

If all this was too much for the Hymers' sensibilities – and, to be fair, the time they had in the house – they would have been more than willing to contribute their household scraps to the local pig club, or take them to the pig bins that the local council would have started to set up in the streets. Indeed, one of the West Wickham pig clubs, run by a number of ARP wardens on some allotments, brought a poignant reminder of the town's rural past when a haystack was built to cater for porcine needs in the cold winter of 1941.

Kirstie saves kitchen scraps, as a wartime housewife would have done, to put in the neighbourhood pig bin.

CHAPTER 10

'BE LIKE THE KETTLE AND SING...'

'Everyone is fairly gloomy this evening,' wrote Lyn in her diary on Sunday 29 April. 'There's the threat of air raids, food shortages and Michael's forthcoming departure. We had one small rasher of bacon each for breakfast on dry bread, and I allowed the boys a little tomato sauce as a treat.'

Michael had taken three weeks' holiday to join the family as they settled in to their wartime experience, but he now had to go back to real-life work. On Monday the 30th, Lyn got up early to make him cheese and pickle sandwiches for his packed lunch, then walked with him to the station. She stood on the platform waving her white hanky as the train pulled out, taking Michael to London from where he would go back to Otley. He and Lyn had been parted before, of course, in over thirty years of married life, but they'd never been out of phone contact before. Maybe he'd write…

For Lyn and Kirstie, Michael's absence was underlined by Ben. 'I'm the oldest male now,' the ten-year-old asserted as he slipped into the chair at the head of the table where his grandfather usually sat at mealtimes. And it was also brought home to them that after the weeks of Michael's presence around the house they were going to have to deal with the temperamental boiler, the tradesmen, the garden, the blackout and any further restrictions or actions that the 'War Cabinet' might decree had to be observed as the war progressed. How would the two women, living in the same house together for the first time for many years, manage? 'We not merely cope, we care', read an inscription over the doorway of Lord Woolton's Ministry of Food. It could be the Hymers women's motto too.

With Michael away, the Hymers women were left to cope alone, as many of their wartime counterparts would have been.

Michael works just down the road from home in Yorkshire as an engineer with a small firm making aircraft and medical equipment, and other precision engineering products. In the Second World War this would have been a 'reserved occupation' since it was considered essential for the war effort, so Michael would have been exempt from call-up into the forces. In fact, at fifty-two he would have been exempt on grounds of age too. The National Service (Armed Forces) Act had been passed on the first day of the war, making all men between eighteen and forty-one liable for conscription, but it was not until May 1941 that those at the older end of the scale were registered. Men could short-circuit the process by volunteering, and during the course of the war some one and a half million did.

When they registered they could choose between the three fighting services – the army, Navy and air force, or they might be told they were exempt from call-up as they belonged to a 'reserved occupation'. The Schedule of Reserved Occupations had been distributed in November 1938, followed in January by a booklet that listed

'A kiss won't mean goodbye.' Lyn sees Michael off on the train on his return to work in Yorkshire.

all war jobs, both full- and part-time. It was a complicated scheme designed to avoid the problems of the First World War when, in their enthusiasm to enlist, men flooded into the forces, leaving the industries necessary to sustain the war effort perilously short of skilled manpower. The age of reserve was different for different occupations. A lighthouse keeper was 'reserved' at eighteen, whereas a trade union official could still be called up if he was under thirty, but not if he was over that age.

After November 1939 employers could request a deferment of call-up for men employed in a Scheduled occupation, but below the reserved age, and this was later extended to men in non-Scheduled occupations. In addition a man could apply for a deferment himself, and this might be granted if an advisory panel considered the severe personal hardship he pleaded warranted it. There were also tribunals set up to hear the case of conscientious objectors who refused to fight on grounds of pacifism or for political reasons, but by May 1940 these amounted to fewer than six in every thousand men liable for call-up. If their appeals were successful, such men would be put to work on the land, in the merchant navy, down the mines – all essential contributions to the war effort but not directly related to its military prosecution. A few 'conchies', as they were generally and contemptuously known, were given total exemption, and not directed into any war work.

As the war progressed and demands for manpower for the services, the wartime bureaucracy and industry grew, the government widened the net for those who were considered available for war work: the basis of reservation was reconsidered. Until 1941 a skilled engineer could mean a man working in a toy factory: if he was over a certain age, he would be as immune from call-up as a man in an aircraft factory. So the Minister of Labour, Ernest Bevin, created a category of 'protected establishments' where workers employed in organizations engaged in essential work would be reserved at a lower age than those doing inessential work, and the Scheduled age for a number of occupations was revised upwards. By the end of 1941 men up to forty-six were obliged to register and, if in non-essential work, were invited to take up a vacancy in one of the industries where there was a shortfall. Bevin also took to himself powers of direction – workers could be compelled to move from their job to one that was more important to the war effort. He had the power to order them to move away from home for the purpose but this was rarely used until later in the war when large-scale construction projects, such as the Mulberry Harbour for D-Day, involved groups of men working in remote areas.

Not only was it up to Bevin to decide which jobs were essential: if a man worked in such a job he could not be sacked without the consent of the Ministry of Labour, nor could the worker leave without the Ministry's permission. There was an appeals procedure, but cases of persistent absenteeism could be reported to the National Service Officer for the area who had the power to demand that the man worked the stated hours. Anyone who defied such an order could, in theory, be sent to prison.

The state had taken upon itself unprecedented powers to intervene in the life of its citizens in wartime, but this had a progressive aspect too. Bevin was a working man, a former trade union official, and he knew that to force people to work for low wages in primitive conditions could be inflammatory even in wartime. He recognized the war provided an opportunity to improve the lot of working people. He therefore made the EWO (Emergency Work Order) part of a bargain that meant that in return for accepting these unprecedented restrictions on their freedom, the trade unions would be able to negotiate decent pay and working conditions.

So life on the home front with the menfolk away was a usual wartime experience for millions. Women who had previously thought that dealing with the world was 'man's work' found themselves in sole charge of the household, having to make decisions about money, insurance, the children's education as well as those domestic matters that they had always regarded as their sphere. And all this in a context of ever-constant danger, uncertainty, shortages and grindingly hard work. But apparently it was still their patriotic duty to contribute to the war effort by keeping cheerful. As an article in *Mother and Home* urged in January 1940; 'Hang on to your courage, and, if possible, to a laugh. Remember, you used to teach your child to turn up the corner of her mouth to make a pretty smile? Well, do the same yourself today – and every day in 1940.' Morale was all important and women were in the front line in maintaining it. They were particularly urged to keep spirits up at mealtimes, which involved a certain sleight of hand:

- Don't tell the family what the dish is made from until they have tasted – and liked – it.
- Don't moan about the food you couldn't get before you serve it.
- Do praise your cooking in advance to encourage their appetites.
- Do talk pleasant small talk at each meal.
- Don't mention the gas bill until everyone has finished.

There were quizzes asking 'Are You Brave?' which reminded women that 'never was there such a call for the heroic spirit as in these critical times. We may look at ourselves and ask: "Am I made of heroic stuff?" Can you keep cheerful, see hope and even humour where others see only gloom and despair? In temporary defeats can you say, "Well, that's that, it can't be helped," and fight on with your back to the wall? Can you forgo self at a time of dire need for the sake of family, community, nation?'

Lyn made a contribution in her way: in times of acute stress, she would grit her teeth and try to follow the advice of a popular wartime song: 'When you're up to your neck in hot water,/Be like the kettle and sing.'

It was a tough order: as a *Sunday Times* journalist later reflecting on the war recalled, it was a time of 'small, dull, makeshift meals… darkness and drabness and making do, the depressing, nerve-aching, never-ending need to be careful'. And in addition to the usual chores, the housewife often had 'to learn to do-it-yourself' with husbands, sons, fathers and most other able-bodied men away in the forces on essential war work, or putting in hours in the Home Guard or the ARP. Women needed all the advice they could get.

The Board of Trade was on hand with a useful leaflet: 'Why not be your own "handyman" now that skilled labour has so many calls on it? Odd jobs like these are easier than you would think – don't send out for someone to attend to them till you have had a good try yourself.' It came up with instructions for driving in nails, then extracting them with a claw-headed hammer, fixing hooks and screws ('tap a hole with a cold chisel' – no power drills then), unblocking a sink, repairing a stepladder, soldering a saucepan, replacing a fuse, repairing a frayed electrical flex.

Women in charge. Lyn and Kirstie walking with Ben and Thomas.

Wash day 1940s style: 'First you scrub...'

As Caroline Haslett, founder of the Women's Engineering Society in 1919 and the Electrical Association for Women in 1924, and editor of *The Electrical Handbook for Women*, recognized, 'Many women have a nervous dislike of anything to do with electricity, but there is no need for this; as long as you take proper precautions when doing repairs or handling apparatus you will be quite safe. Think how useful it is to be able to do any little job yourself without having to send for an electrician [who was probably not available anyway] and how much cheaper.'

Lyn was worried. 'I really don't know how I can fit much more in. If I'm lucky I get a maximum of six hours sleep a night – and that's a good night. I just don't know if I can do any more and I'm going to have to when Michael goes, because of the jobs he normally does, lighting the boiler, keeping it going, helping put up the blackout, doing jobs outside – though to be honest we haven't done all that much in the garden yet, and we haven't got an allotment to worry about.'

The washing was a particular chore. With five people living in the house, including two active young boys, there were a lot of clothes, bed linen, towels, tablecloths and tea towels to do – and no washing machine. 'Monday wash day' was a long day and sometimes it stretched to two. First the clothes had to be steeped in water and a little soda overnight, or at least for a couple of hours in the morning to 'loosen' the dirt. Then the water had to be poured from the sink in a big enamel jug into the electrically heated tub and the clothes put in with soda crystals and whatever shavings of household soap could be garnered from the Hymers' ever-depleting

rations. The always-helpful Ministry of Food recommended collecting rainwater for 'washing smalls and woollies – much less soap is needed'. There was no agitator in the tub so once the water was hot Lyn had to stand over it stirring the clothes with a dolly peg, a long wooden stick with a brass end that pummelled the clothes clean.

It was hot and steamy work, and Lyn often wished she could take off her warm clothes and stand clad just in the wraparound pinny she always wore when doing housework. Once the clothes were as clean as she felt she could get them, Lyn had to rinse them several times, then drag the mangle from the shed and, with her foot wedged against the bar at the bottom, wrench round the handle to squeeze as much water as possible out of the clothes. At first she did not realize that the screw on the top controlled the pressure on the rollers, so buttons flew off shirts and dresses as the screw was too tight. Then it was a job to get the flapping wet sheets on to the lines where, secured by wooden pegs (which Lyn never seemed to have enough of), they blew in the wind – if it wasn't raining. It was suggested that while this was happening the wash-tub suds could be used to mop the floor and wash dusters and floor cloths to save further

'... then you mangle.' Lyn at her usual Monday morning chores.

precious soap. Another learning curve came for Lyn when she realized that it was nearly impossible to iron the heavy cotton sheets dry, so washing and ironing had to be done on the same day, and the sheets were frequently put on the beds by an exhausted Lyn just before she crawled into them at the end of a tiring day and fell into a deep sleep.

It wasn't just the hard work, it was the ingenuity needed to cope with entirely different circumstances in the 1940s house with no modern conveniences, food shortages and a very different diet from that which the family had been used to. And Lyn felt she didn't have any signposts. 'I need someone to tell me what they did, how they managed. But there isn't anybody. I am having to think on my feet all the time and rationing is getting worse.' The family were in 1941 by now, a time of the greatest shortages before the US Lend Lease programme had been agreed in March 1941. By this agreement, America – which did not enter the war until after the Japanese had bombed Pearl Harbor on 7 December 1941 – supplied munitions, petroleum products, food and services to the Allies on the analogy of 'lending a garden hose to put out a neighbour's fire'.

'After every meal I have to sit down and work out what's left and what we can manage for the next meal. It's very wearing and I feel very responsible. Living here in wartime conditions has changed my priorities in life quite drastically. They are now keeping the home together, looking after the family, making sure that their needs are met, their health, their food, their safety, their home comforts, as much as possible. I don't really aspire to anything else at the moment. Though I'm not really living in the 1940s, of course, it does feel like it and it feels that life is different. It's very hard work, but in return there's a certain kind of family closeness, all of us pulling together. A feeling of safety, somehow, which I've never felt so strongly before. It's odd because a few years ago the Major government made a big deal about family values, and failed. Well, of course they failed, I thought, you can't put the clock back like that. But this experience has shown me that in a way you can. I seem to be living a calmer life, much more focused, what's really important to me seems much clearer.'

The women also found that when Michael was away, their relationship changed. For a start Kirstie had 'taken on the responsibility of trying to keep the boiler going. My dad's given me instructions, but I haven't actually managed to light it from scratch yet, I am just keeping it going basically, but we'll cope, my mum and me, because women had to in the war with their husbands away.'

> 'Mrs Bostock of Loughborough finds that now clothes pegs are difficult to get, she can do without them. She doubles the clothes line equally, and twists the two ropes fairly tight before hanging the washing line up. When putting out the washing, she separates the twists and slips in a corner of the garment. The line holds the clothes safely, and they are easily removed when dry.'
>
> **One of the winning entries in the August 1942 Housewife competition 'Your Wartime Hints'**

Next you peg your 'smalls' on the line so they can dry in
the fresh air – until it rains.

'Kirstie has got a lot stronger, more confident. I'm really proud of her,' Lyn professed. 'When Michael's away we work like a proper team.' The women decided to have 'some sort of rota, because the jobs were piling up, the pressure was on us, and it seemed that the way forward was to divide the work as equally as we could, or more importantly divide the time when we weren't working, so we could spend some time with the children, which they need.'

'Keeping to a routine' was a key concept for women in wartime. It was largely to do with practical things: the need to get to the shops in the morning, having cooked breakfast and washed up, to collect your rations, and then maybe queue for some unrationed delicacy or something on points that word spread like wildfire had just come into the shops. Then it was back home to cook lunch, or prepare the evening meal which was usually three courses, almost always including a cooked pudding, plus teatime in between with cakes or tarts or scones. Making sure that the evening meal was eaten and washed up before the family retired to the shelter for the night as hundreds of thousands did during the blitz. Fruit had to be bottled, jam made, preserves and chutneys produced too.

Household management: surrounded by ration books Lyn and Kirstie work out their coupon allocation.

It was partly to do with high house-wifely standards and inadequate means to fulfil them. Women's magazines set demanding 'work sheets' for (middle-class) wartime housewives, which kept them going hard at it all day (9.30 p.m. 'sit down with a cup of tea' was generously scheduled). *Housewife* even ran a competition inviting readers to put 'Mrs Feckless' back on track: she'd spent too much time playing with her children, or talking to her friends on the phone so she 'made' her husband miss his bus. Women were advised to clean their main rooms every day (open coal fires and solid fuel boilers distributed generous amounts of dirt), and 'turn out' a room a week. Then there was the washing, ironing, dressmaking, mending, household repairs, gardening – and all to be done on their own since their 'help' was now doing more important (and better paid) war work.

A moment of domestic contemplation for Lyn.

But it was partly psychological. In this world nothing seemed certain: no one could predict what might happen next. Control was obvious in the issuing of ration books, but by no means so in the direction or success of the war. There could be no certainty about the future as there had been in peacetime; husbands, lovers, sons might not come home again, and that home could be flattened anyway. In this world it seemed very important to create a domain where order reigned, where a woman could try to reassure herself that if she busied herself organizing the domestic space aright, that might be a talisman against the vagaries of the world at war.

It was during the first week Michael was away that Lyn's serenity began to crack. A video camera had been fixed up in a bedroom cupboard for the Hymers to record their daily impressions of life in the 1940s house. In fact it was used most by Lyn for whom it became a safety valve. Bereft of her friends at home, whom she'd phone in moments of crisis, or whom would call round for a glass of wine and a cigarette, and feeling isolated in her neighbourhood among people she did not yet know and who in any case were carrying on a twenty-first-century life with all its conveniences, Lyn would often unburden her feelings on camera. Wednesday 16 May was such a night: 'Kirstie and I are feeling pretty low, mainly due to an escalation in the withdrawal of

things from the shops,' she confided. Authentic to the wartime experience of 1941, 'greaseproof paper, soap, washing powder, matches, coffee, lots of different things have all disappeared from the shelves. At the end of the day, as darkness fell, once the children were in bed, we both got very, very gloomy. It was so bad that we just sat at the dining room table. I didn't want to wash up, or mop the kitchen floor, or listen to the radio, or do some mending, or write letters, or do any of the things I knew I should have been doing. I just wanted to go home to Yorkshire. I wanted to go back to 2000. I wanted to throw in the towel.'

Kirstie felt bleak too, but she analysed the problem as being largely due to the absence of cigarettes. Both she and Lyn were long-time heavy smokers and it was a habit both knew they would not be able to kick in the conditions of 1940. At first they had been able to get packets of Capstan Heavy Duty, Senior Service and, if they could get nothing else, they smoked – or at least Kirstie did – the ubiquitous Woodbine, or even tried to roll their own. Cigarettes were not rationed in the war, but they were restricted by limits on shipping space and the priority given to supplying the Forces. The quota of packets of both cigarettes and tobacco from wholesalers was tight and local shops would ration the supplies they could get to spread them as fairly

as possible – and also, most likely, save some under the counter to reward the loyalty of regular customers. It was entirely feasible, the 'War Cabinet' decided, that Mr Lovegrove could let Lyn and Kirstie have only one packet each in a particular week, and he might ask them to empty the cigarettes out of the packet so he could reuse it. The following week things might have improved, but that was little consolation to such nicotine addicts as Lyn and Kirstie Hymers.

At the lowest point that evening there was a knock at the door and there stood their neighbours from a few doors away, Peter and Nina Tilling. The Hymers had met the couple the previous week when Peter Tilling, mindful of always having felt cold in the war, brought a bundle of kindling he'd been chopping for their boiler. That

'My feet are agony and cigarettes are in short supply.' Lyn at the end of wash day.

evening Kirstie had called at their house for any ideas they might have about getting some cigarettes. Did they think that a black market in such commodities had existed in West Wickham? Now the Tillings stood on the doorstep of 17 Braemar Gardens proffering two

Kirstie enjoying a cigarette. By the end of the war nearly half the women of Britain smoked.

packets. 'It often was possible to get cigarettes,' maintained Nina. 'You might know someone who didn't smoke, who'd get some for you, or of course soldiers could buy them at the NAAFI and they might swap cigarettes for something they wanted. And a number of factory canteens sold them too. There was a regular barter economy going on and cigarettes were often valuable currency. Then don't forget that there were Canadian troops stationed here living at Coney Hall, and like the American GIs they always seemed to have plenty of "smokes" and they could be very generous.'

Lyn and Kirstie were extremely grateful but, as Lyn said, in the end it wasn't the cigarettes so much as the camaraderie the Tillings brought that night that mattered. 'I explained about our feeling of isolation, with no wartime neighbours to help us along. They said that they understood and that from now on they'd be our wartime neighbours. And that felt good. We talked for two hours and the Tillings managed to help us get everything back into perspective again. What on earth were we doing whinging about not having this and not having that, when after all we were only doing it for nine weeks and in wartime people had been going through greater hardships by far for years. It turned the whole thing round for us and we were full of British wartime spirit again and determined to stay and see things out properly to the end.'

Michael was due back from Yorkshire the next evening for a weekend at home. While away, he had been living in the family house in Otley, but was surprised to find that it no longer felt like home. 'West Wickham feels more like home now,' he said. 'I can't wait to get back to the 1940s. I keep wondering how the family are managing while I'm away. I do feel that I am deserting them. I think it's very hard for the women. They are the ones who have to keep everything together. The burden of the work does fall on them and I am concerned to see how much Lyn and Kirstie are having to work just to keep the family fed and the house clean and organized.

'That was one of the things that came as something of a shock to me. Somehow I always thought of the 1940s as a more leisured age. Of course I knew there was a war on, but I had this picture of the family sitting round every evening, listening to

the wireless, playing board games, the women knitting or sewing. But so far it hasn't worked out like that. There is just so much for Lyn and Kirstie to get done. I've had more time with the boys, I've kicked a football round with them and we made a pair of stilts the other day from some wood I found lying around. But that's about as far as it goes. Everything seems to take so much longer to do. I am amazed at how long a simple job like lighting three fires can take. It takes longer to get dressed with all those buttons and braces, shaving takes half an hour instead of the two minutes I am used to with an electric razor. Even the bath fills at half the speed, and of course there is no such thing as a power shower.'

While Michael was in Yorkshire he stuck to the 1940s regime too: he ate at the house of friends but he was served with the sort of meal he would have had in a British Restaurant. Restaurants had not been rationed when the system was introduced in 1940. They received a quota of food on a scale related to the number of their customers and domestic rations, but there were soon complaints that restaurants were snaffling expensive unrationed fare like lobsters and chicken and out-of-season fruit. As the number of meals they served went up, this in turn

Boys' retreat. Michael reads as Thomas and Ben play cards.

pushed up their quota of meat and other rationed items. This was clearly not in the spirit of equal sacrifice for all, so in the spring of 1942 a regulation was introduced imposing a maximum 5s charge on all meals and permitting only one main course to be served. But this hardly helped the working man or woman; and during the blitz many small cafes were destroyed while, conversely, people needed more than ever to get a hot meal away from home.

The government planned 10,000 British Restaurants to be provided by local authorities; these would be self-service, providing good, plain food priced at between 10d and 1s a meal. They were very popular and opened in all sorts of unlikely places – the Victoria and Albert Museum was one – and there was a British Restaurant in West Wickham High Street too. The enterprise also helped the family rations, since no coupons were required for British Restaurant meals. Sadly, the lassitude of some local authorities and the opposition of commercial catering establishments meant that by September 1943 less than a quarter of the government target for the non-profit making enterprises had been met. But they provided the model for Michael's meals of corned beef hash and bread and butter pudding, or sausage casserole and apple pudding, when he was working away from home.

The pattern of Michael's week was not unlike that of a war worker required to move away from home, except that he had a rather shorter working week. Instead of working on Saturday mornings – or even all day on Saturday – he was home by Thursday night. And at no station did a poster demand 'Is Your Journey Really Necessary?' though it was a question he sometimes asked himself as he battled through the Underground.

Lyn and Kirstie had been really looking forward to Michael's return that first week. Not only would he be able to help them with the heavy chores, but he would, they

One of the 10,000 British Restaurants in Britain.

hoped, be sympathetic about their hardships and offer Lyn uxorious comfort and support. But that is not how it was: when Lyn and Kirstie recounted their stories of hard work and acute shortages, Michael seemed to find it amusing. He laughed and laughed and then asked where his supper was. 'I'm appalled at him,' Lyn said. 'I told him he could make his own bloody supper. My husband just cannot get used to how things have changed round here. He sits at the breakfast table waiting for me to pour his tea out.' But by now, as part of the wider wartime experience, Lyn had started to do some voluntary work outside the home in addition to her household duties, so, as she declared, 'I am no longer going to wait on him hand and foot.'

Lyn's perception of the widening gulf between her and Kirstie's experience and that of Michael increased. 'He just does not get rationing. He does not get frugal living. He keeps saying, "Oh, let's have that," he's made no effort to understand the points system at all. When we went to the shop, he wanted to have Spam and he just couldn't understand when I said that I hadn't got enough points for a tin of Spam. He thinks he can help himself to condensed milk when we've been saving it all week for the children. He was the one who was all nostalgic for the 1940s, but I don't think he will lose his rose-tinted spectacles because I just don't think that the men saw the full extent of the home front battle. My husband goes to work, he comes home at the end of the week, there's food on the table, we save the week's meat ration up so he can have really good meals at the weekend, and then he thinks that we live like that all the time. He doesn't realize what sacrifices we've made. Often our lunch is dry bread with a scraping of marmalade. So did men come home from war and get just what they wanted while the women had been living so frugally? Probably.'

Kirstie was more conciliatory: 'I think with our experience women are sacrificing more than men but I wouldn't say that was necessarily true of the war. I mean, far more men in the forces, in the Home Guard, the Fire Services, the ARP sacrificed their lives let alone their rations. I think it's just that the experiences were different. But here, in this house, the women are certainly sacrificing more than the one man.'

It was a volatile situation: sometimes Lyn deeply resented Michael's presence 'I don't want to bring cups of tea to this man. I don't want to cook his meals. I don't even want him to be here if he's going to waste my coal and my soap.' Other times she was prepared to put on what she called her 'Mrs Miniver' mode, the idealized comfortable wartime housewife of Jan Struther's 1940 novel and William Wyler's multi-Oscared 1942 tribute to the British home front, and welcome him home with a fire burning in the grate and a shepherd's pie in the oven. And Lyn was warm in her praise of Michael's hard work in erecting the family's Anderson shelter, which was soon customized with pictures and even a jam jar of flowers on the small table. But her resolve went deep: 'If there is going to be a fairy godmother after the war to magic away my war-ravaged face and stringy hair, there had better be a Prince Charming on offer too.'

CHAPTER 11

GO TO IT! GO TO IT!

'Dear Mrs Hymers, Thank you for your recent letter in which you enquire about voluntary work for you and your daughter,' started the note on paper headed 'The 1940s House War Cabinet, Whitehall, London,' which Lyn found as she opened a parcel that was delivered to Braemar Gardens in mid-May. 'Members of the local community will be in touch with you shortly to advise you of the jobs that we have chosen for you.'

Lyn and Kirstie had decided that though their days seemed full already with shopping, cooking, cleaning the house and looking after the children – frequently interrupted by dashes to the Anderson shelter in the garden when the air-raid siren sounded – they wanted to contribute more directly to the well-being of the local community. They wanted to 'do their bit' as women all over Britain had done in the Second World War.

'At the moment I don't want to leave the house,' explained Lyn, 'I feel that my whole day is geared to making the 1940s house a home for the family, but I do feel that I should be doing something outside the home too, even if I can't quite see how I can physically manage everything I am doing now, and work as well. I never sit down before ten o'clock at night and then there's the sewing and mending and letter writing to do, and I am up again by seven the next morning. But women did manage, and so must we. We can't just sit around playing house here all day when we remember what women contributed to the war effort in the 1940s.'

> 'I feel that any woman who does not give up her leisure will regret it so forcibly that she will feel ashamed for not doing so,' said Lady Reading, founder of the WVS in 1939. Kirstie adjusts her WVS hat.

There were a number of things that women who were in Lyn's and Kirstie's position could have done on a voluntary basis in the Second World War. Apart from taking as much responsibility as possible for their own families by observing blackout regulations, filling the bath with water and having a stirrup pump at the ready to deal with incendiary bombs, digging for victory and sharing any spare produce with less well-placed friends and neighbours, they could have provided comforts for the troops. Toothpaste or foot ointment was always welcome, as were cigarettes, gramophone records and books – 'not just old ones you have no use for, but good, popular novels'. They could carry on the tradition of the First World War (indeed the Crimea and Boer Wars before that) and knit – socks, scarves, gloves for sailors manning minesweepers, balaclava helmets, squares for blankets. They could have contributed home comforts for the parcels sent by the Red Cross to prisoners of war in Europe and the Far East, or helped organize a group of knitters who could then have obtained wool at a specially reduced price through the voluntary organizations. The whole family could have joined a savings group since 'all the pennies you can save now to lend to the government will buy steel and bullets and help to win the war. Ask at your local Post Office or Bank for details.'

How the war effort would have been helped. The 'Saucepans for Spitfires' campaign in 1940 and collecting household goods for salvage.

The family would certainly have resolved to salvage waste paper, scrap iron, bones, rags, bottles, tins and kitchen waste – though, as Lyn pointed out, they were generating only a small amount of waste. 'At home we have a big metal waste bin in the kitchen and it fills up every day, but here it takes a week to fill one small bin.' It was partly that under the Control of Paper Order (1940), 'No person shall in connection with any sale or retail wrap or pack with paper any article which does not reasonably require such wrapping or packing for its protection', so Lyn and Kirstie came back from the grocer's with their baskets full of loose vegetables, and might have taken their own greaseproof paper to the butcher's. And it was also the absence of modern pre-cooked food and the tinfoil and cardboard containers they

Kirstie sews together crocheted squares, today's equivalent of knitting blankets for the troops.

came in before they were stuffed into paper bags and then plastic carriers.

It made Lyn decide to contribute a couple of aluminium saucepans that she could ill afford to spare to Beaverbrook's appeal. 'We will turn your pots and pans into Spitfires and Hurricanes, Blenheims and Wellingtons,' he had promised on 10 July 1940, asking that 'everyone who has pots and pans, kettles, vacuum cleaners, hat pegs, coat hangers, shoe trees, bathroom fittings and household ornaments, cigarette boxes, or any other articles made wholly or in part of aluminium, should hand them over at once to the local Women's Voluntary Services… The need is instant. The call is urgent. Our expectations are high.' Lyn would have felt proud every time she saw a plane overhead that 'her' saucepan might have been used to construct its wing or tail. However, she might have felt a little perplexed when she noticed that aluminium saucepans were still on sale and that scrap merchants had considerable stocks. And perhaps somewhat disillusioned to learn later that, strictly speaking, it had been a pointless sacrifice since the metal was not of a sufficiently high grade for aircraft – even though the campaign had been a monumentally successful propaganda exercise in making people feel that they were helping to win the war.

Beaverbrook's next initiative was also massively successful: the 'Spitfire Fund', which 'priced' a Spitfire somewhat arbitrarily at £5,000. An individual, a factory or organization, a town or city could 'buy' a new plane for the war effort by contributing

Woman at work: Kirstie scours the bath.

that amount. By April 1941, £13 million had been raised, and soon every town in the land had 'bought' a Spitfire (which were always more popular with the public than Hurricanes); even Durham, where unemployment rates had been high, had 'paid for' two Spitfires. The enterprising Minister of Aircraft Production and the National Savings Movement then issued a 'price list' so that those of more modest means could contribute a bit of the plane – 6d pocket money bought a rivet, the engine cost £1,750 and a small bomb would set you back £20.

Had they had more room, the family could have offered shelter to a refugee from an invaded country – a number of West Wickham families accommodated refugees from Belgium and France after they had fled in 1940. The town had been designated a 'neutral' rather than a 'reception' area, so children evacuated from London under the government schemes were not sent to West Wickham; but it is possible that relations or friends from the big cities might have sought respite from the bombing in this less pummelled Kentish town during the worst of the blitz. Or, if they had been deemed to have 'surplus accommodation', they might have had billeted on them someone drafted to work away from home in a munitions factory, or a girl in the Land Army working on a Kentish farm nearby.

The women could have attended one of the local Red Cross centres each week to make bandages or anything that was required, or helped organize whist drives, beetle drives and sales of work to raise money for the Red Cross or another wartime

charity. (This is one of the things that Nella Last had done, Lyn noted.) They could have attended the instruction classes in first-aid that the Red Cross and St John's Ambulance organized, enabling them to volunteer as a VAD worker at a first-aid post and help with air-raid victims. Or they could (and almost certainly would) have spent one night a week as a firewatcher, patrolling the road on the lookout for incendiary bombs (the most common type, which did not explode but could ignite a property if not extinguished quickly with sand or water); they'd have been armed with a whistle to rouse householders, and a photographic memory for where the street's stirrup pumps were located. From January 1941 in all areas considered at risk, which eventually meant most of the country, it was made incumbent on everyone who was not already a member of the ARP or Home Guard to undertake firewatching duties near their home or place of work. Or they could have responded to an appeal such as the one that appeared in a Stockton-on-Tees newspaper: 'Housework may be horsework, but it's war work too, especially if you mind a bairn whose mother's on munitions', and invited volunteers willing to undertake this task to apply to the Health Department.

Lyn took great pride in keeping the 1940s house immaculate.

Although they were living a 1940s life in all practical essentials, Lyn and Kirstie were living it in 2000 and they wanted the work they did to be of some benefit to the community as women's war work had been. They decided that service with the WVS would be appropriate. There were a number of nationwide women's voluntary organizations that they could have joined, including the Women's Institute, the Townswomen's Guild and the Red Cross, all of which made a great contribution to the war effort, but the WVS was particularly focused on war work.

The Women's Voluntary Service (now the Women's Royal Voluntary Service, 'royal' having been added after the war) was founded in 1938. The Home Office had asked Stella, Dowager Marchioness of Reading, the energetic and practical widow of a Viceroy of India, specifically to find a way of involving women in ARP work, and of preparing them for wartime emergencies – whatever these might be. So great was women's response that a one-way traffic system had to be introduced along the headquarters' corridor in Tothill Street, Westminster. In West Wickham the WVS had opened five canteens at ARP wardens' posts and put out appeals for clothes for victims of possible air-raid attacks before war had even been declared. By August 1939 the WVS had 336,000 volunteers nationwide and by May 1941 this had risen to a million.

Lyn in her WVS uniform.

Whoever volunteered was accepted: no one was to be deprived of 'doing their bit'. The WVS simply did what was required, where it was required, when it was required. Initially the preserve of better-off women with time on their hands, very soon thousands of women throughout the country, who were over the age of conscription or directed war work or had family commitments, proved tireless, courageous, innovative, cheerful and ubiquitous. They would greet returning troops with tea and buns, distribute emergency clothing, staff rest centres and organize transport and voluntary car pools (often driving themselves). They would provide cups of tea, blankets, mobile canteens and comfort for blitz victims, escort evacuated children – in one case writing a pamphlet about dealing with bedwetting among the small displaced evacuees – or help at nurseries set up to look after children whose

mothers were working in the war industries (as the WVS had done in West Wickham) or who had lost one or both parents in the bombing. Even those with onerous domestic responsibilities could join the WVS Housewife's Service. A card in their windows advertised that the services of sensible women in every street would be utilized to provide hot drinks, care for old people and invalids during raids, shelter casualties before the emergency services arrived, help out at local public shelters and do anything else that needed doing.

The service responded to the request of their founder: 'Please do not hesitate to take such lead as is demanded of you.' At the end of the war Lady Reading reflected that, in the past seven years, 'We have learned that it is no good talking about things, we must do them, and… to do that we must take pains, dislocate our lives and our comfort… We have done work we never thought to approach and have carried burdens heavier than we knew existed.' (These burdens included, after 1943, setting up Incident Enquiry Points at major incidents, often having to break the news to people that among the dead or grievously injured were members of their family.) Lady Reading continued: 'We now know that in life no obstacle can block, it can only impede; that tiredness is an incident, not a finality.'

Aware of all this, Lyn was determined that she and Kirstie in their turn would do what was asked of them in very different circumstances. 'The WVS members couldn't say, "Well, we don't want to do that, we don't like taking the wounded to hospital, we don't like ferrying little evacuees away from their parents into the country" – they did it all and, as I saw in the letter from the Cabinet, quite a number of them, 241 I think, lost their lives during the war. So whatever we are asked to do today – cleaning toilets in a hospital, or whatever unpleasant job the Cabinet comes up with, we'll do it because we'd be letting those wartime WVS workers down if we didn't. I don't want people to think that we're playing at this, because that would be disrespectful to the WVS, who throughout the war did some amazingly brave and heroic things and risked their lives many times. So whatever we do in 2000 it has to be at least useful too.'

It was decided that Lyn and Kirstie would work at Glebe Court, an old people's home in West Wickham that provides sheltered housing and residential care. They would help in the restaurant and do what they were asked in the nursing home. In that way they would be doing a useful job as well as meeting a number of West Wickham residents who had lived through the war. At last Lyn looked likely to get her wish to meet people who had been roughly the age she was now, or a bit younger, during the war and would have recollections of how it had been for housewives bringing up a family in those years.

'As soon as I stepped into my green WVS uniform I felt efficient and ready for action,' wrote Lyn in her diary for 22 May 2000. 'It's strange how a uniform can make you feel so different.'

At first the elderly residents did not quite understand what the women were doing there. 'I think a lot of them thought we were actresses, which is nowhere near the mark. If we were actresses we would be off home after we had been filmed in our uniform, instead of coming home to dry bread,' Lyn reflected ruefully as she nibbled on a slice of National Loaf scraped with jam at the end of a tiring day, having resisted the temptation to help herself to a spoonful of the whipped cream or one of the roast potatoes that she had served at the restaurant. 'It's ironic, they seem to throw away more food in a day than we have to live on for a week!'

Gradually, Lyn and Kirstie gained the confidence of Glebe Court residents and realized that the sight of their uniforms brought back all sorts of memories of the war – some of them painful – that they wanted to talk about. They met Ivy Crier, who had lived in Layhams Road as a young wife and mother and had taken in a Belgian couple who had fled from atrocities in their homeland in 1940. 'They were very nervous of the bombs, so my husband built an Anderson shelter in the garden and they slept there every night. But we never did. We slept in our beds. I used to say, if we go we all go together in our own home.' She served as a regular fire watcher for her street during the war, and also befriended a number of the young Canadians who were billeted at Coney Hall. 'They would come in for a cup of tea and a talk. Some of them were very young – eighteen or nineteen – and I think they missed home a lot, though they had a pretty good time with the girls round here. There were lots of dances up at the hall, and then they'd take them to shows in London. I only ever met one Canadian who admitted to being married. All the others claimed to be single. But I rather doubt it.'

Mrs Crier's hospitality brought its rewards. 'I made an apple pie for some of the boys once, and they thought it was marvellous and asked why I didn't open a stall to sell my home cooking. I had to explain that the pie was a rare treat. We couldn't usually get the rations to make as much pastry as that. After that they would bring me great drums of dripping from their cookhouse. They said it would go to waste, but it was a wonderful bonus for me. And then their mothers back home would send me parcels. Once I opened one and it contained three tins of golden syrup and I thought that was pretty good, but when I opened them it was even better. Rolled up inside were pairs of nylons. My stepdaughters, who were teenagers at the time, were so thrilled.'

And Lyn met Reg Long, who talked to her about his time in the AFS in West Wickham. 'He approached me. He wanted me to know about his wartime experiences. He wanted recognition, not for himself at all, but for the work that the AFS had done. He wanted me to know what an input the AFS in West Wickham had had in the Second World War and how brave some of the deeds were that the men performed as a matter of course. Many of them were conscripted into the AFS

and, though they did have some training, they had to learn very quickly. In wartime there just wasn't the time for months and months of training. And then they'd be sent into burning buildings to save people's lives.

'He had some wonderful tales to tell, some very sad and tragic, but they were all incredibly interesting and moving. He's seen so many terrible things in the war. He was very unassuming, he just told me the facts. But some of things he told me about were so dreadful that he got very distressed, and I just can't bring myself to repeat them. But he did tell me about the AFS officers who were killed in Poplar in 1941 and how terrible that had been. He'd been on leave at the time, or he might well have been one of them. He showed me photographs of his friends, all healthy, fit young men, some with families, twenty-one dead in a single incident. And when he had to tell one of the men's widows what had happened she just said, "Well, that's what happens in war." As Reg said, if something like that happened now, if there is a tragedy on a major scale, then the services involved would have trauma counselling afterwards. But there was nothing like that in the war. In those days they just had to get on with it. Go on to the next incident, not knowing what they might find there. Reg thinks that counselling is one of the great advances of the twentieth century, because in the war, he said, people might carry on after a horrendous incident, and seem quite normal, and then some time later they might suddenly have a breakdown or become seriously ill.

'I don't suppose my generation will ever know the full trauma of war and the effect it had on people,' reflected Lyn, 'but by talking to people who were there, we learn something, maybe we can understand better.'

After a while Lyn became aware that her presence was increasingly distressing for some of the residents. 'I feel I am stirring up memories that they can't deal with. If you put yourself in the shoes of someone who's well over eighty and they suddenly see someone who's dressed in 1940s clothes, some of them get very confused, and perhaps they can't sort out where they are, they may think they are back in the war. My uniform brings it all back to them and while at one level they do want to talk about the war, it really upsets them too much. They can't seem to change the subject, but many of them are over ninety so I don't think that I can do this for much longer. It's too hard on them and too difficult for me.'

But before she left Glebe Court Lyn was able to bring Reg Long together with Bertram Rayfield, who had been a fellow fireman with the AFS. The men had shared dangers during the war, but, with rooms on different floors, had no idea they were in the same nursing home. It was a great pleasure for both men to be able to sit together and share memories of these times.

Lyn was delighted too, but her experience had left her with a resolve. 'I have worn my WVS uniform with a great deal of pride because to me it represents the tremendous

1940s HOUSE

work the WVS did in the Second World War, and are still doing today, but it bothers me that during the war there was a culture of shared social responsibility, of which the voluntary services were an expression. I don't think that has been entirely lost in the year 2000, but because my generation and those that come after do not have direct experience of the war, of the hardships, of the need to pull together, I wonder what will happen to the service. Will there be the same motivation – or the time – to carry on these voluntary services? I hope that maybe in some small way, people seeing me wearing this uniform on television might raise the profile of the WVS. People might realize what they do, and it might attract some new recruits. Anyway, I've worn the uniform, and when I get back home, I'm going to apply to actually join the service. I've thought about it before, but now I'm determined to do it.'

Kirstie felt that she had benefited from her WVS experience too: 'I have an admiration for the older generation which perhaps I didn't have before, because

'In this country… the war could not have been won without [women's] help,' said the Queen.

London shopgirl attacks Nazis—

1. With the shop half empty and so little to sell, my old job began to seem pointless and useless.

2. My boy is in the R.A.F.—so they arranged at the Employment Exchange for me to train for War Work.

3. Soon I was passed to a factory, for a worthwhile job helping to make big bombers—those that go to Berlin.

4. And Jim has just got his wings. Who knows? I might have worked on the plane he flies.

Is YOUR work vital to the War Effort? Go to your local office of the Ministry of Labour and National Service. They will tell you how best to serve your country.

Your duty now is

 WAR WORK

ISSUED BY THE MINISTRY OF LABOUR AND NATIONAL SERVICE

38

JOIN THE ATS

ASK FOR INFORMATION AT THE NEAREST EMPLOYMENT EXCHANGE OR AT ANY ARMY OR ATS RECRUITING CENTRE

Women, many of whom lived in a nearby hostel, assembling time fuses at a shelling factory.

now I have more understanding of what they went through. They survived then and they're survivors now, they are memories of that time for us today.' But there was to be a new challenge for Kirstie.

By the beginning of 1941 Ministry of Labour and National Service adverts had begun to appear in newspapers and magazines urging women that their 'duty now is war work'. There was a 'London shopgirl' who 'with the shop half empty and so little to sell' had begun to find her job 'pointless. My boy is in the RAF – so they arranged at the Employment Exchange for me to train for War Work. Soon I was passed to a factory for a worthwhile job helping to make big bombers – those that go to Berlin. And Jim has just got his wings. Who knows? I might have worked on the plane he flies.' But as *Housewife* pointed out, 'Some women who are free to take a war job may yet be hanging back, waiting for the official call-up to reach their age group, on the natural assumption that they will be asked for when needed. The government has not been very clear on this point so far…'

Indeed they hadn't. On the one hand there was the feeling that it would be detrimental to men's wartime morale if the jobs they'd left when they went into the forces were being taken by women – a revival of the old First World War fear of 'dilution' of the work force – and also that they weren't fighting to see the end of the domesticity that many so enjoyed in peacetime. On the other hand, it was becoming clear how great were the manpower demands of the country at war – which would also have to be met by women.

A survey in July 1941 had indicated that 2 million men and women would be required for the forces and munitions industry within the next year – and there was going to be a shortfall of some 300,000. In addition to extending the age of

call-up for men at both ends of the age range and tightening up on the schedule of reserved occupations, it was clear that despite the government's reluctance to do so, women would have to be conscripted – the first time that any country in modern times had compelled women to go into the fighting or labour force. It had not happened in Germany or Russia and Churchill was extremely reluctant, while his Minister of Labour, Ernie Bevin, still clung to his belief that sufficient volunteers would come forward without the need to introduce compulsion. They were concerned how men would feel if the women they were supposed to be fighting to protect were 'militarized'.

Conscription for women was announced on 2 December 1941 and became law two weeks later. It did not, however, as Angus Calder has pointed out, herald a force of pugilistic 'grandmothers firing machine guns'. Only unmarried women between twenty and thirty (nineteen-year-olds were included in 1943) were called up. They were given a choice of auxiliary services, the ATS, the WRNS or the WAAF. None of

these would involve active combat (though women did staff anti-aircraft batteries), but would be in the clerical or catering departments. Or they could work in industry. Part-time service in Civil Defence and the Home Guard now became compulsory, and those who had volunteered were no longer allowed to leave, unless they did so within a fortnight. By mid-1943 it was estimated that of women aged between eighteen and forty, nine out of ten single women and eight out of ten married women were in the forces or industry. Those who weren't, were looking after the nation's young children – and even among those women, thousands were doing some sort of part-time work, maybe as outworkers in their own homes. (In the aircraft industry, for example, it was deliberate policy to disperse the manufacture of parts, so that if a factory was demolished, production would not cease entirely.)

By 1943 it had become almost impossible for a woman under forty to avoid some sort of war work, unless she

Worker's playtime. Women in an armaments factory take a break.

was exempt because she was pregnant, had children under fourteen, or was deemed to have exceptionally heavy family responsibilities, including evacuees or war workers billeted on her. Under the Employment of Women Order, which came into force in 1941, women from nineteen to forty were required to register so that younger women could be forced to move from non-essential jobs to work in war industries. By mid-1943, this had been extended to women up to the age of fifty and to part-time as well as full-time work. Women were considered to be 'mobile' and therefore liable to be sent to 'districts where labour is scarce in relation to demand' – often munitions factories, which for reasons of security were in remote areas – unless they were living with their husbands, or were married to servicemen. 'Immobile' women were drafted into local jobs, often to release younger 'mobile' women.

There were complaints of course: factory work often meant living in hostels, long journeys to work with inadequate transport provided, working long monotonous hours – a twelve-hour shift was not unusual – sometimes in fairly primitive conditions. They sang:

> I'm only a wartime girl
> The machine shop makes me deaf,
> I have no prospects after the war
> And my young man is in the RAF
> K for Kitty calling P for Prue…Bomb Doors Open…
> Over to you…

Women whose only experience before the war might have been with a sewing machine were now working on precision lathes. As the Labour leader Clement Attlee declared in 1942: 'The work that women are performing in munitions factories has to be seen to be believed.' But they often earned around half of what men doing the same job were paid: in the metal industry in 1944 men took home £7 a week, women £3 10s, and a Ministry of Labour survey of 6 million workers in July 1943 revealed that on average men over twenty-one were earning £12 1s 4d a week (including overtime) to the £3 2s 11d that women over eighteen received. If women were injured at work, they received less compensation than a man (as they did if they lost a limb in an air raid); though this changed in 1943, it still linked compensation rates to wages, so women continued to be worse off.

Complaints from married women included the difficulty of shopping if you worked in a factory all day, and the shortage of food left in the shops if you could manage to get to them before they shut, and the lack of child care provision. By the end of 1943 despite a great deal of campaigning by women, there were still fewer than 1,500 day nurseries provided by local authorities.

As a mother of two children under fourteen, Kirstie could not have been compelled to work, but government exhortation, moral pressure and the attraction of wages would probably have led her to look for a war-related job. With Lyn at home to collect the children from school, she could have been expected to take a 'part-time' job of up to thirty hours a week, within a reasonable distance of home. On 3 June she received a letter from the Cabinet informing her that she would be working in an aircraft repair and maintenance factory at Biggin Hill, and a parcel arrived containing her work clothes of boots and khaki overalls. She would receive £3 a week.

'I had this image of myself working a factory in a boiler suit and a headscarf, perhaps a bit like Patricia Roc in *Millions Like Us*, which is a film we've all watched lots of times. I knew that's what women of my age would probably have been doing and it would have given me a sense of independence as well as feeling that I was doing something that would have contributed to the war effort.' The dutiful daughter played by Roc in the film had told her sceptical Home Guard father (who thought that his home comforts constituted sufficiently 'heavy domestic responsibilities' to keep his daughter at home), 'I hear that Mr Bevin needs a million women, and I don't think we should disappoint him.'

The Ministry of Labour tried to make it sound appealing. Under the heading 'War Workers Stay Womanly', it intoned, 'You'll probably be given brown or navy dungarees, with jockey cap to match. They are very becoming to most figures. I've seen mothers of families look just as attractive as young girls. Some girls wear bright hankies

Looking after the children: Ben and Thomas in Lyn's care while Kirstie works.

round their hair and scarves to match… A lot of factories are installing hot air plants for drying hands. This saves the grubby towel business and actually keeps hands well. As a matter of fact a lot of girls had the best kept hands I've seen this war.' The reality was not always so beguiling.

The work that Kirstie was doing was similar to that which ground crews would have done repairing small holes and tears in the fabric of aircraft damaged in operations. During the war Biggin Hill was an operational fighter base so no factories were located there. However, RAF ground crews (riggers and fitters) did carry out running repairs to aircraft during the Battle of Britain. Keeping fighters in service often meant that maintenance crew had to work right round the clock: they had to cope with extremely long hours often in very difficult circumstances and, at the height of the Battle of Britain, had to work outside as all the hangars had been destroyed by enemy action. Any aircraft that was deemed to be BLR (Beyond Local Repair) was sent to a maintenance unit for comprehensive repair and rebuilding.

By 1943 women made up around 40 per cent of all employees in the aircraft industry, which was the most insatiable of all the wartime industries for labour, and the one that Churchill prioritized.

The owner of the factory where Kirstie worked, Mr Cobb, explained that, 'Without women there would have been a terrible shortage of labour in the aircraft industry.' Women tended to start off working in the 'dope shop' where rolls of linen were stitched on to the trailing edge of the wing. The 'dope' was then painted on to stiffen the fabric and make it waterproof. After they got proficient at this, women went on to do every type of job from riveting to precision engineering. A Blackpool dress shop worker directed into the local Vickers Armstrong factory in 1942, had to sew 70 feet of Irish linen, after it had been treated with 'dope', at eight painful stitches to the inch. She recalled: 'Repair work was awful on our hands. Dope was a sickly smelling paint – it smelled like pear drops and was highly flammable.'

Fuel for workers: Kirstie serves supper after finishing her shift at the aircraft factory at Biggin Hill.

Mr Cobb felt that Kirstie did very well: 'For a person who had never seen a machine like this before, she soon picked it up. It was exactly the same during the war – thousands of keen but untrained women ended up doing a fantastic job.'

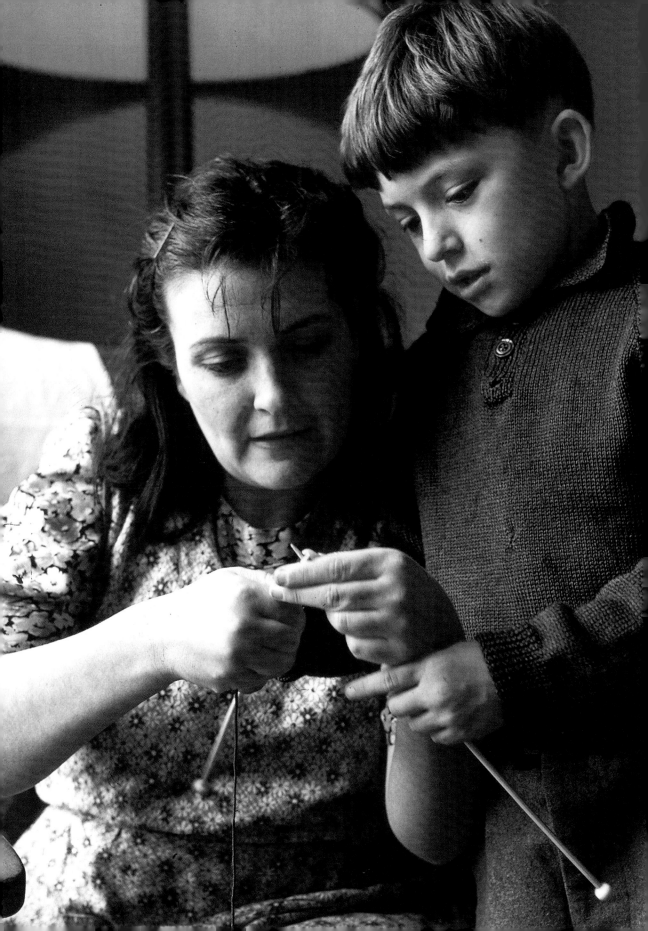

'BEAUTY AS DUTY'

'No Surrender' read the advert for Yardley cosmetics in 1942 showing a woman in uniform. 'We are proud to work with men for victory. But we must achieve masculine efficiency without hardness, without surrender to personal carelessness. With leisure and beauty-aids so scarce, it is very creditable to look our best. Let us face the future bravely and honour the subtle bond between good looks and good morale. Put your best face forward…' Yardley was a tangible example: at one end of the factory's cosmetics and toiletries production line, women were assembling small parts for machinery, while at the other they were putting cream into pots and face powder into boxes – though this represented only a quarter of their pre-war output.

The link between 'beauty and duty' was a potent weapon in the battle for morale. It was part of the encouragement to women to look (and be) 'gay' as their contribution to the war effort, with coiffeured hair, 'pretty' dresses and a generally fragrant presence around the place. An article in the November 1939 issue of *Woman's Magazine* pointed out that 'Anxiety is a dreadful ravager of loveliness, and no man wants to come home to a wife or sweetheart who shows in her face how much she has worried about him.' 'Looking lovely for his leave' was yet another responsibility laid on to the wartime wife: articles pointed out that 'the wise woman realizes what a tonic she can be to men on active service – and so she looks her best'.

Equally, the promotion of facial artistry worked to counteract the androgynous nature of the war effort when an increasing number of women – and particularly

'Make-do and Mend'. Wartime housewives were asked to use their ingenuity in a time when clothing was rationed.

185

young women – were in uniform or wearing overalls or dungarees, their hair stuffed under caps or tied back in snoods or hairnets to keep it from tangling in the machinery they were operating. It might be practical, but it wasn't necessarily very alluring, and it meant that the only individuality allowed was in make-up and hairstyles. Before the war, it had been considered rather 'fast' to plaster your face with make-up, but the drabness of wartime changed that. According to a wartime social survey, two-thirds of all women used cosmetics, and over 90 per cent of women under thirty did so. Magazines tried to be helpful as usual: 'If you have to stay in khaki, don't despair – there is a new lovely make-up for you especially created for this rather trying colour. Its name is "Burnt Sugar". It is a warm, glowing shade that goes beautifully.'

But finding your 'red badge of courage' (as Lyn called her lipstick, adopting wartime magazine terminology), your face powder, rouge or lavender water was not easy. Although the Board of Trade recognized that cosmetics were an important part of women's wartime armoury, as 'luxury' items their manufacture was subject to a labyrinth of quota controls and regulations designed to concentrate productive capacity on war matériel manufacture. The chemicals and labour required to produce make-up were needed in munitions manufacture and consequently were in short supply. A black market trade in cosmetics flourished, and enterprising chemists experimented with home-made substitutes – as did women who also eked out their pre-war cosmetics as best they could. Lipstick ends were crumbled into an egg cup that stood in a bowl of hot water or a double boiler to melt them together; cold cream or almond oil was mixed into the stub of a favourite lipstick to produce matching rouge; eyelashes were brushed with castor oil, burnt cork or shoe polish or even soot when no mascara was available; used tea leaves in muslin bags were used as a face mask; while a 'teaspoonful of unperfumed eau-

No surrender . . .

We are proud to work with men for victory. But we must achieve masculine efficiency without hardness; without surrender to personal carelessness. With leisure and beauty-aids so scarce, it is very creditable to look our best. Let us face the future bravely and honour the subtle bond between good looks and good morale.

PUT YOUR BEST FACE FORWARD.. *Yardley*

'England Expects'. Lyn at her nightly beauty routine.

de-Cologne, poured into an almost empty perfume bottle, will give you that much extra perfume'. (After the fall of France scent was an almost undreamed of luxury – no more 'Evening in Paris' or 'Ashes of Roses'.)

Girls in aircraft factories sometimes used the 'dope' from the paint shop as clear nail varnish, while a drop of witch hazel was added to cold water as an astringent. Powdered camphor blended with cold cream 'will make a whitening hand cream' and desperate women would smooth the greaseproof paper that had wrapped the margarine over their faces – if they hadn't already used every smidgen for cooking.

In the 1940s house Lyn found that 'this beauty for duty routine takes up an awful lot of time. Every night there is an hour in front of the dressing-table mirror smoothing in whatever creams were available. Then I pat my skin vigorously because it was recommended that women of a certain age should do that to keep their skin firm. I've been given what looks like a hammock for a mouse, which I'm supposed to use as a chinstrap to keep my jaw line firm. Then Kirstie and I do each other's hair. We pin it up and I put curlers in and then I cover mine with a hairnet, and by this time I am beginning to look *really* glamorous. I feel twenty years older. I wouldn't expect anybody to fancy me in a million years. Perhaps it's just as well that we've got twin beds. Celibacy is the order of the day here because I don't feel like a woman and Michael doesn't fancy his granny.'

Nevertheless Lyn was assiduous in putting on powder and lipstick every time she went out, even to do the shopping, 'to frighten Mr Lovegrove', though 'it's not what I'm used to, it's second nature now'. Though she doesn't usually wear make-up at home unless she's on a night out, Kirstie wore a 1940s lipstick most days, and she too 'tried to do this beauty thing as a woman would have done it in the 1940s. I could quite easily get up tomorrow and leave my hair straight and not put any make-up on, but that isn't what they would have done, so I think that I should make the effort and put pins in my hair and sleep in a hairnet.'

Soap and their hair were the women's two preoccupations in this context. When austerity was at its wartime harshest in February 1942, soap was rationed in the same month that the domestic petrol allowance was abolished (though it was still possible to get petrol if you needed your car for work or official purposes). 'The oils and fats used in soap occupy so much shipping space, and some of this must be saved for food,' the Ministry of Food announcement explained. People were issued with four coupons for use over a four-week period and they could use them either on soap or soap products. Four coupons entitled each person to a maximum of 4 ounces of hard soap (household soap in bars), or 3 ounces of toilet soap (a small-sized tablet), or 6 ounces of soap powder a month. So personal hygiene was in competition with household washing – though, as Lyn noticed ruefully, shaving soap was not rationed, despite often being in short supply, as was scouring powder. It made bath time, already a perfunctory affair since you were only supposed to bathe in 5 inches of water, a lick and a promise matter, and at the end of a long and tiring day both women longed for a long, soapy soak. But this was denied to them.

Kirstie made a sore place on her leg, which took some time to heal, trying to rub away her body hair with an unshaped pumice stone. There was also the delicate matter of BO, since modern-day expectations are for a daily shower or bath. But in the 1930s, with so many homes lacking an inside bathroom, bathing was often a weekly, rather than daily, ritual. Indeed, when the GIs started to arrive from America in 1942, one of the complaints they had about British girls was that they often 'smelt' and that their teeth were bad, which before the introduction of free (or heavily subsidized) dental care was hardly surprising. Deodorants were hard to come by in wartime too, but women were advised that bicarbonate of soda patted under the armpits should help.

Shampoo was also scarce and often hair had to be washed in soap if there was enough of that. Kirstie had read somewhere that if you left your hair for long enough, it would somehow begin to clean itself, but that didn't seem to be happening and both women, concerned to save the dwindling supply of shampoo for the boys, went much longer without washing their hair than they would have dreamt of doing in 2000. An article in *Housewife* took the government to task about this in 1942: 'We women have a legitimate grouse [about the shortage of shampoo] and I very much

hope that the Board of Trade will enable more shampoos to be released. A clean head lessens the risk of infection, and it is not easy to achieve a fastidiously clean head unless shampoos are more plentiful, for few of us have either the time or the money to pay regular visits to the hairdresser.'

Then there were their hairstyles. Both Lyn and Kirstie had had their hair cut and professionally styled before they moved into the 1940s house and both were anxious to maintain the look. It wasn't easy as they struggled with hair pins and bobby grips, Lyn winding Kirstie's long dark hair round her finger and setting it in a series of curls on top. 'I'm spending much more time here trying to get my hair right, because at home all I do every day is just pull a comb through it,' said Kirstie. Perfecting their hairstyles was something they could do to pass the time in the Anderson shelter during an 'air raid', and practice made them both more adroit hairdressers, particularly after Jackie Whybra, a local 1940s enthusiast, had visited them. With her dextrous fingers, Jackie showed them quick ways of recreating a 1940s style using kirby grips, curlers, rags or, best of all, a pair of curling tongs that she heated in the fire. And she advised Kirstie that if she ran out of setting lotion she could use sugar and water as 1940s women sometimes had.

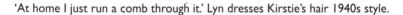

'At home I just run a comb through it.' Lyn dresses Kirstie's hair 1940s style.

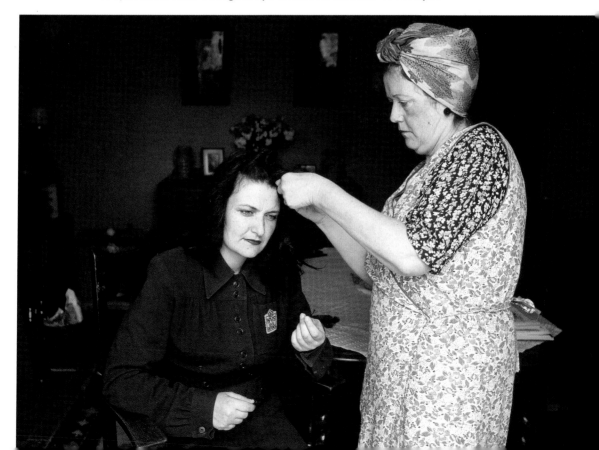

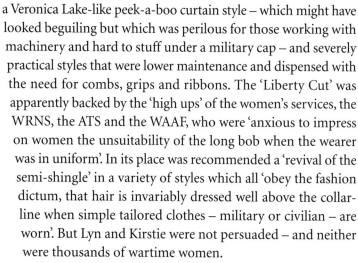

After this tuition, Lyn even felt confident enough to attempt a 'victory roll' for Kirstie, who had been a blood donor in response to an appeal earlier in the day. Taking the bandage that had been wound round her arm (wartime women would have used a roll of muslin, a stocking stuffed with cotton wool, a scarf or even a sanitary towel), Lyn painstakingly pinned Kirstie's hair around her head in a sweep of burnished halo.

In wartime, women's magazines veered between the glamorous look for hair in a Veronica Lake-like peek-a-boo curtain style – which might have looked beguiling but which was perilous for those working with machinery and hard to stuff under a military cap – and severely practical styles that were lower maintenance and dispensed with the need for combs, grips and ribbons. The 'Liberty Cut' was apparently backed by the 'high ups' of the women's services, the WRNS, the ATS and the WAAF, who were 'anxious to impress on women the unsuitability of the long bob when the wearer was in uniform'. In its place was recommended a 'revival of the semi-shingle' in a variety of styles which all 'obey the fashion dictum, that hair is invariably dressed well above the collar-line when simple tailored clothes – military or civilian – are worn'. But Lyn and Kirstie were not persuaded – and neither were thousands of wartime women.

If shampoo was in short supply, so was setting lotion, perm solution, tints and dyes. And this hit Lyn hard. She had hennaed her hair auburn for many years and, after a month or so in the house, the roots were beginning to show through. She wrote to Trevor Sorbie, who had created her 1940s hairstyle, for advice about 'my very noticeable white regrowth'. But none came. There were no suitable products on the shelves of Mr Lovegrove's shop and in desperation Lyn turned to home remedies. First she tried painting on a little dilute Camp coffee, but though that made a difference, it gave a two-tone effect that washed out the next time Lyn shampooed her hair. Beetroot juice was no more successful, nor was carrot juice. She toyed with the idea of pickled cabbage juice, then, deciding that henna was produced from privet leaves, was almost on the point of clipping her neighbour's hedge and boiling down the cull. Had she had grey hair she might have found Reckitts blue starch a useful colorant, but help for redheads was there none, until a mysterious well-wisher tracked down a small packet of black market henna. It wasn't quite the right shade, but it would do, and Lyn was prepared to face the world again.

Clothes rationing was introduced in July 1941. There had been restrictions on the manufacture of clothes prior to that as an increasing number of factories went over to war production and prices rose alarmingly. The restrictions were severe. All clothing was rationed except for industrial overalls and hats. Every civilian was issued with sixty-six coupons a year (when the restrictions were introduced the coupons weren't ready so shops accepted margarine coupons instead). This was supposed to be approximately half the amount of clothes that the average consumer would have bought in a pre-war year. A man could buy pretty much what he stood up in: a suit took twenty-six coupons, a shirt five, socks, three and shoes, seven, a tie, one. Vest and pants took eight, leaving sixteen that could be used for handkerchiefs at one coupon each, pyjamas or a dressing gown, each of which took eight. A woman's suit or outdoor coat would mean the surrender of eighteen coupons, an unlined mac was nine, a took eleven if it was made of wool, or seven if it was made out of cotton or rayon or some other fabric, blouses and jumpers were five each, shoes were five (but went up to seven), a pair of stockings two, vests and knickers three each and bras and suspender belts one apiece. Clothes for children under four years old did not need coupons until August 1941, when they were brought into the scheme. Clothes for children over that age took fewer coupons than comparable adult garments – which meant that children could have more. Pregnant women were given first fifty then sixty coupons to buy maternity clothes and then a layette.

Thomas does up the buckle of his rather worn 1940s sandal.

Generally speaking, second-hand clothes did not require coupons, but prices were fixed. Air-raid damaged stock could be sold at reduced coupon value provided it did not exceed a certain price, and the coupons required fluctuated somewhat in response to supply and seasonal demand. Wool was also on ration, but it required fewer coupons to knit socks and jumpers than to buy them. Blackout material was coupon-free, but in

September 1945, when it had not been required for four months, it was rationed in case anyone took it into their head to do something creative with it.

Special 'industrial' coupons were shared out by works committees to people in particularly dirty occupations, but it was found that this concession was being abused, the term being used to cover a surprising number of garments, and it transpired that those not engaged in industrial work were prepared to dress as if they were if it meant ration-free clothes and an opportunity to save their other garments 'for best'. Thereafter industrial clothes were distributed directly and a low number of coupons given in by the worker.

Clothes rationing, which came as a surprise, though not a particularly unwelcome one, to most people, proved tough. A survey at the end of the first year indicated that the average person had only three coupons in hand while many had run out altogether. In 1943 the coupon allowance fell from sixty-six to only forty, and in 1944 it rose slightly to forty-eight.

It was obvious that those who had a commodious wardrobe of good quality clothes on the outbreak of war fared better than the poor who had to skimp on their apparel, and there was no coupon distinction (though of course prices varied) between good quality and shoddy garments. Partly to deal with this, and with the very steep increase in clothing prices, which rose 72 per cent between September 1939 and April 1941 and a further 23 per cent the following year, and partly to further restrict (or divert) factory production, 'utility clothes' were introduced in 1942. For women's clothes, the Board of Trade asked members of the Incorporated Society of London Fashion Designers such as Norman Hartnell, Hardy Amies, Victor Stiebel, Digby Morton and Worth, to submit four specified basic garments – a top coat, a suit, afternoon dress and a cotton overall dress. These designs were pooled, and the most suitable selected by the Board. They were mass-produced to be in the shops by the following spring, bearing the 'gouda cheese with wedge cut out' CC41 label denoting their status.

The WVS ran clothing exchanges where, in times of rationing and shortages, mothers could barter the clothes their children had outgrown.

The specifications were very strict: the fabrics were dictated, the number of buttons on a jacket or coat was prescribed, as was the depth of hems and the number of pleats and tucks was severely restricted; there were to be no superfluous trimmings of velvet or fur fabric or decoration such as embroidery, appliqué or lace. For men, trouser turn-ups were banned (which some men seemed to have minded terribly), the width of the jacket lapel was specified and no double-breasted suits were allowed; the number of pockets was restricted to three for coats and jackets and two for waistcoats (which did not go down too well either). The clothes were, as *Vogue* put it, 'fighting trim' and Kirstie simply adored the smart utility suit she was provided with. 'I am not really a dress person,' she had explained when she first arrived. 'At home I just live in trousers.' She was unenthusiastic about the four floral print 1930s frocks she wore day in, day out, but the suit was something else altogether, as were the red suede wedge shoes she teamed with it.

Utility fashions: 'an outstanding example of applied democracy'.
This blue flecked tweed suit took eighteen coupons.

Two eras meet: Lyn and Kirstie dressed in their 1940s clothes shop in West Wickham High Street.

Lyn, who at home was a T-shirt and leggings wearer, took to her 1940s wardrobe like a duck to water. She confessed that she soon began to find her 2000 contemporaries 'sloppily dressed' as she went out wearing a smart dress, polished leather shoes, a hat, rayon stockings and gloves, while they hung out in sweatshirts, trainers and leggings or cargo pants. Her main trouble was shoes. Used to wearing flat shoes, Lyn found standing all day in medium-heeled leather court shoes tiring. Her slippers had shrunk in the wash after she had got them caked in mud in that first night-time dash to the shelter. Soon she had developed bunions and calluses; the soles of her shoes had worn thin, which made walking on rough ground painful. Her greatest luxury at the end of the day was to take her shoes and stockings off and soak her feet in a mustard bath.

Women's magazines were full of adverts for shoes ('walk the Barret way'), and for Philip's stick-on soles, which were supposed to prolong the life of shoes and so save their wearers money. 'Go in search of a shoemaker who takes real pride in mending shoes,' women were advised, but Lyn's neighbour Nina Tilling told her that actually getting the right size during the war had been no easy matter: 'You just took what you could get got and either screwed your toes up if they were too small, or stuffed the ends with newspaper if they were too big. I knew a nurse who took size 9 shoes. She could never get any that big, and she ended the war pretty well crippled.'

'Trim, but comfortable too': read an article in a 1942 *Housewife* about the importance of choosing the right corset – advice Lyn wearily endorsed.

Corsets were another bane of Lyn's life: dresses did not fit properly if she was not wearing a corset, but hers had not been bespoke and never seemed to fit properly, and they were hot and sticky as soon as the temperature outside rose. Soon Lyn had sore places and weals under her arms where the boning rubbed. She followed advice to wear a vest under her corset, but that didn't help much, nor did the bra she tried to fashion from two silk scarves – 'It just kept slipping off.' Mrs Miniver's armour seemed more attack than protection.

'Looking better on less is going to be our duty in 1942,' *Housewife* announced in March, 'but it can be a pleasure too.' The only way it could be achieved for duty or pleasure, however, was to fall in with the Board of Trade's scheme to 'Make-do and Mend'. Launched in 1943, the campaign was 'intended to help you get the last possible ounce of wear out of all your clothes and household things'. Its aim was 'not merely to revive the lost art of darning and patching, but to raise morale by showing how old clothes can be turned into really smart and attractive new ones'.

Working with officials at the Ministry of Education, local authorities and women's voluntary organizations, the Board of Trade instigated some 5,000 classes that met regularly to be instructed in this essential austerity art and to share best practice. Exhibitions of the most successful examples were held in village halls and

Housewives model the clothes that they have made.

department stores, advice centres were opened in works canteens, and evening classes arranged in factories. The Ministry of Information produced a booklet that was a steady best-seller with over a quarter of a million copies sold; and adverts featuring an irritatingly doll-like and bright-eyed seamstress, Mrs Sew and Sew, appeared in newspapers and magazines.

The previously untapped – or at least unpublicized – resourcefulness of British women, and their educators, was truly awe-inspiring: gloves from ribbons; slippers from felt hats (and no doubt someone somewhere did it the other way round); women's skirts from their husband's trousers (and in the case of Connie Purkiss from West Wickham, from his favourite plus-fours); buttons from string, leather, cord, knitting or work basket scraps ('now that zips have gone and snap fasteners are going'); dressing gowns from candlewick bedspreads; sandals from too small shoes with the toes cut out; a new blouse from half one worn blouse plus half another; jumpers knitted with the front that shows in contrasting stripes, the back in any wool you could lay your hands on (but do remember to keep your jacket on); hats refreshed and refurbished with muslin, net, ribbon, feathers, lace; stockings re-footed; knickers re-gusseted; sheets turned sides-to-middle; 'patriotic patches' on the knees and elbows of worn clothes; cuffs re-turned; sleeves re-set; collars replaced; underarms reinforced; brassières from 'quite small scraps of satin and other substantial material left over from worn slips and knickers using an old, well-fitting brassière as a pattern'; men's jackets transformed into small boys' or girls' coats or

jackets; men's shirts into children's pyjamas; nightdresses into petticoats; then those petticoats turned into cami-knickers; skirts from dresses; skirts into a child's play suit; woollen stockings with worn-out feet into an infant's jersey 'bound at the neck with ribbon'; women's summer skirts into children's knickers; pyjama legs into babies' vests; an old mac into a child's pixie cape and hood; a woman's winter coat into a Churchillesque 'siren suit' for a toddler.

The list was endless – and daunting, particularly for someone like Kirstie who confessed that when the children tore their clothes, or buttons came off, she put them in the ironing basket and they rarely saw the light of day again; when the boys ripped their jeans she either cut them down for shorts or 'chucked them out'. Or like Lyn, who admitted that while her sister-in-law, on a visit to the house, had fashioned a useful kettle holder out of scraps of material she had found, the extent of the enthusiasm that Lyn had absorbed from Mrs Sew and Sew had been to unpick some lace from a dress because it scratched. Since then she had been unable to wear the dress any more since its now plunging neckline made it 'unsuitably tarty for round the house'.

A practical suggestion from the *Housewife*. Kirstie learns the lost art of darning.

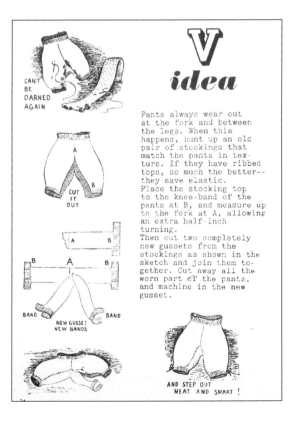

CAN'T BE DARNED AGAIN

V idea

Pants always wear out at the fork and between the legs. When this happens, hunt up an old pair of stockings that match the pants in texture. If they have ribbed tops, so much the better-- they save elastic.
Place the stocking top to the knee-band of the pants at B, and measure up to the fork at A, allowing an extra half-inch turning.
Then cut two completely new gussets from the stockings as shown in the sketch and join them together. Cut away all the worn part of the pants, and machine in the new gusset.

CUT IT OUT

BAND   NEW GUSSET   BAND
NEW BANDS

AND STEP OUT NEAT AND SMART !

CHAPTER 13

THE CHILDREN'S WAR

By 1942 even the *Beano* had been conscripted into the war effort. In the pages of the children's comic, sandwiched between the exploits of 'Lord Snooty and his pals', 'Pansy Potter, the strong man's daughter' ('In two weeks see the best of scraps – it's Pansy Potter 'gainst the Japs') and a crudely drawn Mussolini ('Musso the Wop – He's a big-a-da-flop'), was a drawing of a boy looking rather like Richmal Crompton's William poring over his stamp collection. 'His hobby is collecting little bits of coloured paper,' the caption ran. 'Make YOUR hobby collecting big bits of waste paper – the bigger the better! Every scrap you get helps to make more planes and shells and bullets. Start your new hobby right away – you'll find it's great fun – and SAVE WASTE PAPER!'

Children had been in the front line for many months prior to the declaration of war. Plans had been laid for the evacuation of mothers and children since 1934. At first, there had been debate about whether the evacuation of children should be voluntary or compulsory, but by July 1938 a report had recommended that it should always be voluntary and so it was to remain throughout the war.

A government leaflet was distributed in July 1939:

There are still a number of people who ask, 'What is the need for evacuation? Surely if war comes it would be better for families to stick together and not go breaking up their homes?' It is quite easy to understand this feeling,

An awfully big adventure: Thomas and Ben prepare to leave their Yorkshire home.

because it is difficult for us in this country to realize what war in these days might mean. If we were involved in a war, our big cities might be subjected to determined attacks from the air – at any rate in the early stages – and although our defences are strong and are rapidly growing stronger, some bombers would undoubtedly get through.

We must see to it that the enemy does not secure his chief objects – the creation of anything like panic, or the crippling dislocation of our civil life. One of the first measures we can take to prevent this is the removal of children from the more dangerous areas.

The first large-scale exodus took place on 1 September 1939 (there were to be two more during the course of the war: one at the start of the blitz in 1940, then when the flying bombs started to land in 1944). There had already been a stream of privately arranged evacuations throughout the summer of 1939, as children were sent to stay with friends and relations in the country or even abroad; and some nervous adults found themselves 'funk holes' in Wales or the West Country and sat round 'drinking, smoking and waiting for war'.

The whole country had been divided into 'evacuation', 'neutral' and 'reception' areas. It was, of course, a fallible division. The designated evacuation areas were large urban centres where heavy raids were expected but some places like Bristol, Plymouth and Swansea, which in the event were to experience intensive bombing, were not scheduled for evacuation.

As a small town on the edge of London, West Wickham was designated as a neutral area, which meant that officially it neither sent nor accepted evacuees – though many families in so-called neutral areas made their own arrangements. So in 1939 Kirstie would not have been called upon to make the agonizing decision about whether to send Ben and Thomas away. 'I felt very emotional listening to the radio about the evacuation of children. It must have been very hard as a mother to say goodbye to your children, but being told that it was the best thing for them. It's not something that I could ever have done. I would have kept them with me at all costs. I can't even begin to imagine what it must have felt like for mothers having to make that decision.'

Lyn found the appearance of Ben and Thomas in their 1940s clothes 'very emotional. It reminded me of all those photographs I've seen of little evacuees with their caps on, clutching their gas masks, and the worst bit was the labels tied on to their jackets. I find it so moving because today we have absolutely no conception of parents sending their children into the care of someone who they've never met in some strange place miles away. When those little boys, my grandsons, came into the room that first time in their 1940s clothes they encapsulated all that, and it made me cry.'

Those to be evacuated in 1939, it was decided, were schoolchildren – usually an entire school went in the charge of the teachers – children under school age accompanied by their mother 'or by some other responsible person', expectant mothers who were sent somewhere safe to have their baby, and 'adult blind persons and cripples whose removal was feasible'.

However much a mother might miss her children, she could convince herself that their safety was paramount, but that was hard when parents received pathetic cards and letters scrawled by their offspring pleading 'please tak me home' or 'I dont lik it here' or 'the man has a orrid face and shouts'. And there was the money: a householder received 10s 6d a week for the first child boarded on them, and 8s 6d for subsequent children. Although this charge was waived for the poorest families, the government later required a contribution based on a means test. This uncertainty, among other things, contributed to the gradual drift back to the towns and cities that characterized the 'phoney war', with mothers and small children in the vanguard, preferring to take the dangers of urban life to the restrictions and boredom of a rural existence.

The children's war: children arrive in the country to continue their journey to their wartime billets, part of the mass evacuation from cities that started on 1 September 1939.

On that Friday, schoolchildren, teachers, mothers with young children, pregnant women and the blind and disabled had been instructed to present themselves at assembly points for evacuation. Children met in the school playground and were marched to railway stations and packed into trains – 'destination unknown' so as not to give 'useful' information to the enemy. During those first few days of war, 827,000 schoolchildren, 103,000 teachers and helpers, 524,000 mothers with children under school-age, nearly 13,000 expectant mothers and some 7,000 either blind or in some other way disabled people – a total exodus of nearly one and a half million people – left the cities.

It was the children leaving on their own who were the most heart-wrenching. In the event, under half of all London schoolchildren left the capital in September 1939, while the figure was nearer two-thirds in Lancashire, much less in the Midlands and around a third in Scotland. Parents who were convinced that it was perilous for their offspring to remain at home tried valiantly to hold back the tears as they waved their children off. A woman who had helped with the evacuation of children from Bow in East London recalled 'most vividly' that while the 'children were wild with excitement… most mums were pale and drawn, no doubt wondering when they'd see their sons and daughters again. It was certainly the first time the mothers had been parted from their schoolchildren. Very close families were the order of the day in Bow. No one had to tell you about the value of family life in the East End then because, quite frankly, we didn't know anything else.'

The official historian of the civilian aspect of the Second World War, the sociologist Richard Titmuss, wrote: 'Many reports testify to the general confusion and unpreparedness which characterised the reception of the mothers and children in September 1939.' Trouble was caused by a number of factors, including train delays, lack of pre-knowledge about the evacuees, and the ban on spending – local authorities had been asking for months to be allowed to spend money on providing hostels, maternity homes and so on. Such expenditure was refused until six days before the outbreak of war, even though the government had predicted that 4 million people – including a large number of children and pregnant women – would need to be evacuated. As Titmuss described, these troubles were 'piled higher when many of the parties travelling in crowded trains, sometimes without lavatories and adequate water supplies, arrived in a dirty and unco-operative state. It was not a good start. Town and country met each other in critical mood.'

It had been decided that the only solution to providing accommodation for the estimated 4 million evacuees was to billet them in private homes. It was clearly undesirable to house children in huge hostels, and anyway by January 1939 it was obvious that there would be no time to erect the network of rural camps such a policy required. But it was recognized by the government that this 'invasion of family life on

such a scale was unprecedented, and that such a policy would have to fight in every village and town of the country a centuries-old dislike of billeting in private homes' – indeed one MP complained that for his constituents 'compulsory billeting would be far worse than the war'. Eventually a limited number of camps was built, mainly for children who were physically handicapped or in some other way hard to place, but 90 per cent of evacuated mothers and children were billeted in private homes.

The billeting officers faced a daunting task. In cities and towns local authority officials took on the task, but in rural areas the officers were usually volunteers and of course these varied hugely in organizational ability and the gift of persuasion – though while evacuation was voluntary, billeting was a statutory duty on householders who were deemed to have the room and had no valid reason for refusing. Some areas had done a splendid job in planning for their evacuees: they'd had plenty of rehearsals, had organized to meet the mothers and children at the railway station or bus stop and take them to a dispersal centre, and everyone knew exactly what they were supposed to be doing. But it was not the same everywhere and many arrangements were much more haphazard. The situation was not helped by the speed with which evacuees had been shovelled out of the cities into the countryside: school parties being broken up and pupils dispersed, groups had arrived in the wrong place or got lost – and most reception areas did not get what they were expecting.

In a Norfolk village, 'evacuated mothers and children arrive… from Shoreditch and Hoxton. Wrong trainload arrive – only children expected. Organizers have great difficulty in getting people to take them in. Three families taken to a country mansion buried in trees. Two families refuse to get out of car because of weird atmosphere of place.'

It was not much different in Margery Allingham's Essex village where the evacuee reception committee had waited most of the day for the ninety children they were expecting. She was 'frankly fascinated by the evacuation scheme, and had been from the beginning because it seemed to me to be the most revolutionary of all the government's measures, not excluding conscription'. Finally, 'eight big red double-decker buses, the kind that carries thirty-two passengers on each floor, and as far as we could see they were crowded. They pulled up in a long line all down the road… it was a difficult moment. We locals were all doing arithmetic. Twice thirty-two is sixty-four; eight times sixty-four is five hundred and twelve: and the entire population of Auburn is under six hundred and fifty. We hoped, we trusted, there had been some mistake. It was at this point that [we] made the second discovery. They weren't children. They were strange London-dressed ladies, all very tired and irritable, with babies in their arms. When the committee rang to find out if there had been a mistake, the authorities sounded a bit rattled also, and we gathered our difficulties were as nothing beside the trouble of others, and that we'd kindly get

An apprehensive Thomas with Kirstie. As a neutral area West Wickham was not part of the official evacuation scheme.

on with what God and the German Chancellor had seen fit to send us. So we said, "All right," and went back. It was the beginning of the war for us.'

The wartime guests of country towns and villages were further aggrieved when, in many areas, they were walked or paraded around while householders took their pick. 'Scenes reminiscent of a cross between an early Roman slave market and Selfridges bargain basement ensued.' One boy likened it to 'a cattle show', for farmers picked 'strong-looking lads', and the presentable, nicely dressed children were quickly chosen. The method of billeting seems generally to have been either direct selection by householders or haphazard allotment.

The hardest to place were mothers with young children, and there were poignant stories about the wrench it had often been for them to decide on evacuation. A north London woman 'washed and cleaned everything in sight' in those last days of August 1939 and, as her daughter later recalled, took her three children 'on more visits than usual to see our grandparents. On the morning of 1 September we rose early and got dressed in several layers of clothes including our winter coats, even though there was no sign that the good weather was about to break. We left the house laden with rucksacks and gas masks… As we walked down the steps of our house in De Beauvoir Square, my mother said, "Goodbye, home." On 20 October 1940 the house was bombed.'

There were many successful evacuation experiences, with children loving the freedom of the countryside and staying happily with their host families for the duration of the war and keeping in touch for years afterwards. But there were horror stories too, of cruelty and abuse, neglect and humiliation. And in between there were innumerable accounts of misunderstandings, culture mismatches, low-level unhappiness, homesickness and sheer boredom. City kids often found the countryside dull – 'everyone curls up at seven o'clock' – and country people slow and lacking the joshing warmth they were used to at home. The playwright Bernard

Kops, who was evacuated with his sister, never saw his host put his arm round his wife or pinch her cheeks so doubted if they were really married. And if this was true for children, particularly teenagers, it was so in spades for evacuated mothers and pregnant women who had nothing to do all day and were often made unwelcome in the billetor's house, or treated as an auxiliary housemaid. To get away, all they could do was to push the pram or pushchair disconsolately round the village green for hours or scandalize their rural hosts by spending opening hours in the pub.

There were complaints about dirt, bad language – and even fights – and there were plenty of reasons for domestic friction with such evacuees paying 5s a week for board but being expected to purchase their own food – and cook in the householder's kitchen. A Norfolk garage owner's daughter recalled that in her village 'three women said they were starving themselves in order to pay their fare home. Many evacuees returned to London because on the night of Sept. 3rd and on the morning of the 6th there was an air raid warning. They said they thought they had been sent to safety areas but they decided they were no safer on the east coast than in London especially as they have air raid shelters in their gardens and in the parks. There are none here... They grumbled at the inconveniences of travel, now only one bus each way every two hours and three trains a day... Some said there was no cinema and one wanted to know where she could get her hair permed... They found the country very quiet and lacked amusement. One woman said, "I'd rather be bombed on me own door step than stay here and die of depression."'

Evacuees in the country in 1940. 'They have spring every year down here.'

For their part, those in the reception areas were often horrified at the condition and behaviour of the evacuees they were being asked to take into their homes. In the absence of the expected news of raids and battles, the papers were full of stories of filthy and verminous children, bedwetters, vandals, hooligans and petty thieves. Host families were appalled to find some children were not house trained and defecated on the floor and in beds, had clearly not seen a bar of soap for months and were literally sewn into brown paper for the winter. Some were reported to sleep under rather than in the bed (beds being for laying out corpses on). Many had never worn night clothes, were not used to sitting down for a meal but ate bread and dripping or jam on the run and hungered for chips and cake and pop rather than nutritious green vegetables, home-grown apples and fresh milk. They swore like small troopers and came piteously ill equipped for life in the country – Liverpool was known as 'plimsoll city' on account of the flimsy footwear of its evacuees, and the 'rags' that some children arrived in had to be burned.

These criticisms revealed the gap between the two nations that comprised 1930s Britain. The evacuees came from heavily populated, industrial inner cities often with appalling slum housing. Wages were low and unemployment high, and there was simply no money to dress or equip children to a standard that was remotely acceptable to the those who took the children into their homes – who were often middle class, since it was they who were more likely to luxuriate in 'surplus accommodation'. Though the incidents of extreme deprivation, the extent of anti-social behaviour – and of the dreaded head lice and nit infestation – were exaggerated, the government was provoked into action, providing clothing grants for the most 'necessitous cases, mackintosh sheets for persistent bedwetters' and setting up an official inquiry into the prevalence of 'head infestation'.

As the Boer War had shocked the public by the revelation of the sickliness and puny physical standards of many of the recruits, in the Second World War evacuation was a salutary and for some a politicizing experience, as evacuees and their hosts each came to realize what divisions lay deep in a nation that must be united if it were to win the war. It was an awareness that would influence many when they started to think about what they wanted from a post-war world.

The government's imperative had been 'to get the children away' from danger. Evacuation was 'a military expedient, a counter move to the enemy's objective of attacking and demoralizing the civilian population'. It was not, as Titmuss says, 'a scheme planned to operate in peacetime conditions' and speed was regarded as of the essence. Had the expected bombs rained down on the cities of Britain as the trains pulled out from city stations, as had been feared, the administrative problem that evacuation presented would have seemed trivial indeed in comparison. If it is possible to draw up a balance sheet in such matters that involve separation, loss and

psychological trauma, in the credit column must be entered the fact that the figures for London show that twenty-seven evacuated children were killed in the course of the war, while it was estimated that the expedient saved the lives of some 4,500 children.

Children from West Wickham took part in the Overseas Evacuation Scheme under which free passages were offered to Canada and the USA, and others made private arrangements. The first contingent under the government scheme arrived in Canada in August 1939, but some West Wickham children en route for Canada were on a ship that was torpedoed, and it was several agonizing days before parents learned that all were safe. But for those children who were not evacuated, the outbreak of war was a time of disruption, and a certain amount of joyous freedom. 'I've talked to a number of people round here who were Ben and Thomas's age, or perhaps a little older, during the war,' said Michael, 'and they all seemed to have had a whale of a time. Obviously there were hardships and bravery and probably family sadness, but it seems to have been very interesting for them, never a dull moment, a real adventure. Plus the fact that in those days children seemed to have had more freedom. They might be out playing in the fields all day and not come in until it got dark. It's not like that any more, I'm afraid. You can't let your children just wander off like that these days. Which is a shame for them.'

'A is for air raid.' A south-east London teacher and her class in their gas masks.

War had broken out as the autumn term was about to start; schools were closed and did not reopen until they had shelters built to accommodate all their pupils if necessary. One of the first schools to reopen was St David's College, where Ben and Thomas were pupils during their 'wartime' in West Wickham. It had a large shelter in the grounds, which was deemed safe – though it frequently filled up with water. A number of the school's pupils had been removed to the country by anxious parents and the school roll had fallen sharply, but soon the numbers were up again by the expedient of accepting students who, for whatever reason, wished to continue their education – and this meant that St David's soon had a full roll call of pupils aged between three and thirty-three.

THE
SCIENTIFIC
HEIGHT
FINDER

SILHOUETTES IN THE SKY

WELL-KNOWN AIRCRAFT
QUICKLY IDENTIFIED
INCLUDING

Scientific Height Finder

Most of the local authority schools remained closed, but a home tuition scheme was introduced, in which children met for lessons in English, arithmetic and current events in private houses. It was not until the spring of 1940 that a number of children were back at school full time. But within weeks their schooling was further disrupted by intermittent dashes to the shelters during air-raid alerts, and often long dreary hours spent confined underground while air battles raged overhead. Joyce Walker, who has written the history of West Wickham during the war, tells of local primary schoolchildren who had practised air-raid drill as a sort of game, being encouraged to see who could get under the desks fastest when the siren sounded. They would file into the shelter carrying their coats, gas masks and a small box containing emergency Horlicks tablets, ear plugs and chewing gum, which they were instructed to place between their teeth during a raid to stop them from them biting their tongues. At first it was pitch black in the shelter, but as the war progressed rudimentary lighting was installed, and the children sat on benches leaning against the shelter walls, often with their feet in a puddle of water, and continued with their education.

Though this routine must have been wearisome and often anxiety-inducing to teachers, the war had its moments of excitement for children. A bomb crater could make a perfect camp to play in, as well as be a source of wonder when layers of fossils were revealed and carefully excavated. Many children – boys in particular – became expert aircraft spotters and could confidently and accurately identify the fighters – Messerschmitt 109s and Focke-Wulf 190s that screamed overhead – and the bombers – Heinkel IIIs, Junkers 88s, Dornier 17s – that droned threateningly through the sky. Real enthusiasts kept notebooks recording the numbers and types they had seen, and could confound any grown-up who was prepared to listen with their compendious technical knowledge of aircraft construction and capacity. A 6d Penguin book of aircraft silhouettes was one of the war's outstanding best-sellers.

Then there were the booty hunters who would scour the countryside looking for wartime 'souvenirs': torn lengths of parachute, twisted hunks of metal from aircraft, fragments of shrapnel or even nose cones from exploded bombs. The tinfoil flak dropped by German aircraft in an attempt to confuse the British radar detection was soon discarded as being far too easily found to have any collectable value. It was not, of course, a pastime to be recommended: Peter Tilling recalls that one day at school a policeman came into the classroom to warn the boys about the dangers of such scavenging. 'Have any of you got any shrapnel?' he asked severely at the end of his homily. Every single desk lid shot up as the boys fished out their treasures. But this wartime hobby could have tragic consequences: in March 1942 six West Wickham boys picked up a number of unexploded smoke bombs and 2-inch trench mortar bombs from a local army training ground. As they gathered round to examine their haul one of the mortar bombs exploded, killing three boys outright while a fourth died of his injuries on the way to hospital.

Aircraft spotters: Thomas and Ben at Biggin Hill.

1940s HOUSE

The Hymers family's decision to sign up for the wartime experience had involved ten-year-old Ben and seven-year-old Thomas from the beginning: they had been in on the exhaustive discussions, and the boys had been as enthusiastic as the adults. As Lyn had emphasized, 'There was no way that we would have done this if everyone had not been 100 per cent behind it all the way.' But how would the children – who could have only a hazy idea of the Second World War coloured by Grampy's stories, books and games – fare? It meant going to a new school in a very different part of the country, leaving all their friends behind as well as their aunt and uncle to whom they were very attached. It meant turning their back for a significant length of time on their whole 2000 way of life with its computer games, television, sports and trips, and embracing a world more than half a century back in time where the certainties they had grown accustomed to were challenged and disrupted.

'The children are quite remarkable. They captured the spirit of the 1940s house from day one, and they never really lost it,' Lyn said. 'Of course there were some problems, but that's absolutely how it was.'

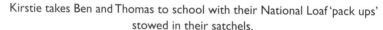

Kirstie takes Ben and Thomas to school with their National Loaf 'pack ups' stowed in their satchels.

'Seeing the house for the first time was quite amazing,' recalled Ben. 'We saw this big house with the green gate and door and window panes and stuff and it turned out to be a really nice house, with two rooms downstairs with a radio, and we went upstairs and there was a bedroom for me and Thomas to share, and we found all these toys in a chest in our room and there was a football for me, a real proper leather one. There's a garden we can play in. I imagined it would be a really small garden, but it's not, it's quite big. It's got a vegetable patch and a lawn and flowers and stuff. It's brilliant. I just love the house completely.'

The clothes they had to wear did not seem to bother the boys at all. They segued from jeans, trainers and sweatshirts into knee-length corduroy shorts, flannel shirts, ties, blazers and caps without resistance, and indeed it is some comment perhaps on educational values that the uniform of the prep school they attended in West Wickham had not changed significantly in that half century. Apart from the material their shirts were made from and the length of their shorts, Ben and Thomas did not stand out from their fellow pupils.

When it came to food the boys welcomed home cooking rather than the 'stuff from the microwave' they usually had at home. Ben thought the rissoles Lyn cooked that first night were 'gorgeous, all crisp like veggie burgers on the outside and mince on the inside'. And they were generous about the pink rabbit-mould blancmange that their mother attempted, even if it didn't quite work the first time. Ben thought that the food they were eating was 'a lot healthier than 2000 food. It hasn't got all that added sugar, but there is more fat, I think.' Both boys recognized that the cooking took a lot of time and appreciated the cakes and puddings Kirstie cooked – they begged her to keep on making them when they got home.

'I think my granny's coping very well too,' Ben opined, 'because actually she's got a lot on. She always cooks a big meal for us all every night and that must be difficult because she's having to think about air raids and things as I know 1940s housewives had to do. But I am proud of her. And I'm very proud of my mum too. She's doing very well. She helps my granny a lot and she's learned to bake and she's never done that before. She's a good cook now and I really enjoy the things she makes like tarts and scones and a treacle sponge she made. That was a really nice pudding. She and my granny are working very, very hard. They never get a chance to sit down until half-past nine or ten o'clock at night and I worry about that.'

At first the boys complained that they were always hungry, and that worried Kirstie and Lyn. As Lyn said, 'Growing boys are hungry all the time but I can't bear it because for the last ten years I have been able to give Ben everything he wants, and it's very hard as a grandmother to deny a child food, but we just haven't got it.'

But Kirstie thought it wasn't so much hunger as habit. 'They get a good breakfast, we see to that, we give them our milk ration if necessary to have on porridge, and

then they take pack-ups to school and always have a good meal in the evening and I make a pudding to fill them up. So when they come in and say they are hungry, I think that it's because they are used to snacking at home. They have crisps or biscuits or raid the fridge, but here they just get a glass of milk and a jam tart when they get in from school and wait for their evening meal. I don't mind if I don't have things to nibble on during the day, but the kids burn up so much energy, and it's hard to see them getting upset and saying they're hungry. But I'm sure they'll soon adjust to the new food routine.' Which they did.

Lunches were more of problem: the boys' 'pack-ups' for their school lunch consisted of rations of dry National Loaf sandwiches of corned beef, or perhaps a little cheese, while other children had lunch boxes crammed with modern-day delicacies – yoghurt, crisps, soft bread or crispbread sandwiches with a variety of succulent fillings, plus a range of fruit. 'Ben really hates the National Loaf. Thomas is eating it quite happily, but Ben won't. He complains that it's so dry and coarse. It's OK to dip in soup, but I agree for sandwiches it's a bit grim. I put lettuce in to try to make it more moist and there is no reason why he shouldn't eat it, it's good nutritious food and I'm afraid he'll have to get used to it.'

'Yes, it's mashed potato again.' Lyn serves Ben his supper.

'At school there is a tuck shop just round the corner from my classroom,' Ben explained, 'and every time I come down the stairs I see it. And at break most of the other kids get crisps and chocolate bars and that's quite hard when I see them stuffing their faces with things that I'd really like to have. I don't go into the tuck shop because I don't have any money [the Hymers did not have modern-day money. Their accounts were kept in accordance with a 1940s budget] and anyway that would be cheating because I wouldn't have had that stuff in the war.' But Ben admitted that he did allow himself little leeway in the authenticity stakes: 'At lunchtime I go and sit with my friends and I open my tuck box and think, "Oh not this again" – all I get is a flapjack or a jam tart, an apple and some horrible

Test-driving the go-cart the boys made with the help of their grandfather.

sandwiches so some of the boys give me a couple of their sandwiches after I've eaten mine.' And Kirstie was chagrined to hear from other mothers that their sons were requesting extra sandwiches each day 'for Ben and Thomas'.

But it was apparent how well the boys were doing when Ben invited a schoolfriend home for tea, 'which wasn't very successful', Lyn recalled. 'He wouldn't eat the wartime sausages I'd prepared, or the lumpy potatoes mashed without milk or butter, so he had to go hungry. We had no alternative. We're lucky that our children will eat most things that we put in front of them here.'

Lyn described Thomas as 'the perfect 1940s child. He's running around outside all day. He gets filthy dirty and rubs his runny nose on his sleeve. He's having a great time.'

But Kirstie was a little concerned. 'Thomas's pattern of play has changed. All he does now is grab a piece of wood and pretend it's a gun and stand on top of the Anderson shelter "shooting at the Germans". That's not something that I want to encourage. At home the boys are not allowed guns, they can't have computer games with anything to do with fighting on, but of course here it's different. Ben and Thomas helped their grandfather to build the Anderson shelter and they knew why we were doing that. And when the siren goes we all have to hurry down into the shelter and the sound of the bombs is relayed to us in there. And they've been to see the Spitfires at Biggin Hill and both boys sat in one and Thomas had the helmet

and the goggles on and everything. The boys obviously know that Spitfires were in battle against German planes all the time, shooting them down and getting shot down themselves. That's what they were built for, after all.

'And one night we went to a beetle drive in the village hall and everyone was talking about the war, and a man showed some home movies of the war here in West Wickham. Thomas was quite anxious when we got home. He didn't want to go to bed in case the Nazis came and he didn't want to go into the shelter. We had to explain that there wouldn't really be any bombs and that he'd be quite safe and Michael gave him a torch and Ben took him down to the shelter and they jumped around and he calmed down after that. But they are in effect living a wartime experience and hearing news about the war every day, so it's bound to affect their behaviour at times. We must take care and never be complacent about how the children are coping.'

The celluloid war: home movies of wartime West Wickham shown at the beetle drive in the church hall in Braemar Gardens.

Ben had particularly enjoyed helping his grandfather to fulfill his dream of constructing an Anderson shelter, and neither boy ever demurred at going in when the siren sounded – even if they had been fast asleep in their beds or if the alert went just as Lyn was cooking supper, as it often did, so they were very hungry as they sat waiting for the 'All Clear'. Indeed, Ben was rather proud when he woke up one morning and realized that he had slept all night in the shelter. 'I like the shelter. It's very homely inside.'

'Shelter time' was time spent with his family, which is one of the things that Ben had really been looking forward to and which had been somewhat confounded by the amount of work Lyn and Kirstie had to do. 'I would be quite happy if there was an air raid every single night, so I'd get more time with my family,' he said. Lyn, Michael and Kirstie would read to the boys and they'd all play games. Michael had brought with him a *Brighter Blackout* book that he had picked up in a second-hand bookshop, and the family played 'blackout bee', testing each other with quiz questions (which were called 'intelligence tests' but were nothing of the sort since they depended purely on circumstantial knowledge). Ben proved surprisingly good at knowing (or guessing) when Coronation year was (1937); when petrol rationing began (December 1939); how to begin a letter to a royal princess (Madam); what the highest building in the world is (in 1939 it was the Empire State Building); whom Goering had married (an actress); and 'who a famous novelist playwright in a high position at the War Office is' (Ian Hay). They tried to complete crossword puzzles and to provide the final line of a limerick that started:

> A young man whose weakness was liquor
> Said, 'I don't like old Hitler's swastika.'
> Then picked up a bomb
> And with great aplomb…

They sang songs such as 'My Bonnie Lies Over the Ocean', 'Polly-Wolly-Doodle', 'One Man Went to Mow' and 'Widdecombe Fair' – or could have done.

Children were encouraged to make a contribution to the war effort beyond their personal bravery and fortitude. As *The Times* pointed out in 1941, 'There are not many things that small boys can do' – but salvage collection was one. One encouraging jingle ran:

> The war is driving Hitler back
> And here's one way to win it.
> Just give your salvage man the sack
> And see there's plenty in it

The Ministry of Supply organized a campaign to ensure that all waste paper, bones, string, rubber and cardboard was put to good use – or recycled as we would say today. *Housewife* ran a competition to find out what made their readers 'salvage conscious'. This was suggested by a woman who had never thought of saving water until her son, who was serving with the army in Libya, wrote to tell her that he had just one pint a day to drink, bathe and wash his clothes in. Women were urged to sort their salvage into separate containers for string, wire, glass, razor blades, rags and paper, and articles were published giving impressive end products for all this diligence: 'One envelope makes 50 cartridge wads; 60 large cigarette cartons makes one outer shell container; one 9-inch enamelled saucepan makes a bayonet; a broken fork plus an enamelled pail makes a tommy gun; and a mixture of leaky garden hoses, old hot water bottles, rubber teapot spouts, bathing caps and golf balls would yield barrage balloons and airmen's dinghies'.

Local authorities had a legal obligation to collect salvage, and certainly in places the size of West Wickham there was every incentive to do so, since the sale of salvage material kept down the rates. Bins marked 'paper', 'rags' and 'glass' appeared on street corners, and the equivalent of salvage 'monitors' were appointed (or self-appointed) to be responsible for assembling their street's waste for the salvage collector. There were 'salvage drives' to parallel savings drives; the Boy Scouts lent a hand, and in March 1940 between 7 and 8 tons of paper had been collected in the Beckenham area (including old sheet music, cheque-book stubs, bus tickets, labels, old card games and jigsaws). A 'Cog Scheme' was started, by which children were recruited through their schools as salvage collectors. There were competitions; the 'cogs' had their own song – 'There'll Always Be a Dustbin' – an official badge and,

in some areas, great success in doubling the salvage haul. Lyn and Kirstie did their bit for a modern-day salvage operation when, dressed in their WVS uniform and riding three-wheeled tricycles pulling a small trailer, they distributed and then collected bags for the cerebral palsy charity Scope, which householders filled with discarded clothes.

But Ben took on another wartime responsibility. One morning a letter arrived at 17 Braemar Gardens addressed to him. He tore it open and read:

> I am writing to you about the Fuel Saving Scheme which was launched in 1942 and continued until the end of the war. It was part of every family's wartime effort to which you can make a special contribution. The government needs to control supplies of fuel to local coal merchants, but rather than rationing this like food is rationed, it is appealing to families to use as little as possible. It is suggested that every family should set itself a target according to its size. (That's not a target to aim for, of course, but the absolute maximum amount of fuel that they must use.) You could be the fuel warden and make it your job to ensure that everyone in the house sticks to this target. You will need to listen to radio broadcasts and read adverts in the newspaper to learn how to read the electricity and gas meters and put up cards showing how much your family is using.
>
> Something else that was widely done was to paint a plimsoll line round the bath tub so that no one had a bath with more than five inches of water so as to save fuel [and a small tin of pint and a brush was enclosed so Ben could do just that].
>
> Best of luck for your role in what was called the 'Battle for Fuel'.

The letter was signed 'Norman Longmate'. Ben was thrilled both by the letter 'from a famous writer' who wrote lots about the home front, and also by his new responsibilities – which he took very seriously. He mastered the tricky task of setting and monitoring fuel targets by learning to read the meters. 'We're in a 1940s house and we have to do 1940s things now, and that's what they would have done. The reason why I am doing this fuel monitoring business is because fuel was needed for ships for transporting war matériel and troops to places where the army needed to fight, and the factories needed it too. And if we used up all the coal in people's homes, then they wouldn't be able to fight a war and Britain would soon have been under Hitler's rule.

'I've got a badge and I read the meters every morning. I have a gas meter page and an electricity meter page and I write down the totals and then I read it again at teatime and subtract the previous total and that tells me exactly how much fuel this family has used in a day. I've set the fuel target at 50 units a week, which is Wednesday

1940s
HOUSE

to Wednesday, and last week we did well because we only used 48 units. I was quite pleased with that, but this week might not be so good as we've used 14 units already and it's only day one. If we miss it, it means we have that amount less units for the next week.' (In the event, the week's total came in 'well under the weekly target by 13 units' and the fuel warden pronounced himself 'pretty happy with them this week'.)

Ben also monitored solid-fuel consumption: 'He has decided that we are only allowed to use three shovelfuls of coal a day,' explained Kirstie. 'I think that's a bit on the mean side, but we do stick to it, at least my mum and I do, but my dad comes back and looks in the coal bunker and sees that there's plenty in there, he starts piling it on the fire. I shall have to get Ben to have a word with my dad about it.' Which Ben did when he saw Michael putting 'five shovels on when he knows it's only supposed to be three. He said it was for two nights but I don't believe him. He's got to take it more seriously. It's no point being a fuel warden if no one takes any notice of you.'

'He's very stringent,' Kirstie agreed. 'He's forever going into rooms to check that the lights have been switched off and we often have to eat in the gloom because he says we can see all right and can't have the lights on yet. And he keeps a very close eye on our bathtime routine. Ben and Thomas have to share the same bath water and we adults can only have a bath alternate nights, and even then Ben knocks on the door to make sure that you are only sitting in 5 inches of water. And if you have exceeded that, which apparently Mum did the other night, it means that he is allowed to have the culprit's pudding. I have to say it's really quite a relief when he goes to bed.'

Ben's austerity measures: notices on light switches, a water line painted round the bath tub and only three shovelfuls of coal allowed each day.

CHAPTER 14

THE BEGINNING OF THE END

'Never have holidays been more faithfully earned than this year,' read a leaflet that the Hymers family received from the 'War Cabinet' at the end of May, 'but it's more than likely that the majority of people, both in uniform and out, will only be able to have a short period of leave. In addition transport services are giving priority to moving troops, war matériel, munitions and foodstuffs. Over 90,000 railway men have been called up, and every powerful locomotive is now an engine of war.' And, it could have added, fuel was at a premium and petrol for non-essential domestic use unobtainable. It was another way of posing the official query 'Is your journey really necessary?' and from the summer of 1941 the government urged every patriotic citizen to 'take your holiday at home'.

'Thousands of Londoners are finding that holidays at home can be enjoyable and interesting' proclaimed a London Transport poster and, up and down the country, enterprising councils were laying on programmes of events for holidays at home. In July 1942 Orpington Council, not far from West Wickham, produced a leaflet laying out a tempting range of activities for its citizens who were prepared to take their pleasures locally that summer, and another was promised for August. There were bowls 'from 2 p.m. to 6 p.m. and then again from 6 p.m. to blackout', lawn tennis, swimming, cricket, 'rambles' to nearby beauty spots (one went to Wickham Court), a 'comedy in three acts, *Doctor Knock*', several displays of physical training, dances in the open air on recreation grounds and in the village hall, several concert parties; the 'Fire Force Follies' put on a couple of evenings' entertainment,

'Holidays at home': Thomas sets out on
his bike.

there was a military band concert given by the Scots Guards, a dog show and a gramophone recital, while a number of householders had 'kindly thrown their gardens open to the public.' Appropriately these seemed to promise inspiration in the 'Dig for Victory' campaign, with examples of vegetable gardens appearing to outclass the 'displays of standard roses,' 'pretty fishponds' and 'charming rockeries'.

And on 23 July 1942 ENSA was scheduled to give a concert in the village hall in Orpington. Actually that might have been a mixed blessing. ENSA (Entertainments National Service Association) had been set up just before the outbreak of war at the urging of Basil Dean, a distinguished theatrical producer. It entertained the troops in remote areas in every theatre of war, often within the sound of gunfire, and, at the request of Ernie Bevin, the workers in war factories, usually performing in canteens at lunchtime. By 1946 it had given over two million concerts and was reckoned to have employed four-fifths of the entertainment industry. Which was part of the problem.

Many stars performed for ENSA, Gracie Fields, Sybil Thorndike and George Formby among them, and the genius of Tony Hancock and Terry-Thomas was first recognized when they appeared in ENSA concerts. But Dean was very concerned with the quality of other members of his massive troupe; he was determined it should not be a giant 'foxhole' for less than adequate entertainers, but, given the ambitious commitment of the programme to go wherever the troops went and entertain war workers in industry wherever they had their factories and no matter what time their shifts, were there simply were not enough good performers to go round. The pay was poor and it was not surprising that some very mediocre talent was also employed – a six-week engagement with ENSA could defer call-up, and for a brief, alarming moment in 1942 it looked as if chorus girls aged between twenty-one and twenty-four were liable to be conscripted.

The material was often 'smutty' despite Dean's strictures, and unfunny. A Manchester man leapt on the stage after an ENSA concert to call for 'three cheers for the audience', and a woman who had worked in a radar factory during the war told Norman Longmate that her factory had to 'endure ENSA about once a month, and endure it was'. But while for these people ENSA lived up to its alternative name of 'Every Night Something Awful', for many others it was a 'tonic' and a morale booster. As the war progressed Dean introduced a more serious (or 'igh brow as Bevin dubbed it) range of concerts including the Hallé orchestra in Wigan and the London Symphony Orchestra in Stepney – though, for different reasons, these sometimes had a struggle to get the appreciation they deserved from tired war workers on short breaks.

Ever ready to help, women's magazines supported the 'holidays at home' initiative by suggesting that families should save 'fun' money for these occasions, shroud rooms not in regular use with dust sheets to save on the dusting, have breakfast outside which will be 'thrilling because it is so different', and on fine days 'use the garden as a living

room from noon to night' where you can 'read out of doors in the morning and fuss about hats' and 'all wear your newest and nicest clothes as you would on every holiday'.

But Lyn, while she welcomed the programme drawn up for the family for 'Holiday at Home' activities in West Wickham, particularly as it was Ben's and Thomas's half-term, had a certain scepticism. Ben understood why: 'Holidays at home were a really nice time. It wasn't exactly like a normal holiday because you're in the same place – I mean at home – all the time, but we went to different places every day. We played pitch and putt, and we saw this brilliant Punch and Judy show, and the whole family went for a bike ride and had this great picnic in a field and played games. And as we were sitting there this Spitfire went over and we all got up and waved our handkerchiefs because we thought it might be Lee. I'd never been on a picnic with my whole family before. I think it was the best bit of holidays at home. But,' he added thoughtfully, 'it wasn't much of a holiday for my granny because she had to do lots of preparing stuff before we could go out.'

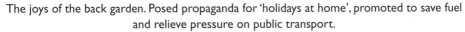

The joys of the back garden. Posed propaganda for 'holidays at home', promoted to save fuel and relieve pressure on public transport.

Lyn agreed. 'Holidays at home, I don't think so. I was up at six o'clock this morning to get ready for our "holiday at home" day. The shopping still has to be done, holidays at home or not, points have to be sorted out. Then I had to do some washing, prepare the vegetables for the evening meal and make what seemed like a thousand sandwiches. And then you come home, and you're always late home when you've had a day out, and then have to make dinner, and that takes a couple of hours, and then there's the washing-up, and it starts all over again the next day. And I didn't get any new clothes, which you usually do for a holiday. I fancy a yellow swing coat and matching hat, but here I am still in my dreary workaday clothes with a corset that cuts into me. They certainly knew how to holiday in the 1940s!

'When our children were young we didn't have a lot of money, so we decided to try this holiday at home lark just for a week and I found it exhausting and I vowed that I'd never do that again. It was a proper holiday or nothing. And here I am again and I certainly don't think that it's any less tiring in 1943, which is the year we've now reached in our "wartime" experience, than it was twenty years ago. I think it's just another bum deal for the wartime housewife. Holidays at home, my foot! For the

'It was one of the best days.' The Hymers family on a 'holidays at home' picnic.

Rare wartime treats: Michael enjoys a cigar and Lyn drains a glass of beer.

men and the children yes, for the wartime housewife, no way. A *real* holiday would be for somebody to take the whole family off somewhere, drop them in a park for three hours, and let me read a book. Now that *would* be a holiday!'

But there were aspects of her 'holiday' that Lyn greatly enjoyed: 'We found an idyllic spot in a field by West Wickham church for our picnic. The sun shone and we played ball games with the children. The only thing that would have improved it was a Spitfire going overhead, and then, unbelievably one did. It was a perfect afternoon.'

And the whole family found their visit to nearby Chislehurst caves breathtaking. 'I was speechless,' said Lyn. Strictly speaking, these are not caves at all, caused by running water, but passages carved out of the Kent hillside for mining chalk and flint.

The first reference to the caves is in the thirteenth century, and in the early twentieth century they became a popular tourist attraction, with electric light installed, picture postcards on sale, the site of occasional concerts and a dog trained to track down visitors who had got lost in the miles of underground caverns. In the First World War, the caves were taken over by the government as part of Woolwich Arsenal and, used to store ammunition. After the army finally relinquished them in 1920, the caves were turned over to mushroom growing. In 1938, during the Munich crisis, they were temporarily used by troops, but military thinking in the 1930s favoured the dispersal of ammunition to local stores rather than have a huge central dump, so Chislehurst caves lost that function in the build-up to war.

It might have been thought on the outbreak of war that the extensive caves would have been requisitioned for deep shelters, but government thinking was very much opposed to mass deep shelters, fearful of the potential tragedy should panic break out underground, and also concerned that 'deep shelter mentality' would mean that an intimidated population might simply refuse to come out from their subterranean hideouts and order would break down.

For this reason – and the need to keep the lines open for troop movements – the use of Underground stations was banned at the beginning of the blitz. But Londoners were having none of it. For those in flimsily built terraced houses with no cellar or garden for an Anderson shelter, deep in the labyrinth under the capital instinctively felt the place to be when bombs began to fall. Every night thousands would buy a ticket (or vault over the barrier) and make themselves as comfortable as possible on hard concrete platforms without sanitation for the night. It was something of an illusion. A direct hit from a high explosive bomb could penetrate 50 feet of solid ground: when Marble Arch station received a direct hit on 17 September 1940, two

Sweet dreams? Thousands of people crowded into Underground stations every night.

people were killed; in October four tube stations were hit in three nights, and at Balham sixty-four people died. In January 1941 at Bank station 111 travellers and people taking shelter were killed.

The government relented: the branch line to Aldwych station was closed and three disused stations were opened to the public. Some 10,000 people sheltered nightly in an unfinished extension line that ran from Liverpool Street under the East End; and by the end of September 1940, 177,000 people were sleeping in the Underground system. Many in fact lived there, and queues formed for a place as early as 6 a.m. with the constant worry of whether you would find a space for the night – with 'spivs' charging half a crown for a pitch as the raids grew worse. White lines were painted on the platforms: until 7.30 p.m. shelterers had to stay behind the second line to allow passengers to get on and off the tubes; after that, until 10.30 p.m., they could advance to the second line, painted 4 feet from the edge of the platform. Then the electricity was switched off and the station was theirs, as were the tunnels for informal use as public conveniences and the escalators for sleeping once every square inch of the platform was jam-packed. Hammocks were slung up, mattresses laid down and committees formed to press for improved sanitation, first-aid posts and the provision of proper sleeping accommodation.

By April 1941 conditions had greatly improved, 600,000 bunks had been installed, food was provided at the larger shelters often by the WVS or Salvation Army, and the government realized that it had found itself a cheap alternative to building the hundreds of thousands of shelters that would have been required to protect the population of the metropolis.

A very similar 'people's occupation' happened in Chislehurst caves as soon as the blitz started – and predictably neither Trust Houses, the hotel chain that owned the caves, nor the local council were any happier with this than the government had been with the colonization of the Underground, but the local MP, the WVS and the Red Cross could see the sense of it. By the end of November 1940 the caves were full to capacity and, according to Dr Eric Inman's guide to the caves, 'a clergyman, a mushroom grower and a retired rubber planter masterminded the creation of an underground town'.

At first living conditions were fairly primitive with the shelterers living their troglodyte existence on bare earth (or a deckchair they had brought in with them), with only candles or torches for light, a single tap and an oil drum containing creosote for sanitation. Soon electric lighting was installed; the Red Cross opened a medical centre; church services were held with a choir; the local council supplied bunk beds; and the caves even boasted their own Scout, Guide and Brownie packs. In November 1941 (when the blitz had effectively been over for some six months) the caves were designated as an official public shelter.

1940s
HOUSE

'I had never heard of the caves before, and certainly had absolutely no idea that at one time they sheltered more then 15,000 people,' Lyn said, 'I found them amazing. As far as I am concerned they are a most impressive piece of social history and an important portrayal of an aspect of life on the home front. The ticket office is still there, and you can imagine people queuing up for an overnight pitch. Apparently the temperature rose to 80 degrees when they were full. Walking round the caves you could see traces of people's lives, somebody's bunk bed, a candle holder hewn out of the rock face. I could have stayed in there for hours reading the inscriptions on the walls and trying to imagine how it was for all those people living there. I had so many questions, I really want to know their stories.'

Unsatisfied by the tour of the caves, which concentrated on 'spooks and ghosts' when what the Hymers wanted to hear about were the wartime conditions, they were very pleased to meet Alex Gilham, who had been one of those who had sheltered in the caves.

'My wife and small son had been evacuated to Oxford,' he explained, 'and my house was badly damaged in the blitz, so I was invited along to the caves by a friend who was the projectionist at the local cinema and his wife to see for myself what it was like. When I went in it was already pretty full with people settling down in deckchairs

Saving on fuel: Thomas and Ben on their bikes outside 17 Braemar Gardens.

trying to make themselves comfortable for a long night. I was so engrossed with looking at the barber's shop, the first-aid post, a church organ in a corner reserved for church services, as I walked from cave to cave, that by the time I was ready to leave, a red light near the entrance showed that there was an air raid going on. So I had to stay and I wandered around looking for somewhere to sleep. At intervals the corridors widened into alcoves and in one a woman had laid a table with a meal for her family – there were rugs on the floor and a couple of pictures on the walls. It was a real home from home, just like walking into someone's living room.

'We finally got to what was known as the "druid" section. All the space was taken up by sleeping children and the warden told us that the only place that was vacant was what was known as the "druid's altar" since people were superstitious about lying down on what they thought was a sacred place.' (In fact the druid theory was strongly disputed by the Archaeological Association at the beginning of the century, who insisted that the raised platform had a more prosaic use – to allow miners easier access to the roof.) With some misgivings Mr Gilham and his friend bedded down on the 'altar' and in fact 'it became our bedroom for three months and two beds were installed later'.

Mr Gilham used to cycle to work at Woolwich every day, ditch his bike in a nearby wood and seek safety in the caves. He remembered, 'They really came into their own as a shelter in May 1941. After two disastrous raids on London with massive loss of life, hundreds started trekking out from the East End to sleep in the caves.'

Lyn was enthralled with Alex Gilham's recollections. 'There was a WVS canteen in the caves, a cinema, a theatre, a hairdresser, a medical centre with an operating theatre and at one time a whole ward of a children's hospital was evacuated there. At Christmas 1940 it was decorated with hundreds of tiny, twinkling fairy lights to bring a little joy to the sick children in the midst of the blitz.' (The local belief is that the hospital was Great Ormond Street, but there is no mention of it in the hospital's records since it relocated to Tadworth Court in Surrey and Hemel Hempstead in Hertfordshire.)

'Apparently,' Lyn continued, 'you couldn't hear a thing once you were in there. In fact once the cave suffered a direct hit and no one heard – or felt – anything. All that happened was that the lights flickered momentarily, and some chalk flaked off the walls. The caves became so popular that houses nearby offered rooms to let at very high rents because they provided easy access to shelter. So there was some profiteering going on too.'

There were rules: 'No admission (or re-entry) to the dormitory section after 9.30 p.m. (10 p.m. in double summer time)'; 'Children should be in their pitches by 9 p.m. and stay there'; 'Music must cease by 9 p.m.'; 'Lights out and absolute silence by 10.30 p.m. in the dormitory section'; 'Pitches must not be changed, exchanged or sold'; 'Four days absence may involve loss of pitch'; and the final injunction was 'Arrive early and stay put'.

At 9.32 on the morning of 6 June 1944 the newscaster John Snagge, speaking from London, broadcast the momentous news: 'D-Day has come. Early this morning the Allies began their assault on the north-western face of Hitler's Europe.' During the night US airborne troops followed by Allied landing craft had landed on the beaches of Normandy. The 'second front' urged since 1942 had opened. By nightfall on 6 June 156,000 troops had landed in France.

It had been obvious for weeks that a major operation was about to take place, with conveys of tanks, lorries and bulldozers heading to the invasion ports along the coast and troops massed in camps and billets awaiting orders. Secrecy was imperative: the Germans suspected an invasion was being planned, but they must not know when or where it would take place. But from early that morning of 6 June the inhabitants of southern England had realized what was happening as streams of planes droned overhead and gliders silently swooped towards France. Despite extensive advance reconnaissance no one had any certainty that the Germans would not be able to throw the Allied offensive back into the Channel, so the relief when it was confirmed that the troops had secured a foothold in occupied France – albeit at a high human cost, particularly of US troops on Omaha beach – was intense. Expectations ran high that the war 'would all be over by the autumn'. But it was not to be: the fight through Normandy was slow and harrowing; there were delays at Falaise and a shattering reverse at Arnhem in September 1944.

But within less than a week of D-Day Britain was under attack again from a devastating new German weapon. Hitler had boasted in the early days of the war that Germany possessed 'a weapon with which we ourselves could not be attacked'. He was probably thinking of the Luftwaffe, but Hitler's 'secret weapon' became one of the great wartime jokes as it failed to materialize. In fact Germany was soon developing two secret weapons.

At 4.08 a.m. on 13 June 1944 a greengrocer and a builder, part-time members of the Observer Corps, were keeping lookout atop a Martello tower on the Romney Marsh that had been constructed as a defence against Napoleon some 140 years before. They saw something the size and shape of a small fighter plane surrounded by a red glow emanating from the fuselage hurtling towards them. It was the first of four flying bombs launched from the French coast to land in England. Three fell in the countryside causing little damage but the fourth fell on a railway bridge in Bow, East London, killing six people, seriously injuring thirty and rendering 200 homeless.

Rumours circulated like wildfire about this new weapon, but the government was particularly anxious that the Germans should not learn that at least one of their missiles had reached its intended target: London. As a consequence no official announcement was made and people were left to speculate about this new terror. On 16 June Herbert Morrison stood up in the House of Commons and announced that

'the enemy… has now started to use this much-vaunted new weapon against this country… it is important not to give the enemy any information which would help him. All possible steps are, of course, being taken to frustrate the enemy's attempt. Meanwhile the nation should carry on with its normal business.'

It was a pious hope as the grim litany of death and injury mounted: in an attack on the Guard's Chapel in Birdcage Walk during morning service on Sunday 18 June, 119 people (most of them servicemen) were killed and 182 so seriously injured that several died later. On 30 June, forty-six were killed when a flying bomb came down in Aldwych, 399 received serious injuries and a further 200 were allowed home after hospital treatment. On 28 July one of the twenty bombs that were to fall on Kensington exploded at a cluster of cafes, killing forty-five and seriously injuring fifty-four, with 116 sustaining minor injuries. Earlier the same day fifty-one were killed and 124 seriously injured in a flying bomb 'incident' in a street market in Lewisham.

South London suffered the worst, but the effect on the morale of an already war-weary population was devastating. Anyone who could leave the capital did, and although the government had decided against a mass evacuation of schools, thousands of children were sent to what was hoped was safety. It was an eerie time: the exodus made London like a ghost city full of empty, boarded-up and often damaged properties. The capital 'belonged to the brave and the few' in the words of a Frenchwoman living in Mayfair's Shepherd's Market; theatres were half empty and most closed down; the Proms were abandoned – though Myra Hess's lunchtime concerts at the National Gallery continued despite damage to the building. The Tate Gallery had also been damaged, along with the National History Museum, the British Museum, the Royal Observatory, Greenwich, the magnificent hall of Staples Inn, Buckingham Palace – twice – and the War Office. Nearly a million private homes were damaged and 23,000 destroyed.

There was soon pressure on Morrison and the Ministry of Information to identify where the bombs were landing and the true extent of the effect they were having since 'public morale is very much… lowered, not so much by the bombs themselves, as by the secrecy that surrounds them'. It was not, however, until 6 July 1944 that Churchill described the flying bombs' devastating effects. London had become, in Evelyn Waugh's phrase, 'a city infested with venomous insects' with 'lighted cigars cutting the darkness'. It had been subjected to what the Air Chief Marshall in charge of the Air Defence of Great Britain – successor to Fighter Command – described as 'this intermittent drizzle of malignant robots'. They had, the Prime Minister reported, killed… almost exactly one person per bomb… the latest figures are 2,754 flying bombs launched and 2,752 fatal casualties sustained… up to six o'clock this morning… The total number of injured detained in hospital is about 8,000.'

Though the target was London, the south of England suffered grievously too from the flying or buzz bombs – Morrison had counselled against the use of the term 'pilotless planes' since 'it implies a mechanical monster impervious to human interference' and recommended the use of 'flying bombs' as being 'more accurate and less alarming'. Soon, though, the British either took to using the German designation V1, an abbreviation of *Vergeltunngswaffe* ('revenge weapon') or, somewhat confusingly, nicknamed these projectiles 'doodlebugs' – which was odd as unfortunately the last thing they did was to leisurely trace an indeterminate path through the sky.

Anti-aircraft defences were moved from London to the North Downs and then in mid-July to the coast; aircraft patrolled the skies above Kent and Sussex, which soon became known as 'Doodlebug Alley', attempting to shoot down the V1s before they reached the capital. The Germans were aiming at Tower Bridge (and one actually succeeded in hitting the bull's-eye), but they were aiming blind and British Intelligence was remarkably successful in keeping their achievements from Colonel Watchel, who was in charge of the operation. In fact many V1s did reach central London, but most fell short. If, however, the Germans could be persuaded that their missiles were overshooting they might shorten the range still further, so that more flying bombs fell on the less densely populated suburbs. 'A policy of trying to push the bombardment south' was therefore pursued, though it was kept secret even from most members of the government and Herbert Morrison himself was unhappy about deceiving the enemy so that one person died instead of another. 'Who are we,' he asked, 'to act as God?'

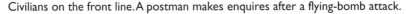

Civilians on the front line. A postman makes enquires after a flying-bomb attack.

Nevertheless the deception policy was adopted and as a direct result Croyden, nine miles to the south of London, and Shirley and West Wickham, six miles away from Westminster, found themselves at the heart of the target instead of on its edge. As a result the borough had the unwelcome distinction of suffering more flying-bomb incidents than anywhere else in the country. One hundred and forty-one V1s fell on Croydon. The *Croydon Times* produced a map. In the eighty days that the main attack lasted, nearly 1,500 homes were completely destroyed and 54,000 damaged (some more than once).

Audrey Thompson, who was on fire watch duty at Hawes Down School, West Wickham, the night the first 'doodlebug' came over, 'knew this was something different and very terrifying. The All Clear did not sound until well into the next day, making it difficult to get home for breakfast and back to work.' On 16 June, 1944 houses in Links Road were hit and a householder killed, and six members of the Heavy Rescue Squad were killed in their lorry on their way back from an incident nearby where a wardens' post had been hit and three wardens were killed. So dreadful was the destruction that a Mobile Medical Unit was instigated and it worked round the clock treating victims who might otherwise have died before reaching hospital. For the first time West Wickham lost its neutral status and was designated an evacuation area; numbers of pupils from local schools were sent north to Yorkshire and Leicester-shire, out of range, it was hoped, of this new, pre-programmed and deeply demoralizing menace.

Salvaged belongings are piled in the street after a V2 attack.

Further bombs that summer fell in the High Street; a bus was thrown off the road and into a pond outside the White Hart pub and thirty passengers required treatment. Soon the incidents were so numerous and destructive that ARP reinforcements arrived from Yorkshire, while Marines, drafted in to help clear up the damage, were billeted in local homes. The numbers seeking refuge in Chislehurst caves, which had fallen so dramatically at the end of the blitz that the caves were being used to store official local authority records, now climbed rapidly and soon 2,000 were sleeping in the caves every night, with special rush hour trains laid on to bring others seeking a safe berth. ARP wardens controlled the crush at the station,

and a special section was reserved for WAAFS from Biggin Hill so that they could get an undisturbed night's sleep.

By September it seemed, according to the Chairman of the Counter Measures Committee against the German secret weapons, Churchill's son-in-law Duncan Sandys, that 'except possibly for a few last shots the Battle of London is over' – with a final toll of 6,184 civilians dead and 16,000 more seriously injured – . But it wasn't: between then and March 1945, more than 750 V1s were launched, of which seventy-nine reached London. Isolated bombs fired at Manchester travelled as far north as Yorkshire and as far west as Shropshire; on Christmas Eve 1944, twenty-seven people were killed in Oldham.

Furthermore, on 8 September, another terror struck when a huge explosion occurred in London: it was heard all over the city. The terrible explosions continued and increased with as many as six a day by November. At first there was no official word about the cause. It was different from a V1, which made an unforgettable noise like a 'badly tuned motor cycle engine'; this noise grew louder, until the engine cut out as the fuel ran out, leaving you fifteen seconds or so to dive for cover. This new device, which was 45 feet long and weighed 14 tons, travelled so fast that it was impossible to hear it before it exploded in a supersonic bang and a blinding flash of white light. There was no time to take shelter or any avoiding action. It was a game of deadly bagatelle – a case of 'if your name's on it…'

Not until 6 November, almost two months after the first explosions in Chiswick and Epping, did Churchill finally admit to the House of Commons that the devastatingly loud bangs and flashes were not caused by 'flying gas mains' as popular rumour or sceptical humorists suggested, but another 'secret weapon', rockets or V2s as they were called. Over a thousand – 1,115 – of these rockets landed on British soil; 518 reached London: 2,274 people were killed, over 6,000 badly injured and an almost inestimable number of houses destroyed or damaged – the four V2s that fell on Croydon damaged 2,000 houses.

The V bombs proved more disturbing to many than the blitz: it was not just , after almost five years of war, having your hopes of imminent peace dashed, nor the high toll of human life and property. It was also that the raids came at any time of the day or night so that daily life was permanently disrupted and nerves on edge. The authenticity of the Hymers family's wartime experience meant that after nearly two months in the 1940 house Lyn described 13 June as 'the day from hell'.

The family had had four raids so far that day and had been in and out of the Anderson shelter. After the first one Lyn had gone back into the kitchen to make curry for that night's supper. Tired from a busy day at the old people's home, coming home to do a load of washing, she inadvertently put ginger rather than curry powder into the meal she was making and was attempting to wash it off when the siren went again.

'Everyone else rushed into the shelter,' Lyn said, 'but I continued to try to rinse off the ginger because I know that if I didn't it would soak into the vegetables and make them inedible. We were going to Ben's school play and we had to have a meal before that. I couldn't give them a sandwich because with Michael being home at the moment we don't have any spare bread, so there would be nothing for them to eat. I felt guilty about not being in the shelter with the rest of them, so as soon as the food was OK, I rushed down there. I was so tired and I still had so much to do that I felt very agitated in the shelter. The children were starving so I got out of the shelter to see to the meal. The others were angry with me, but I was past caring.

'Then when the All Clear went, we managed to bolt down our meal. I went upstairs to get changed (fifth time today – dress for housework, dress for shopping, dress for work, dress for going out – it was so different in the 1940s!) and Kirstie and I and the children rushed off to see Ben's play, which was excellent – *The Lion, the Witch and the Wardrobe*, a very good choice for a 1940s family. My feet were really hurting as we walked home and as we got near the house we heard the bloody siren go again. Michael was at the gate looking out for us and we all rushed straight through the house and into the shelter. Luckily the All Clear soon went, but I was feeling so low that I just went up to the bedroom and started to cry. Then that bastard siren went again. I really did not want to go into the shelter again and Michael and the children were asleep. But we knew we had to, so Kirstie went to wake Michael, and she and I

Hole in about fourteen. Thomas and Ben putting in the park.

1940s HOUSE

packed up the boys' breakfast to take in there because we had no idea how long the alert might go on for. It might be over in minutes – after we've woken everyone up – or it might go on all night. But I guess that's what it was like for a 1940s family, never knowing when you could sit down and relax, or have a bath or make a meal. And the doodlebugs must have been terrifying, That period of deathly silence after the engine cut out, not knowing where it was going to fall. I never thought we'd get back to this once the blitz was over.'

'I stuck my head of the shelter at one point and it was a beautiful calm moonlit night and I did begin to feel privileged then. No fighter planes overhead, no sound of bombs exploding, not even any ack-ack [anti-aircraft] guns. All we have are relatively minor discomforts to complain of – tiredness, a hard wooden school chair to sit on. This *is* playing at it. I have to be honest. We'll all be alive at the end of the night and our house will be safe, as will the houses of our friends. I feel almost guilty sitting here in an Anderson shelter with no bombs. And then I thought this is why we're going down to the shelter two, three, four times a night. We're not doing it for us, we're not doing it for a television crew. We're doing it for the men and women of Britain who suffered so much during the Second World War, and whose stories we've heard while we've been doing this project. Their experience has really touched us all and been an inspiration. None of us will ever forget them. But I *do* feel tired and cold and hungry

Lyn listening to sounds of an air raid, transmitted to the Hymers' shelter.

too, and I would give *anything* for a cup of tea. It's now 4 a.m. and Michael's snoring is reverberating round the metal walls. I may have to wake him. How *can* they all sleep?'

Lyn found the incessant air raids wearing, but also isolating. 'I would love to invite the Tillings in for an evening, but knowing that the siren could go at any minute I can't do that. It's just too distressing for people who lived with it, to hear that awful wail again. They find it brings it all back to them and I can't do that to them. It's just not fair.'

But the next night it was back to an uncomfortable night in the shelter: 'It's even more cramped now. Michael has moved a bed in which takes up all the floor space. He says it's for me, but I can't help noticing that it's he who is lying sprawled right across it fast asleep. He's suspended the candle from the roof for safety, but now I can't see to read and am having great difficulty writing. It's very hot down here and I'm the only one awake even though there are tremendous bangs being relayed into

the shelter. I feel trapped and shut in. I am desperate for a cup of tea and the toilet. I just want the All Clear to go.'

It went at 7.30 a.m. but as Lyn scrambled out, she realized that the house had suffered bomb damage. 'It must have been a V2,' said Ben. 'We didn't hear a thing.' It had not been a direct hit – there was no structural damage – but there was broken glass, crockery and plaster dust everywhere, And the water, gas and electricity were off.

'It was a bitter blow at that stage,' said Lyn. 'I just went to sit outside and try to collect my thoughts. My husband managed to make me a cup of tea by suspending an empty baked bean tin on a long piece of wire into the embers of the boiler. That made me feel better, and I set about organizing the tasks that had to be done to get the house straight again. The children had cereal in the garden and went off to school and I got going on the house, though the lack of a vacuum cleaner, any detergent, or even any water, made clearing up all the plaster dust very arduous. The more I swept, the more it seemed to swirl around the room and settle in places that I'd already cleaned. Kirstie came back from the shops to find me in tears on the dining room floor. I felt that I had worked hard for nine weeks to keep Braemar Gardens immaculate and it would never be the same again.

'I'd just finished cleaning the dining room and put a wet towel round the door to make sure no dust could get in and Kirstie and I were having a sandwich – no cup of tea of course since there was still no water – when we had a message that we three adults had to listen to a very important broadcast.'

It was the voice of Richard Dimbleby, then a war correspondent, who had flown on bombing operations over Germany and was now with the army as it advanced into Germany. On 19 April 1944 he stood outside the charnel house of Belsen concentration camp, and in a low voice told listeners to *War Report* about 'the most horrible day of my life… it is hard to describe adequately what I have seen… there are 40,000 men, women and children in the camp, German and half a dozen other nationalities, thousands of them Jews… In the last few months alone, 30,000 prisoners have been killed or allowed to die… I wish with all my heart that everyone fighting in this war, and above all those whose duty it is to direct the war from Britain and America, could have come with me through the barbed wire fence that leads to the inner compound…

'I've seen many terrible sights in the last five years, but nothing approaching the dreadful interior at this hut at Belsen… The dead and dying lay close together. I picked my way over corpse after corpse in the gloom. A terrible sickly, thick smell of death and sickness, corruption and filth hangs over everything… We were on our way down to the crematorium where the Germans had burned alive thousands of men and women in a single fire... Those officers and men who have seen these things have gone back to the Second Army [the US liberating force] moved to such an anger as I have never seen before.'

CHAPTER 15

GOODBYE, MRS MINIVER

'Of all the people that I have talked to here about their war experiences, not one of them has ever mentioned VE Day,' wrote Lyn. 'No one has talked about it. We know there were big parties, but it's almost as if it wasn't that important to them.'

Nella Last, whose diary she had been reading as a vade-mecum to the life of a 1940s housewife, bore out Lyn's perception. She recorded that when she went to the shops in her home town of Barrow-in-Furness on 7 May 1945, 'All the shops had got their rosettes and tricoloured buttonholes in the windows; and the multiple grocer's had ladders out and men putting up lengths of little pennants and flags. There seemed a curious expectancy about, but to many of my enquiries for MO [Mass Observation, for which Mrs Last was an observer], "What will you do on VE Day?" I got disappointing answers: "I don't know" and "What *is* there to do?" were the chief ones.'

Mrs Last put this down to the fact that 'the tide is running out so swiftly and unnoticeably that the actual cease-fire will be shorn of excitement and any of the wild "whoopee" of the last armistice. It's a very dreadful thought: I'm not very old, but can clearly remember three wars – and at the rate they have been, could yet see another.' The 9 o'clock news that night announced that the next day would be VE Day and that Churchill was to speak at 3 o'clock, and though she felt remarkably unexcited Nella Last thought to herself, "'Well, dash it, we *must celebrate somehow* – I'll open this tin of pears," and I did.' On 8 May, 'bonfires were lit… in one street a piano was being pushed out, as if a dance was contemplated later, but no real "let go"

'I only have eyes for you.' Lyn and Michael Hymers dancing to celebrate VE Day.

signs anywhere, not even a merry soldier or sailor… we got in to listen to the King's speech, and we drank a toast in beer and cider… I still feel that curious "flat" feeling.'

After six long years the war came to an end with a whimper rather than a bang for most people. The Civil Defence outside London had been partly disbanded in September 1944 and the same month blackout restrictions were reduced to a 'dim out', or 'half lighting' as it was officially called, though few private citizens bothered – or dared – to make the change. The Home Guard stood down in December; the last V2 fell on 29 March 1945; and on 1 May Hitler's death in a Berlin bunker was announced.

At 7 p.m. the next day a news flash announced that Germany and Italy had surrendered. People listened every hour for an announcement on the BBC, but the government 'with barely credible stupidity' (or at least a certain disregard for the feelings of its war-weary citizens) had agreed not to make the announcement until a time that suited both the Americans and the Russians. At 3 o'clock (double summer time) speaking from the same room at 10 Downing Street where Chamberlain had announced the outbreak of war on 3 September 1939, Churchill broadcast to the nation – loudspeakers had been rigged up in local town halls up and down the country.

'Yesterday morning at 2.41 a.m. at General Eisenhower's headquarters, the representative of the German High Command… signed the act of unconditional surrender of all German land, sea and air forces in Europe to the Allied Expeditionary

'This is your victory,' Churchill told the crowds on VE Day, 8 May 1945.

'There's a land of begin again.' Crowds in the London streets celebrate Victory in Europe after nearly six years of war.

Forces. Hostilities will end officially at one minute after midnight tonight... but in the interest of saving lives, the cease-fire began yesterday to be sounded along all fronts. The German war is therefore at an end... We may allow ourselves a brief period of rejoicing, but let us not forget for a moment the toils and efforts that lie ahead. Japan, with all her treachery and greed, remains unsubdued... Advance Britannia! Long live freedom! God save the King.'

Crowds gathered outside Buckingham Palace, chanting, 'We want the King,' and George VI appeared with his family again and again on the balcony while in the streets below people cheered and sang and danced. Buildings were floodlit, ships in harbours and on rivers hooted a V sign and searchlights cut Vs in the sky as darkness fell. All over the country bonfires were lit, church bells pealed out and fireworks exploded. But another MO diarist, Naomi Mitchison, noticed that 'almost everyone was tired and wanting to look rather than do. They were sitting when possible, lots of them on the steps of St Martin's [in the Fields, a church in Trafalgar Square]. Most people were wearing bright coloured clothes, lots of them red, white and blue in some form... Most women had lipstick and a kind of put-on smile, but all but the very young looked very tired when they stopped actually smiling.'

In West Wickham there were services of thanksgiving in the churches attended by representatives from the ARP, the WVS, the Women's Institute, the Home Guard, the Royal Observer Corps, the Red Cross, the Boy Scouts and Girl Guides and many more of the organizations that had been involved in the defence of the country. Numerous street parties were held and victory bonfires lit in public spaces. A few weeks later the West Wickham pig club was formally closed and it was announced at a farewell social evening (for the owners) that a total of a thousand guineas had been raised for the Red Cross Prisoner of War Fund, while a local rabbit club also ceased its activities.

Atomic bombs were dropped on Hiroshima and Nagasaki in early August: on the 14th, Japan surrendered and on 15 August VJ Day was celebrated, again with flags, bunting, bonfires, parties and parades. Gradually servicemen were demobbed, POWs started to arrive home – Ivy Crier's stepson Jack was so weak when he arrived at Waterloo Station that a porter had to hurry down the platform with a trolley to carry him and his luggage back to his waiting family. And rationing continued into the 1950s.

The cost of war to West Wickham, as to most of the country, had been high: forty-one civilians and twenty Civil Defence workers had been killed, while at least sixty-two deaths were recorded of men and women serving in the forces. Nationwide the total was 335,000 British citizens dead by enemy action at home and abroad.

'It seems wrong somehow to party,' wrote Lyn in her diary. 'My war has not been easy, and it's not really over yet.' That morning Thomas had excitedly burst through the front door shouting 'Victory Boy' and handing his grandmother an invitation for the family to attend a VE Day dance at Keston Village Hall, which is close to Biggin Hill. But Lyn felt fragile, marooned in a complex space between her 'wartime' life – which the day before had included the experience of clearing up the house in the way that thousands of her wartime contemporaries had in the wake of the devastation caused by the V weapons – and the family's return to Yorkshire and the year 2000.

As usual the family conferred on the issue and decided that though it might seem to trivialize their recent experiences to have fun, in fact it had its own authenticity. 'I am sure that social events like that would have been particularly important in wartime,' Michael suggested. 'It would have been very necessary to have a break sometimes, to let go for a bit, enjoy yourself and meet some new people.' And like everything else that they had done in the 1940s house, the Hymers were determined to get as much as possible out of the occasion. That afternoon Dean and Jackie Whybra, their guide to the fashion and music of the period, came round and they rolled up the carpets, turned on the gramophone and tried to teach the family to jitterbug.

'Michael and I were less than average but Kirstie and Ben really got into it,' said Lyn, who was also concerned that the knee-length bloomers she wore would make her look ridiculous as she cavorted to the big band sound.

'You'll have the world on a string.' Kirstie and Ben cutting the rug at the dance held in celebration of VE Day.

When the family arrived at the hall that evening, they were overwhelmed. It seemed almost like a panorama of what VE Day would have been like. The hall was decorated in perfect 1940s style, everyone was in the right clothes, many were in uniform, the music was perfect – 'Watch the Birdie' (Dean's particular favourite), 'Don't sit under the apple tree with anyone else but me' and of course 'We'll meet again, don't know where, don't know when', which Lyn found particularly poignant that night. 'The Yanks gave Ben and Thomas Hershey bars and gum which after the frugal time they'd been having was wonderful for them. I kept thinking how tremendous it must have been on VE Day to know that after nearly six years you were safe again, your home was safe. Of course shortages and rationing continued, but at least the people were safe, and they were free. That was something worth celebrating, surely.' For Kirstie, the VE Day dance was 'probably one of our best evenings. I think we all needed to let off steam, let our hair down as the saying goes. I danced with a different partner for almost every dance, servicemen from all three forces, GIs – and

Ben and Thomas, and I can understand why these dances were so important to people during the war. It must have been a time when they were able to forget about what was happening in their daily lives, at least just for a couple of hours.'

Michael was reflective: 'I'm sure that on VE Day even when people were celebrating, they would also be thinking about the uncertainties that lay ahead, what life held in store for them, how they would be able to rebuild their lives. A lot of people who were having fun that night might have been bombed out or living in temporary accommodation, they might not have known whether they had a job to go back to. Rationing was still acute [in May 1945 the weekly bacon ration was down to 3 ounces rather than 4, and lard from 2 ounces to 1: in September the clothing allowance fell to thirty-six coupons a year] and it continued for some time after the war – in fact it got worse, bread was briefly rationed in 1946,

and that never happened during the war. And of course Britain had massive debts to the US, all its gold reserves were gone, its industry had been turned over almost entirely to war production, there was a tremendous shortage of housing after the bombing and devastation everywhere.

'It took a long time for Britain to get back on its feet again, and people must have suspected that would be the case. They must have had very mixed feelings as they celebrated the end of war. The costs both human and financial were enormous and they must have wondered, as they had after the First World War, will it really be a better world – for *everyone*?'

'Will it be so again,' the poet C. Day-Lewis had written, 'A poppy wreath for the slain/And a cut-throat world for the living?/That stale impostor played on us again?'

The Beveridge Report had been published on 1 December 1942 to enormous public interest: the report and its brief official summary sold nearly three-quarters of a million copies, and it even featured on *ITMA* when Tommy Handley explained that he'd been up for the last three days and nights reading the first chapter of the (very dense) report, 'a book called *Gone with Want* by that stout fellow Beverage'. (*Gone with the Wind*, was the hit film of 1940 when cinemagoers braved the blitz to see it.)

The report was an attack on the 'five giants on the road to reconstruction: Want, Disease, Ignorance, Squalor and Idleness', and proposed an overall social insurance scheme for all that would cover every crisis in life from the cradle (maternity benefits) to the grave (funeral grants) and give security through child allowances, sickness and unemployment benefits and pensions.

A month after VE Day Winston Churchill, the inspirational wartime leader, confessed to his doctor, 'I am worried about this damned election. I have no message for them now,' and in a war-torn economy promised to cut taxation *and* implement the Beveridge report's recommendations on social insurance and its concomitant, a National Health Service. But a majority of the electorate recalled the dole queues of the 1930s and preferred Labour's slogan, 'Let Us Face the Future', to the Conservative plea 'Help Him Finish the Job'. After a three-week delay while the 'khaki vote' came in from what had been theatres of war all over the world, Labour was returned with a majority of 117 seats, and the modest Clement Attlee replaced Churchill as Prime Minister, setting off in his stead to negotiate the future of Europe with Stalin and Truman at Potsdam. On 26 July Churchill's doctor railed against the ingratitude of the British people in rejecting their wartime hero the moment that peace came. 'Oh no,' Churchill demurred generously, 'I wouldn't call it that. They have had a very hard time.'

It was over for the Hymers too: 'The End. Mrs Miniver is no more,' Lyn wrote on the last page in her 1940s house diary. 'I got up early to clean and tidy the house and pack my belongings. I was sad, of course I was sad. This had been our home for

nine weeks and so much had happened to us here.' She was to find the time travel forward to her former life painful. 'It was too soon to be part of the year 2000. I felt that I had only just finished the war… My house seems cluttered – a land of plenty, indeed of excess, confronting a woman who has had to live without side plates for nine weeks! The children were clamouring for takeout pizzas but I couldn't cope with that yet. Fortunately Michael and Kirstie understood and we settled on a compromise, fish and chips, which would have been available in the 1940s.

'I found the thing that upset me most was Kirstie's appearance. She looks so stark now in jeans and black T-shirt. Where has my lovely feminine daughter with her curls and floral frocks gone? The boys' trainers look so big and clumsy after seeing them in their brown Startrite sandals for so long, and when I saw Thomas in his black and red *Star Wars* pyjamas I wanted to weep for my little 1940s boy. At least I made a mental note to buy a beaded milk jug cover and try to find a wraparound pinny like the one I'd worn day in, day out at Braemar Gardens.'

The family returned to Leeds University for medical tests to see how they had fared on an austerity diet: were the claims justified that despite food shortages wartime families were healthier than they are today in more affluent times? Lyn was delighted to find that all that National Loaf, no chocolate, pizzas or chips (well, only once) and little alcohol meant that she had lost a stone. Kirstie had shed nearly half a stone and even Michael, with his British Restaurant meals, was down by four or five pounds. But the other results were less conclusive. Susan Jebb explained that the weight loss was most probably due to the changes in diet but also to the fact that without modern appliances in the home Lyn and Kirstie in particular had been having to do much harder physical work – all that washing and cooking and walking to the shops every day. No opportunities to be couch potatoes in front of the television brought its rewards!

Dr Jebb explained that whilst nine weeks was a short period to be able to measure the impact of a changed lifestyle on a family's health and well-being – after all a wartime family would have lived that way for nearly 300 continuous weeks – the results act as a useful reminder that although food was rationed during the war, the intake of essential vitamins and minerals was preserved and the nutritional well-being of the population as a whole was good. Today the health of our population is much more varied as it depends on a number of factors including personal choice, income and the region of the country in which we live. Lyn could count the benefits herself which included decreased breathlessness, eyes no longer red and bloodshot, hair no different for not having been properly shampooed for eight weeks – in fact it was less dry. Her skin did not seem to have suffered from the absence of a battery of expensive face creams, and the rough toilet paper that the family had so feared had been no problem. It was just her feet, tired, callused and sore, that bore the scars of battle.

What she had also gained was the knowledge that 'I can push the perimeters a lot further than I thought. I can do more mentally and physically than I had realized. I found I could manage with shortages and rationing and I have resolved never to throw away food like I used to. I hope I won't rely so much on convenience foods, or have as many takeaways, because I have found that I can cook some nice meals myself.

'There were many occasions when I thought, "I can't do this, too much is being expected of me – the housework, cooking, the laundry, plus voluntary work on top, the sleep deprivation when we were in and out of the Anderson shelter all the time. I am a 2000 woman, I don't work eighteen-hour days." But then I'd stop and say, "Hang on a minute. I am here for the wartime experience and in the war women didn't say they couldn't do it. They just got on with it." But I have realized my own strengths in this "war" and I have rediscovered my independence and I'll never let that slip again. I am convinced that women won the war on the home front, not the men. I've had to do so many things without my husband's help or intervention that I've become much stronger, and I can't go back. I think that many women did find that hard after the war when their husbands came home. They were pleased to see them, of course, but they'd grown used to coping alone, and they found it hard to pick up the old ways, what I'd almost call the subservience again, and maybe give up jobs they'd enjoyed, and start being just a housewife again, having to let someone else make the decisions.'

Her 'wartime' had had an unexpected – and disturbing – legacy for Lyn: 'It changed people, of course it did. Even those who you might think just had a good time. I've been reading stories of children who were evacuated and the effect that had on the rest of their lives. And even the next generation, those people like me who didn't directly experience the war, our childhood was sometimes made dark by it. Of course our parents wanted a better life for us, but sometimes because they had been through so much they somehow wanted us to know about it. To experience some of the pain and hardship they had felt, maybe without even realizing that is what they were doing. It's a very complex legacy and I'm not sure that we understand the half yet: the war cast a very long shadow in my view.'

What about Michael's rosy view of the 1940s that his family had been so anxious to disabuse him of? Had that survived? 'The project enabled me to do a lot of things that I had been wanting to do for a very long time – build an Anderson shelter, sit in a Spitfire, that sort of thing. But just about everything about the experience, the things we did, the people we met, all enabled me to get a better understanding of life at the time. And yes, it has pointed out a few flaws in my perceptions. I learned that people had a lot harder time than I imagined, just in their day-to-day living. I have seen the amount of work that Lyn and Kirstie have had to do. There is always something for them to do. There is never any time when they could just sit and relax and listen to the radio. They'd be darning, or sewing or shelling peas at the same time.

'It all takes a great deal more time and effort than I had appreciated – putting the blackout up every night, checking it all, thinking ahead all the time – will the coal run out? You couldn't even take a proper bath when you were tired. The daily hardships. All the queuing and then when you finally got to the front of the queue whatever you had been queuing for might have sold out. Were you going to be able to get to work? I know that when the train lines and the stations had been bombed it could take half a day or more to get into work, but people still did it. The frequency and duration of the air raids and the uncertainty and the daily fear people must have felt. All of that I appreciate much more now, I think.

'And I am sure that men had difficulties too. I often think that it must very hard for them to readjust, particularly if they had been away fighting. I am sure they would miss the comradeship and perhaps even the heroics. One day you were up there in the open skies flying a fighter plane, or on a bombing raid, and the next you were stood down with all the uncertainties about the peace and fitting back into civilian life. Having lived in barracks or whatever with your mates, it would be hard having to readjust to family life after having been away for maybe years. Your family would have changed, your children growing up, perhaps they'd been babies when you went away, or not even born, maybe your wife would have a job. Having spent six years fighting for your country, would there still be a place for you now?'

But as Michael and his family had coped with their ersatz war he had no doubt that today's young people would have risen to the challenge of another war too – 'though God forbid that they'll ever have to go through anything like that again. I think that given the same set of circumstances, the same reason for fighting for freedom, they would do the same. All over the world it's the young people who are in the front line opposing dictators. It's youth that fights for freedom and resists oppression. Look at Tiananmen Square – I didn't see that many fifty-year-olds in front of the tanks, it was the students. And the First World War was so much a young man's war, young people volunteered to go to Spain to fight in the Civil War, and when we went to the graveyard here and looked at the headstones of the pilots – young men every one. I have no doubt that if anything like Nazi Germany threatened now, the young people would respond just as they have always done.'

Kirstie had 'mixed feelings about going back to my previous life. Obviously I missed my sister and my best friend. But I have considered Braemar Gardens to be my home for the last nine weeks and I think that I'm probably going to find it difficult to go back to what I think of as "normality". I hoped that the experience here would help me gain confidence and it has. Rather than saying that I don't want to do something, I just get on and do it. I don't rely on anyone else like I used to. I give it my best shot. I used to find it very hard to go into a roomful of strangers and make conversation, but here I've had to talk to all sorts of people, and do things that

I didn't think I was capable of. At home, if someone important was coming to the house, I wouldn't have risked cooking for them, I'd have got a takeaway. But here I thought "I'm going to have to do it" when Marguerite Patten was coming for tea, and just got on with it. And it was fine.

'So one of the lessons I've learned from the experience is to have a go at something, rather than saying no, and it tends to work out OK. It's a question of having the confidence. It was like that at the aircraft factory too. OK, I've learned a few things about how an aircraft is made. But I have also learned to come into an all-male environment as the only woman and I think that I handled that quite well and that gave me confidence. I'd even like to go up in the aircraft that I've been working on. I am a bit of a coward about things like that, but at least I hope that I can come back to Biggin Hill and watch it take off. That'll give me a lot of satisfaction.

'I think that my dad is quite proud of me – and perhaps even a little bit jealous because he's always tinkering around with model aircraft and things and here I was working on the real thing. But I want him to be able to say, "My daughter did that. She stuck it out" – and realize what a lot it took for me to do that. And my relationship with my mum has changed too. I thought that we'd have some terrible arguments stuck in the same house together for nine weeks. But we haven't really, and as I've got stronger we've learned to rely on each other much more. I think that's because we've both helped each other come through the difficulties we've had. We've supported each other, and maybe that's not something we've done before when we've had so many other distractions. It's one of the best things that's come out of this experience. I am really proud of her, how's she's managed everything so well, how hard she's worked, and I think she's very proud of me too.

'I think that women would have come through the war with a tremendous sense of achievement and I think that I've got as close as possible to the experience that a woman would have had in the war. Obviously I can't begin to imagine what it was really like because I haven't had the fear of being killed, or losing my family, or my home, but in the practical, everyday things I think it was pretty close. And I've come back with a sense of achievement for the things that I've done too.'

But the people that Kirstie was proudest of all of were her two sons: 'I think that Ben and Thomas have done remarkably well in everything that they have been required to do. They had to settle in to a new school, make new friends and now they are going to have to leave them again. Both boys have had very good school reports and that makes me very proud. I have very much enjoyed watching the children go through this experience, though initially I had huge guilt for the first week or so. I kept thinking, "What have I done bringing the children here and putting them through all this?" – particularly when they were complaining all the time that they were hungry. But they have adapted. It's become a way of life for them. They have given up television and all

their games and Ben has taken a lot of responsibilities, particularly with my dad away and being the fuel warden, and he's taken it all very seriously and stuck with it. And Thomas has really entered into the 1940s life even though he's only seven. He's been so imaginative and inventive, making up games and painting pictures. I'm so proud of them both, and it makes me wonder if children really need all we give them. Maybe it's we who spoil them because here they've amused themselves much more, gone off and created their own entertainment. They have been so energetic, outside playing all the time, never worrying about television and their computer games. And it can't have been easy for them when they saw other children having all the treats they are used to – sweets, ice-cream, crisps. And they never even ask me for them. That makes me very proud. I just hope that we might be able to carry that on when we get home!

'It's been a vital experience for them and it is something that will stay with them for the rest of their lives. I think that they have been very privileged to have been able to do this. I think we all were. It was a learning experience. I learned something new every day and so the kids must have been learning things all the time.'

All the Hymers would have liked to be able to transport Braemar Gardens right back home to Otley. They felt there was nothing from the house that they weren't going to regret leaving – except maybe the washtub and mangle. 'I'll miss every room, every piece of furniture, every ornament,' sighed Lyn. In the event they were each given a souvenir: Lyn was awarded her wraparound pinny that had come to symbolize her struggles as a wartime housewife; Kirstie had the red shoes that she coveted so much; Michael was given a War Savings poster to remind him of the hours spent calculating the budget; Ben was allowed to keep his leather football; while Thomas took home the 1940s teddy bear that had kept him company in the shelter.

What the family would really like to have packed up as a memento of their 'war years' was the Anderson shelter – Michael partly because he had built it, and that was something that he had always wanted to do, but also because, as Lyn put it, 'It's a popular icon. I associate an Anderson shelter with the home front. And that's exactly what it was for us. We've argued in it, and cried in it and laughed in it, but above all that's where we've really felt we've been a wartime family. That's where our best moments have been. I know it sounds strange but it has, because that's where the war has seemed most real to us. It's brought us closer together and I think that it's in the Anderson shelter that we have been best able to envisage what it must have really been like for people in the Second World War.

'And that has increased our admiration for them hugely, not only for all the people who we have met while we've been here who have shared their experience with us and told us how it was for them and helped us to understand – given us a living history lesson really. But for *everyone* who went through that terrible war, to whom we'd like to pay tribute with our experience.'

SUGGESTED READING

ANDERSON, Verily, *Spam Tomorrow* (Rupert Hart-Davis, 1956).

BRIGGS, Asa, *Go To It! Working for Victory on the Home Front,* 1939–1945 (Mitchell Beasley, 2000).

BRIGGS, Susan, *Keep Smiling Through: The Home Front, 1939–45* (Weidenfeld & Nicolson, 1975).

BROAD, Richard and Suzie Fleming (eds), *Nella Last's War: A Mother's Diary 1939–45* (Falling Wall Press, 1981).

BROWN, Mike, *Put That Light Out! Britain's Civil Defence Services at War, 1939–1945* (Sutton Publishing, 1999).

CALDER, Angus, *The People's War: Britain 1939–1945* (Jonathan Cape, 1969).

CALDER, Angus and Dorothy Sheridan, *Speak for Yourself: A Mass-Observation Anthology, 1937–49* (Jonathan Cape, 1984).

CALDER, Ritchie, *The Lesson of London* (Secker & Warburg, 1941).

CC41: Utility Furniture and fashion, 1941–1951 (Geffrye Museum Trust, 1995).

COSTELLOE, John, *Love & Sex & War: Changing Values, 1939–45* (Wm Collins, 1985).

CROSBY, Travis L., *The Impact of Civilian Evacuation in the Second World War* (Croom Helm, 1986).

Davies, Jennifer, *The Wartime Garden: The Home Front, 1939–45* (BBC Books, 1993).

DAVIES, Jennifer, *The Wartime Kitchen and Garden* (BBC Books, 1993).

EDOM, Robert, *A Great Life If You Don't Weaken* (Minerva Press, 2000).

FITZ GIBBON, Constantine, *The Blitz* (Allen Wingate, 1957).

FITZ GIBBON, Theodora, *With Love: An Autobiography, 1938–46.* (Century Publishing, 1982).

FAVIELL, Francis, *A Chelsea Concerto* (Cassell, 1959).

FELTON, Monica, *Civilian Supplies in Wartime Britain* (Ministry of Information).

Few Eggs and No Oranges: The Diaries of Vere Hodgson, 1940–45 (Dennis Dobson, 1977; Persephone Books, 1999).

HANCOCK, W.K. and M.M. Gowing, *British War Economy* (HMSO, 1949).

HARRISSON, Tom, *Living Through the Blitz* (Collins, 1976).

HARRISSON, Tom and Charles Madge (eds), *Mass Observation: War Begins At Home* (Chatto & Windus, 1940).

HARTLEY, Jenny (ed.), *Hearts Undefeated: Women's Writing of the Second World War* (Virago, 1994).

HARTLEY, Jenny (ed.), *Millions Like Us: British Women's Fiction of the Second World War* (Virago, 1997).

HICKMAN, Tom, *What Did You Do In The War, Auntie? The BBC At War, 1939–45* (BBC Books, 1995).

HODSON, James Lonsdale, *Home Front* (Gollancz, 1944).

INGLIS, Ruth, *The Children's War: Evacuation, 1939–1945* (Wm Collins, 1989).

KNOWLDEN, Patricia and Joyce Walker, *West Wickham: Past into Present* (Hollies Publications, 1986).

KOPS, Bernard, *The World Is A Wedding* (MacGibbon and Kee, 1963).

LEWIS, Peter, *A People's War* (Methuen, 1986).

LEHMANN, John, *I Am My Brother: Autobiography II* (Longman, 1960).

LONGMATE, Norman, *How We Lived Then: A History of Everyday Life During the Second World War* (Hutchinson, 1971).

LONGMATE, Norman, *The Doodlebugs: The Story of the Flying-Bombs* (Hutchinson,1981).

MACK, Joanna and Steve Humphries, *The Making of Modern London: 1939–1945* (Sidgwick & Jackson, 1985).

MACKENZIE, S.P., *The Home Guard: A Military and Political History* (Oxford University Press, 1995).

McLAINE, Ian, *Ministry of Morale: Home Front Morale and the Ministry of Information in World War II* (George Allen & Unwin. 1979).

McCRUM, Mark and Matthew Sturgis, *1900 House* (Channel 4 Books, 1999).

MINNS, Raynes, Bombers and Mash: *The Domestic Front, 1939–45* (Virago, 1980).

Mrs Milburn's Dairies: An Englishwoman's Day-to-Day Reflections, 1939–45 (Harrap, 1975).

NICOLSON, Harold, (ed.) Nigel Nicolson, *The War Years: 1939–1945 Volume II: Diaries and Letters* (Wm Collins, 1967).

OGLEY, Bob, *Kent At War, 1939–45* (Froglets Publications in association with Kent Messenger Group Newspapers, 1994).

PANTER-DOWNES, Mollie, (ed.) *William Shawm, London War Notes, 1939–1945* (Longman, 1972).

PATTEN, Marguerite, *We'll Eat Again* (Hamlyn, 1985).

SHERIDAN, Dorothy (ed.), *Wartime Women. A Mass-Observation Anthology: The Experiences of Women at War* (Heinemann, 1990).

SINCLAIR, Andrew, *War Like a Wasp: The Lost Decade of the Forties* (Hamish Hamilton, 1989).

STOREY, Joyce, *Joyce's War, 1939–1945* (Virago, 1992).

SUMMERFIELD, Penny, *Reconstructing Women's Lives: Discourse and Subjectivity in Oral Histories of the Second World War* (Manchester University Press, 1998).

SUMMERFIELD, Penny, *Women Workers in the Second World War: Production and Patriarchy in Conflict* (Croom Helm, 1984).

SUMMERFIELD, Penny and Gail Braybon, *Out of the Cage: Women's Experiences in Two World Wars* (Pandora Press, 1987).

TITMUSS, Richard M., *Problems of Social Policy* (HMSO, 1950).

TURNER, E.S., *The Phoney War on the Home Front* (Michael Joseph, 1961).

WALKER, Joyce, *West Wickham in the Second World War* (Hollies Publications, 1990).

WALLER, Jane and Michael Vaughan-Rees, *Women in Wartime: The Role of Women's Magazines, 1939–1945* (Macdonald Optima, 1987).

WALLER, Jane and Michael Vaughan-Rees, *Women in Uniform, 1939–45* (PaperMac, 1989).

SHERIDAN, Dorothy (ed.), *War factory: Mass Observation* (1943, Century Hutchinson, 1987).

What Did You Do In The War, Mum? (Age Concern Theatre Trust, 1985).

ZIEGLER, Philip, *London at War, 1939–1945* (Sinclair-Stevenson, 1995).

ZWEINIGER-BARGIELOWSKA, Ina, *Austerity in Britain: Rationing, Controls, and Consumption, 1939-1955* (Oxford University Press, 2000).

LIST OF SUPPLIERS

FURNITURE, WALLPAPER AND PACKAGING
Trevor Howsam Ltd, The Granary, Grove Street East, Boston, Lincolnshire PE21 6TL. Tel: 01205 356010.

SALVAGE
Jonty Young, Restoration, 26 Wellington Road, Norwich NR2 3HT. Tel: 01603 611833.
Brondesbury Architectural Reclamation, The Yard, 136 Willesden Lane, London NW6 7TB. Tel: 020 7328 0820

KITCHEN EQUIPMENT
Kitchen Bygones, Alfie's Antiques Market, Church Street, London NW8 8DT. Tel: 020 7258 3405.

LIGHT FITTINGS
Christopher Wray Ltd, 600 King's Road, London SW6 2YW. Tel: 020 7751 8650.

GARDEN TOOLS
S Brunswick, Alfie's Antiques Market, Church Street, London NW8 8DT. Tel: 020 7724 9097.

CURTAINS
Chrissy and John Stansfield, 81 Durban Road, Beckenham, Kent BR3 4EY. Tel: 020 8658 4052.

ASBESTOS TESTING
A.A. Woods Asbestos Abatements, Unit 1, Station Estate, Eastwood Close, South Woodford, London E18 1RT. Tel: 020 8491 1001.

ANTIQUES
Nightingales Antiques and Craft Centre, 89–91 High Street, West Wickham, Kent BR4 0LS. Tel: 020 8777 0335.

TOYS
Unique Collections, 52 Greenwich Church Street, London SE10 9BL.Tel: 020 8305 0867.

Artefacts for the house were also purchased at the markets in Swinderby, Lincolnshire; Anderly, Kent and Kempton Races, Newark, Nottinghamshire.

PICTURE CREDITS

While every effort has been made to provide accurate picture credits, the publisher apologises for any omissions.

All photographs © Simon Roberts/Growbag except the following: © Imperial War Museum: 35, 36, 45, 74, 78, 81, 92, 112, 114, 141, 146, 164, 168 (right), 177, 192, 193, 196, 201, 207, 223, 240 and 241. © Topham Picturepoint: 38, 44, 46, 83, 88, 89, 91, 102, 104, 136, 168 (left), 176 (right), 178, 179, 205, 208, 226, 232, 233 and 244. Norman Longmate: 27, 43, 52, 73, 142, 176 (left), 183, 186, 190, 195 and 197 (left). Ben Hymers: 64 and 71. Tessa Cheek: 23. Bromley Central Library: 107. *Kentish Times*: 115. . MAFF: 135. Nature's World: 140.

AUTHOR'S ACKNOWLEDGEMENTS

I would first like to thank the Hymers about whom 'without whom this book could not have been written' has never been truer – so many thanks for the enthusiasm, good humour, fortitude, frankness and hospitality of a remarkable family: Lyn, Michael, Kirstie – and Ben and Thomas too.

Wall To Wall Television have been wonderful to work with and imaginative and tireless in the help and support they have given me. Thanks first to Simon Shaw and to Caroline Ross Pirie, Lia Cramer, Caroline Hecks, Andrew Meyer, Lareine Shea, Emma Slack and Zoë Watkins. Alexander Finch's research help was invaluable as deadlines loomed.

I would like to thank my fellow 'War Cabinet' members Piers Brendon, Guy de la Bédoyère, Susan Jebb and particularly Norman Longmate whose encyclopaedic knowledge of the home front, so generously shared, has indubitably made this a better book. Marguerite Patten has – again – put me right on a variety of 'food facts' with great kindness, and Dennis and Melanie Cornish of Higher Wall Nurseries, Devon were a mine of information about wartime vegetables.

At the Imperial War Museum Terry Charman, Christopher Dowling, Angela Godwin and Phil Reed were – yet again – a source of help and encouragement. Thanks too to the staff at the Mass Observation archive at the University of Sussex and to all at Channel 4 Books, particularly Charlie Carman, who first helped me to envisage the book and Emma Tait whose calm good sense and humour made the challenge of writing a television tie-in a hugely enjoyable experience. Christine King was a sensitive copy editor and Isobel Gillan involved me in her superb design of the book which was made a pleasure by the vivid photographs of the 1940s family taken by Simon Roberts. I would also like to thank my agent, Deborah Rogers, for her help and advice.

Then there are the people of West Wickham whose lively recall of their lives during the Second World War has deepened my understanding. In particular I would like to thank, Ivy Crier, Reg Long, Marjorie Moyce, Bert and Connie Purkiss, Nina and Peter Tilling and Connie Winters. Joyce Walker's history of West Wickham in the Second World War has been a valuable source of local detail. And finally I acknowledge my debt to all the organisations and individuals who answered questions and supplied me with information, to those who have published their memories of the Second World War, and to those historians who have written so authoritatively and interestingly about it. Any omissions or faults of commission are, of course, mine alone.

PRODUCER'S ACKNOWLEDGEMENTS

Wall To Wall Television would like to thank the following people for assistance with research: the staff of the Imperial War Museum, BBC Radio Archive, Human Nutrition Research, Leeds Metropolitan University's Sports and Science Department, the *Daily Express*, the *Kentish Times*, Remember When, Dr Penny Summerfield of the University of Lancaster, Ina Zweiniger Bargielowska, Dorothy Sheridan and Joy Eldridge at the Mass Osbervation Archive, the University of Sussex library, Walter Duncan at the Rowett Research Institute, Judith Laske of the Institute of Family Therapy, Albert Aldred, Joyce Walker, Tessa Cheek and Dr Cox and Patricia Knowlden for research in Kent.

For the restoration of 17 Braemar Gardens they would like to thank art director, Lia Cramer, buyer Nick Scott and site manager John Kenny. Also, Jonty Young at Restoration, Rosemary Williams in Cardiff, Jane Walton of Reading, Phil Reed at the Cabinet War Rooms, AA Woods for advice on asbestos, Trevor Howsam, Sue Toone at Phoenix, Keeleys for help with the shelter and renovating bicycles and The Ekco Collection at the Victoria & Albert Library.

For supplies to the 1940s house shop: Gareth Thomas of Dabounds Ltd, Nanda Hop of Nederlanse Industrie Van Eiproducten, Caroline Rose of Rose and Co. Apothecary, Robert Opie and The Flour Advisory Bureau. For information on pricing and rationing: Bridget Williams, of Sainsburys, Daniella Davies of Boots The Chemists and Claire Tunstall of Unilever. For supply of period clothing: Angels the Costumiers, Studio 4 and Jackie Vernon.

For assistance with the filming in West Wickham: Nigel Lovegrove at Crumbs Delicatessen, Michael Ashenden at L.A. Larratt's butchers, Tony Tibbs at Unigate Dairy, Lincoln Noronha at Loafers Bakers, Peter and Nina Tilling, John and Lisa Farley, Mr and Mrs Fincham, Terry Elliot, Jackie and Dean Whybra, Bill and Jenny at Butt & Co., Daniel Ede at Country Gardens of Croydon, Inspector Drayson and Sergeant Warne of West Wickham Police, Brian Vinall, Biggin Hill Airshow, Chislehurst Caves, Mr and Mrs Alex Gilham, Cob Aviation, St David's College, the Dog Shop, St Mark's Church Hall, Ye Olde Barbers and Win Allison and all the Residents of Ben Curtis House and Braemar Gardens.

Thanks also to Elizabeth Arden, Andy Bowness Carol Churchill, Dennis and Melanie Cornish, Sarah Drake, Eric Gaskin, Emily Grainger, Highroyds Hair Salon in Leeds, Trevor Sorbie, David King Taylor, Andre Leon, Bryan Martin, the National Trust at Chartwell, Produmax, vintage car suppliers, Warren Rushton and Eddie Farrell.

Thanks to the 'War Cabinet': Guy de la Bédoyère, Juliet Gardiner, Norman Longmate, Dr Piers Brendon and Dr Susan Jebb. Special thanks to Marguerite Patten OBE, Gill Brown and Janice Hadlow at Channel 4 Television.